California Fresh

C O O K B O O K

The Junior League of Oakland-East Bay

Foreword by M.F.K. Fisher

Art by Beth Van Hoesen

The Junior League of Oakland-East Bay, Inc.

Oakland, California

1985

The purpose of the Junior League is exclusively educational and charitable and is to promote voluntarism, to develop the potential of its members for voluntary participation in community affairs, and to demonstrate the effectiveness of trained volunteers.

We proudly dedicate this book to Junior League volunteers, past and present, in celebration of the Fiftieth Anniversary of the Junior League of Oakland-East Bay.

The proceeds from the sale of *California Fresh* will be returned to the communities of the East Bay through the projects sponsored by the Junior League of Oakland-East Bay.

To order additional copies of *California Fresh* write to:

California Fresh
J.L.O.E.B.
1980 Mountain Boulevard
Oakland, California 94611

Copyright © 1985 by The Junior League of Oakland-East Bay, Inc.
Foreword copyright © 1985 by M.F.K. Fisher
Beth Van Hoesen retains copyrights on all work reproduced in this book.

"Grilled Summer Vegetable Pasta" from *Chez Panisse Pasta, Pizza & Calzone* by Alice Waters, Patricia Curtan, and Martine Labro, copyright © 1984 by Tango Rose, Inc. Reprinted by permission of Random House, Inc.

Design by Gordon Chun

Library of Congress Cataloging in Publication Data
Main entry under title:
California fresh
Includes index. 1. Cookery, American—California style. 2. California, Northern—Social life and customs. I. Junior League of Oakland-East Bay.
TX715.C15145   1985   641.5   84-28920
ISBN 0-9613744-0-3

First Printing: 15,000 copies June 1985
Second Printing: 20,000 copies August 1985

THE COOKBOOK COMMITTEE

Shelley Frisch and Jane Horn
Editors

Candy Caldwell
Chairman 1984–1985

Committee Members 1981–1985

Suzanne Ainsworth

Sandra Boyd

Christina Cahall

Candy Caldwell

Shelley Frisch,
Co-chairman, 1981–1983

Muffy Gal

Caryn Gregg

Gigi Halloran

Martha Holstlaw

Jane Horn,
Co-chairman, 1981–1983

Anne Johnson

Mary Joan Kealy

Shannon Kirby

Josette McPhee

Gala Mowat

Vicki Pierpont

Sally Pitts

Ruthie Reed

Marsha Servetnick

Betty Shapiro,
Chairman, 1983–1984

Marcia Thomas

Ayn Thorne

Dorothy Trautman

Barbara Westover

Sarah Young

ACKNOWLEDGMENTS

The old saying notwithstanding, the contributions of many cooks made *this* broth so much better. Many thanks and "Bon Appétit!" to the hundreds of League members and friends who donated their favorite recipes, and to the dedicated recipe testers who carried on from there. Our special thanks to: Jean van Löben Sels for her encouragement, ideas, eminently sensible advice, and wine expertise; Frances Bowles for her generosity in preparing the index; Barbara Chaconas; the Advertising Department of the Clorox Company; Maggie Crum; Hooper Printing; Elizabeth Martini; Quest Computers; Marcia Robbins; Thomas Smegal; and Sharon Smith.

SPONSORS

We are grateful for the financial support of the following sponsors:

Mr. and Mrs. Stephen Bechtel, Jr.
Dr. and Mrs. Kenneth M. Caldwell
The Clorox Company
Friedkin-Becker Realty Corporation
Piedmont Grocery Company
Mr. and Mrs. William E. Trautman

CONTENTS

PRINTS AND DRAWINGS BY BETH VAN HOESEN

1. *Jicama,* 1977
   graphite
   7¼ × 8½

2. *Trout,* 1971
   etching, printed à la poupée
   Ed. 25
   6½ × 6⅞

3. *Lea's Lettuce,* 1978
   drypoint
   Ed. 10
   13¾ × 17¾

4. *Torpedo Onions,* 1977
   color pencil
   8⅞ × 11

5. *Bok Choy,* 1977
   graphite
   21½ × 17¼

6. *Hawaiian Bananas,* 1980
   color pencil, graphite
   9⅛ × 11⅜

7. *Sweet Spanish Yellow,* 1978
   drypoint, engraving
   Non-editioned
   10¾ × 13⅞

8. *Jan's Squash,* 1982
   color pencil
   14¼ × 14¼

9. *Brussels Sprouts,* 1980
   ink
   22½ × 17½

10. *Pomegranates,* 1976
    aquatint, drypoint, etching
    Ed. 25
    10¾ × 11¼

11. *Mushrooms,* 1961
    aquatint, engraving
    Ed. 25
    5½ × 6

12. *Squid,* 1978
    color pencil, graphite
    6½ × 8¼

13. *Leeks,* 1960
    drypoint, engraving, etching
    Ed. 25
    9¾ × 7⅞

14. *Chocolate Truffles,* 1982
    color pencil, graphite
    13 × 12¾

15. *Oranges to Cut,* 1970
    graphite
    11¼ × 12

16. *Seven Persimmons,* 1976
    color pencil, graphite
    12½ × 13½

cover:
Fresno Basket, 2nd State
1984
aquatint, drypoint, etching,
watercolor, printed à la poupée
Ed. 12
12¼ × 12¾

FROM THE PRESIDENT

The publication of *California Fresh* by the Junior League of Oakland-East Bay celebrates a milestone in the history of our organization. This year, 1985, marks the Golden Anniversary of our League.

The purpose of the Junior League of Oakland-East Bay—to serve the community with effective, trained volunteers—has remained constant throughout our fifty years. As steady as we are to our ideals, our volunteer opportunities have changed dramatically to meet the expectations of our members as well as the agencies with whom we collaborate. Today we offer our members a wide variety of choices that challenge their creative, resourceful, and professional energies.

California Fresh is a symbol of that challenge, and clearly illustrates the expertise and sophistication that were necessary to the book's production. The proceeds from the sale of *California Fresh* will be returned to the communities of the East Bay through projects sponsored by the Junior League of Oakland-East Bay.

It is appropriate that this contemporary, attractive cookbook, created and produced by Junior League volunteers, commemorates our Fiftieth Anniversary.

Nancy Colbert
President 1984–1985

FOREWORD

A few decades or perhaps I should say a while ago I wrote what was then called an article, but is now called a piece, about a Junior League cookbook published somewhere in the Deep South.

I liked the book because it was what I recognized as genuine. I also thought it was sad and pathetic and truly funny, which I made very plain in my story, and the editors were dubious about publishing it because they felt that it might harm their so-called image. They finally did.

To my real amazement I got a lot of letters about the article, and they were all good. They, and by *they* I mean the Binkies and TDs and Beejos of the Junior League, knew that I knew them and recognized exactly what they and I were, in that social and culinary and even global scene.

Their book was very bad, or rather it was not very good. It was inept. I said so, which was one of the things that bothered the magazine. But *they* knew what I was saying, and they wrote to me and *not* the editors and told me so. I felt fine.

Now I can say I feel even better, for here is another Junior League cookbook, and I am almost unbelieving about how much better it is than the other one I read and criticized.

I know that Binkie and TD will understand this, and even Beejo, who as I remember submitted a recipe for what she called Guzzpatchee that was mostly mashed soda crackers in canned tomato juice with chili powder. (This was during the South Pacific or maybe the Korean business, when wives found themselves stranded in strange places like Santa Laguna. . . .)

Of course all that was a couple of wars ago, at least. But now in *California Fresh* the children and maybe even the grandchildren of our Binkies have produced a handsome book indeed, well designed, well edited, and filled with good recipes that have been tested with the severity that real sophistication demands. In other words, we've all grown up since those dim days when almost any group of well-meaning females could put together a batch of favorite dainties for their "club budgets," and count on a captive audience to hand out money because Mummy (or young Ms. Manell) had her name printed under Fudge Brownies (or Guzzpatchee). . . .

I admit to feeling an almost maternal pride in this big step from naiveté to cool, poised expertise. Perhaps I have always been a little uneasy about my first gentle teasing of these young ladies in Miami or wherever it was. Or perhaps I am simply relieved to see that I too am better able to recognize the rewards of hard intelligent work!

Certainly we all knew, all the Binkies and I, that enthusiasm is forever. There is as much of it in *California Fresh* as there ever was in the old childish, awkward, lovable cookbooks we once bought and tried to forget as soon as possible. By now we know we'll get our money's worth! We'll read and use and finally pass along to Binkie's great-grandchildren this present proof of her own integrity: *California Fresh* is a *good 'un*!

M.F.K. Fisher
Glen Ellen, California

INTRODUCTION

Stretching inland from the eastern shore of San Francisco Bay is a narrow band of dense urban settlement contained by a low range of verdant coastal mountains. Farther east, burgeoning suburbs spread across a classic California landscape of pastoral interior valleys and oak-dotted rolling hills. This is the East Bay.

For more than a century, its expansive parklands, culturally rich city centers, and benign climate have attracted those seeking a comfortable environment in which to raise their families, or a respite from San Francisco's fog.

East Bay life is a lively blend of people and customs. Many generations of immigrants from the countries of Asia and the Pacific, as well as an active commercial port, have forged strong links with the Orient. Proximity to Mexico has added a Latin flavor to many neighborhoods. Shops and restaurants reflect this stimulating diversity in the variety of goods and foods they offer. Ingredients specific to Oriental and Latin cooking are routinely available in most local markets and are used with imagination by cooks of all backgrounds.

The cities and towns of the East Bay took shape amidst orchards and farmland first cultivated by Spanish settlers in the early 1800s. The bounty of the surrounding countryside, including the nearby waters of the bay and the ocean, became the foundation for an indigenous Northern California cuisine that is today nationally acclaimed.

It is a cuisine based on the freshest ingredients, imaginatively combined and attractively presented. Its practitioners, a new breed of adventuresome and creative cooks, acknowledge many influences—earthy, highly seasoned ethnic dishes, unpretentious American home cooking, and refined, elegant haute cuisine. And while these talented men and women pursue a personal culinary style, they share a common goal—to produce food that is light and fresh, simply prepared, and of the highest quality.

With *California Fresh*, we hope to provide a portrait of the exciting variety that is the hallmark of Northern California cooking. From East Bay chefs, restaurateurs, and other professionals in the field who are recognized as being in the forefront of this culinary revolution, we offer recipes that reflect their interpretation of the new style. From home cooks, both Junior League members and friends, we have culled the best of their personal files, the recipes they reach for first to serve their families and special guests.

Wine recommendations accompany some of the recipes in *California Fresh*. They reflect the wines of the nearby Napa, Sonoma, and Livermore valleys. There are hundreds of wineries in this area and each puts its own "print" on the varieties they produce. You are encouraged to experiment on your own to find the ones you like best, using our suggestions as the starting point. Wine does wonderful things to food, and, if correctly paired, food in its turn brings out the best in wine. For the creative cook, this is a never-ending adventure.

We offer *California Fresh* as a glimpse into our kitchens, a peek over the shoulders of cooks whose busy, full lives often demand that their meals be quick to prepare, yet who refuse to sacrifice quality for convenience. Whether you are seeking ideas for your family's meals or want to expand your repertoire of recipes for entertaining—you will find what you need in *California Fresh*.

CHAPTER ONE

Appetizers and First Courses

Sun-dried Tomatoes with Cream Cheese and Basil

Sun-dried tomatoes, packed in olive oil*
Baguette, thinly sliced
Natural cream cheese
Fresh whole basil leaves or tiny sprigs of watercress

Pungent and chewy, sun-dried tomatoes add zest to salads, sauces, and hot foods, especially pastas. Traditionally, the best ones, made from Roma tomatoes packed in olive oil, have come from southern Italy. More recently available are domestically produced dried tomatoes marinated in oil-and-vinegar blends or herb-seasoned oils.

Drain tomatoes and cut in quarters. Spread bread slices with cream cheese. Garnish with a small whole basil leaf or sprig of watercress, and a piece of tomato.

*Available at specialty food stores and well-stocked supermarkets.

Garlic and Herb Cheese

*Makes about
1¾ cups*

12 ounces cream cheese, softened
2 tablespoons butter, softened
½ teaspoon celery salt
1 large clove garlic, minced
1 teaspoon snipped fresh chives
¼ teaspoon red wine vinegar
¼ teaspoon Worcestershire sauce
¼ teaspoon dried marjoram
¼ teaspoon dried summer savory
¼ teaspoon dried thyme
1 teaspoon milk, if needed

Minced fresh parsley or chives for garnish
Unseasoned crackers or melba toast for accompaniment

*Grown
underground,
garlic bulbs or
heads are made up
of many cloves,
each with its own
peel. This pungent,
intensely flavored
vegetable is
extensively
cultivated in
Northern
California near
Gilroy, which
holds an annual
Garlic Festival in
its honor.*

In a food processor or with an electric mixer, combine all ingredients. Thin with teaspoon of milk, if needed. Refrigerate for several hours or overnight.

Garnish with minced parsley or chives. Spread on unseasoned crackers or melba toast.

NOTE: If possible, prepare this spread a day ahead to allow the flavors to blend.

Jicama Piquant

*Makes about
30 appetizers*

8 ounces cream cheese, softened
2 tablespoons finely chopped green chiles
1 clove garlic, minced
½ teaspoon salt
⅛ teaspoon paprika
1 large jicama, peeled

Sweet red or green bell pepper, or pimiento and green onion for garnish

*Jicama is a large,
thin-skinned tuber
or root vegetable
originally brought
to California by
Mexican
immigrants and
now widely
available in local
markets. Eaten
raw as a crudité or
as part of a salad,
its crunchy and
somewhat sweet
white flesh
resembles a water
chestnut.*

Mix cream cheese, chopped chiles, garlic, salt, and paprika. Spoon into a pastry tube fitted with a large star tip and refrigerate if not using right away. When ready to assemble, first bring cream cheese mixture to room temperature.

Slice jicama in bite-sized pieces or cut in decorative shapes with small metal cookie cutters. Pipe cream cheese rosettes on each piece of jicama. Decorate with diamond-shaped bits of bell pepper or pimiento. Refrigerate until ready to serve.

N O T E : To vary, filling can also be piped into blanched snow peas or onto seeded and drained ripe cherry tomatoes, green pepper strips, or zucchini rounds.

1.
Jicama
graphite

Cheddar Curry Spread

*Makes about
2 cups*

2 cups (about 8 ounces) grated Cheddar cheese
1 can (4¼ ounces) chopped black olives, drained
½ cup mayonnaise (page 69)
½ teaspoon curry powder
2 green onions, finely chopped (including green portion)
1 small clove garlic, minced

Crackers or thinly sliced French bread for accompaniment

Combine all ingredients in a bowl with a fork until blended. Refrigerate several hours to allow flavors to blend.

Serve cold or at room temperature spread on crackers or thinly sliced French bread.

Polynesian Dip for Vegetables

Makes about
3 cups

1 cup sour cream
1 cup mayonnaise (page 69)
¼ pound tiny cooked shrimp, chopped
¼ cup minced green onions (including green portion)
¼ cup minced fresh parsley
2 cloves garlic, minced
¼ cup finely chopped water chestnuts
Grated fresh ginger root (at least 1 teaspoon)

1 red cabbage

Assortment of crudités such as carrot sticks, cauliflowerets, cucumber sticks, celery sticks, green pepper wedges, broccoli flowerets, sliced jicama

In a bowl, combine sour cream, mayonnaise, shrimp, onions, parsley, garlic, and water chestnuts. Add grated ginger root, stir well, and refrigerate for at least 1 hour. Taste for seasoning; add more ginger root, if desired.

Slice a lid off the top of the red cabbage. Trim stem end so cabbage will stand upright. With a sharp knife, hollow interior of cabbage, being careful not to puncture the sides of the shell. Discard center of cabbage, or reserve for another use. Fill cabbage with the chilled dip.

To serve, place on a platter, and surround with crudités.

Eggplant Caviar

*Makes about
2½ cups*

1 large eggplant, or 2 small (about 1½ pounds total)
1 cup chopped onion
6 tablespoons olive oil
½ medium green bell pepper, minced
1 large clove garlic, minced
2 large ripe tomatoes, peeled, seeded, and chopped
2 teaspoons salt
½ teaspoon sugar
¼ teaspoon freshly ground black pepper
⅛ teaspoon cayenne pepper
2 tablespoons fresh lemon juice

Pita bread wedges or pieces of Armenian cracker bread (Lahvosh) for accompaniment
Halved ripe cherry tomatoes and chopped fresh parsley for garnish

Preheat oven to 425 degrees.

With a fork, prick eggplant in several places; place on a rack set in a baking pan, and bake for 50 minutes, turning the eggplant every 15 minutes. Skin will be soft and wrinkled. Remove from the oven and cool. Cut in half and scoop out pulp. Chop the pulp well, place in a colander, and drain at least 15 minutes.

In a medium skillet, sauté onion in oil over medium-high heat until soft, but not browned. Add green pepper and garlic and sauté 5 more minutes, stirring occasionally. Stir in eggplant, tomatoes, salt, sugar, black pepper, and cayenne. Simmer, covered, for 30 minutes, stirring occasionally. Remove cover and simmer until moisture has evaporated. Remove from heat and stir in lemon juice. Cool, then refrigerate until chilled.

Serve chilled in a bowl, surrounded by wedges of pita bread or pieces of Armenian cracker bread, and garnished with cherry tomatoes and chopped parsley.

Vegetables Vinaigrette

Serves 8 to 10

MARINADE:

⅔ cup apple cider vinegar
⅓ cup vegetable oil
1 tablespoon fresh lemon juice
1 teaspoon dried oregano
½ teaspoon salt
¼ teaspoon freshly ground black pepper
⅛ teaspoon Tabasco sauce

1 bunch broccoli (separated into bite-sized flowerets)
1 large onion, cut in eighths and separated into strips
1 can (6 ounces) pitted black olives, drained
½ pound mushrooms, sliced

Combine marinade ingredients.

Combine vegetables in a serving bowl. Pour dressing over vegetables and marinate in the refrigerator overnight.

Drain before serving. Provide toothpicks to spear the vegetables.

NOTE: To vary or extend the recipe, add or substitute cauliflowerets, sliced hearts of palm, or water-packed artichoke hearts, drained.

Vegetables in Horseradish Cream

Serves 12

MARINADE:

2 cups mayonnaise (page 69)
½ cup prepared white horseradish
2 teaspoons fresh lemon juice
2 teaspoons dry mustard
¼ teaspoon salt

VEGETABLES:

2 cups raw cauliflowerets
2 cups raw broccoli flowerets
1 pint ripe cherry tomatoes, stems removed
1 can (6 ounces) pitted black olives, drained
1 can (8 ounces) whole water chestnuts, drained
¼ pound mushrooms
½ to ¾ pound large cooked shrimp (optional), shelled and deveined

In a large bowl, combine marinade ingredients. Add vegetables and mix with marinade. Gently stir in shrimp. Refrigerate overnight to give vegetables time to soften.

Drain before serving. Provide toothpicks to spear the vegetables.

NOTE: As a first course, or main course salad, serve on a bed of mixed greens with a sprinkling of paprika for additional color. Makes 6 to 8 servings.

Pâté de Volaille (Chicken Pâté)

Joyce McGillis, Cooking Instructor, Berkeley

*Makes 3 to 4
dozen appetizers*

2 cloves shallots, chopped
1 tablespoon butter
¼ cup brandy
2 whole cooked chicken breasts, skinned and boned
1 egg
1 teaspoon dried basil
Salt and freshly ground black pepper
¾ cup butter, softened
¼ cup whipping cream
8 to 12 slices (5 to 8 ounces, depending on size) prosciutto
Chopped pistachio nuts or freshly grated Parmesan cheese (optional)

*Joyce McGillis
created this pâté
so that it could be
easily made with a
food processor,
one of her favorite
kitchen tools. To
cook tender
chicken breasts for
this recipe, Joyce
suggests placing
the raw breasts in
a pan of boiling
water, removing
the pan from the
heat and steeping
the chicken,
covered, for
twenty to twenty-
five minutes. The
chicken will be
juicy and slightly
pink at the bone.*

In a small skillet, sauté the shallots in 1 tablespoon butter over medium heat until translucent. Add brandy and simmer for 2 to 3 minutes. Set aside and cool.

Cut chicken breasts in 1-inch pieces. In a food processor fitted with a metal blade, chop chicken to ground-meat texture. Add egg and seasonings, then butter and cream, and blend well after each addition until the mixture is very smooth. Add the shallots and their cooking liquid, and process to blend. By hand, stir in pistachio nuts or grated Parmesan cheese, if desired. Adjust seasonings, if necessary.

Turn the mixture onto a piece of plastic wrap and form into a roll, about 2 inches in diameter. Wrap well and refrigerate until firm. This mixture can be prepared a day ahead.

To serve, arrange slices of prosciutto, long edges slightly overlapping, on a piece of plastic wrap as long as the chicken roll (the grain of the prosciutto will wrap around the chicken roll for easier slicing). Place the chilled chicken roll at one end of the prosciutto and roll it up, guiding the prosciutto firmly and tightly against the roll. The roll should be encased in a single layer of prosciutto slices.

With a sharp knife, slice crosswise in thin circles and serve.

Spicy Walnuts or Pecans

Makes about
4 cups

3 tablespoons butter
3 tablespoons Worcestershire sauce
1 teaspoon salt
½ teaspoon ground cinnamon
¼ teaspoon garlic powder
¼ teaspoon cayenne pepper
⅛ teaspoon Tabasco sauce
1 pound walnut or pecan halves

Preheat oven to 350 degrees.

In a 10- or 12-inch skillet, melt butter; stir in Worcestershire and other seasonings. Cook over medium heat for several minutes, or until sauce thickens slightly. Add nuts and toss until well coated. Spread nuts onto a jelly-roll pan or cookie sheet in a single layer. Bake 20 to 25 minutes, or until nuts are brown and crisp, stirring every 5 minutes.

Toss in salads, or serve with cocktails or wine.

Seasoned Prawns

*Makes about
30 appetizers*

MARINADE:

⅓ cup white vinegar
2 tablespoons vegetable oil
4 teaspoons capers, with some juice
1 teaspoon celery seed
½ teaspoon salt
⅛ teaspoon Tabasco sauce

¼ cup chopped celery tops
2 tablespoons mixed pickling spices
1½ teaspoons salt
1 pound large raw prawns
½ onion, thinly sliced and separated into rings
3 to 4 bay leaves

*On the West
Coast, large
shrimp are called
prawns. Although
suggested in this
recipe and in many
others, deveining is
really an optional,
cosmetic
procedure.*

Combine marinade ingredients; set aside.

In a 3-quart saucepan, bring 2 quarts of water to a boil. Add celery tops, pickling spices, and 1½ teaspoons salt. Drop in the prawns; boil 1 to 2 minutes, or until they turn pink. Do not overcook. Remove from heat, drain, and cool. Shell and devein the prawns, and brush off most of the pickling spices and clinging pieces of celery.

In a glass or ceramic bowl, layer prawns with onion slices and bay leaves. Pour marinade over prawns. Refrigerate for 24 hours or longer. Stir once or twice during this time to thoroughly marinate all the ingredients. Drain off marinade and discard bay leaves. Serve prawns in a glass bowl.

NOTE: To serve as a first course, include some onion slices with each portion. Makes 4 to 6 servings.

Radicchio with Pernod-Crab Filling

Serves 8

¼ to ½ pound cooked crab meat
½ cup cooked long-grain white rice
¼ cup mayonnaise (page 69)
1 tablespoon fresh lemon juice
2 teaspoons (or more) Pernod (see Note)
1 to 2 small heads radicchio, leaves separated, washed, and dried

Fresh parsley sprigs for garnish

Red-leafed radicchio is a variety of chicory with a tangy, slightly bitter flavor similar to curly endive. It was first grown in Italy, but is now also cultivated in the United States.

In a bowl, combine crab, rice, mayonnaise, and lemon juice. Add Pernod. Cover and chill overnight to allow flavors to blend. Taste, and add additional Pernod, if desired.

Trim any discolored areas from stems of radicchio leaves, being careful not to split the tender leaves. Spoon 1 to 3 teaspoons of crab mixture into each radicchio leaf.

Garnish with parsley.

NOTE: For this appetizer, radicchio leaves serve as tiny bowls for the rice and crab filling. Use the smaller inner leaves as they are easier to pick up and can be eaten in one or two bites.

Pernod is an anise-flavored aperitif.

Ceviche

Serves 8 to 10

1½ pounds cooked crabmeat, thinly sliced raw scallops, or other raw firm-fleshed white fish such as halibut, cut in ¾-inch cubes, or a combination of these
1 cup fresh lime juice (about 6 limes)
¼ cup olive oil
¼ cup chopped red onion
¼ cup chopped fresh parsley
2 tablespoons chopped canned green chiles
1 clove garlic, minced
1 teaspoon salt
½ teaspoon dried oregano
Dash of Tabasco sauce
Freshly ground black pepper
¼ cup sour cream (optional)

8 to 10 iceberg or butter lettuce cups
2 ripe avocados, sliced in crescents, for garnish

Assure wary guests that the seafood in their ceviche is indeed cooked. The citric acid of the lime juice acts on fish proteins, "cooking" the raw fish just as surely as heat would.

In a bowl, combine fish with lime juice. Marinate, refrigerated, for 3 to 4 hours; stir once or twice. Drain well in a colander or sieve, discarding juices. Return the fish to a bowl and add remaining ingredients except lettuce and avocados. Let the mixture sit at room temperature for 1 hour. Drain again.

For each serving, spoon a portion of the fish mixture onto a lettuce cup set on individual plates. Garnish with avocado slices.

Hearts of Palm Salad

Serves 4

DRESSING:

¼ cup fresh lemon juice
3 tablespoons olive oil
2 cloves garlic, minced
½ teaspoon dried oregano
½ teaspoon salt
½ teaspoon snipped fresh chives or minced green onion (green portion only)
⅛ teaspoon cayenne pepper

1 can (14 ounces) hearts of palm, drained
½ pound large cooked shrimp, shelled and deveined

1 head butter lettuce
2 small-to-medium ripe tomatoes, cut in wedges
1 ripe avocado, peeled and sliced

1 teaspoon capers or caviar for garnish (optional)

Hearts of palm, ridiculed as swamp cabbage and celebrated as the "millionaire's delicacy," are the tender shoots of the Sabal palmetto, also known as the cabbage tree. The description "millionaire's delicacy" is quite appropriate, since a whole tree must be cut down to get to the heart.

In a medium bowl, combine dressing ingredients.

With a very sharp knife, slice the hearts of palm in ¼- to ½-inch rounds; toss with shrimp in the dressing to coat. Refrigerate 1 hour or more to absorb the vinaigrette, stirring at least once.

Serve the salad on a bed of crisp butter lettuce, surrounded by tomato wedges and avocado slices. If desired, garnish with capers or, more extravagantly, caviar. Spoon any remaining dressing over salad.

Avocado Salad with Lobster Dressing

Serves 6

2 lobster tails (about 8 ounces each)

LOBSTER DRESSING:
¾ cup mayonnaise (page 69)
2 tablespoons olive oil
2 tablespoons fresh lemon juice
1 tablespoon drained capers
1 tablespoon chili sauce
¼ teaspoon (or more) dried dill weed
¼ teaspoon salt
⅛ teaspoon freshly ground black pepper
  Pinch of cayenne pepper

3 large ripe avocados
2 heads butter lettuce

Lemon wedges for garnish

Avocados, like tomatoes, have been cultivated since pre-Columbian days. The two varieties most commonly grown in this country are the thin-skinned green Fuertes, available in the winter, and the pebble-skinned black Haas, abundant in the summer.

Drop lobster tails into 3 quarts boiling water. Boil 7 to 8 minutes, or until lobster floats and turns bright orange; check for doneness by cutting into thickest part of the meat (it should be opaque). Drain tails and set aside until cool enough to handle.

Meanwhile, combine dressing ingredients in a medium bowl.

Cut away shell from cooled lobster tails with kitchen scissors and remove meat. Cut in small chunks and add to dressing. Chill well.

At serving time, peel and halve avocados. Discard pits. For each serving, place half an avocado on a bed of butter lettuce. Fill the avocado cavity with Lobster Dressing. Garnish with lemon wedges.

Scallop Mousse with Herb Sauce

Serves 6 to 8

A Dry Semillon is suggested.

MOUSSE:

1 cup fish stock or bottled clam juice
Bouquet garni (3 sprigs parsley, 1 bay leaf, 1 teaspoon thyme leaves, tied together in a square of cheesecloth)
1¼ pounds scallops
3 egg whites
1 teaspoon grated onion
¼ teaspoon salt
⅛ teaspoon ground white pepper
Dash of cayenne pepper
1½ cups whipping cream

HERB SAUCE:

2 egg yolks
4 teaspoons fresh lemon juice
½ teaspoon salt
¾ cup vegetable oil (or half olive oil and half vegetable oil)
2 cups tightly packed watercress
1 tablespoon (or more) white wine

To prepare Mousse: In a small saucepan, combine fish stock and bouquet garni. Bring to a boil and add 8 ounces of the scallops. Reduce heat and simmer 3 minutes, or until scallops are opaque. Strain, reserving stock for another use. Discard bouquet garni. Finely dice the scallops.

In a food processor, puree remaining scallops with egg whites. Season with onion, salt, pepper, and a dash of cayenne. With the machine running, slowly pour the cream through the feed tube and process until it is completely incorporated. Fold in diced scallops by hand.

Preheat oven to 350 degrees. Butter a 1-quart loaf pan.

Turn the mixture into prepared loaf pan. Set the loaf pan in a 9- by 13-inch baking pan and add enough hot water to reach halfway up the sides of the loaf pan.

Bake for 30 minutes, then cover the top of the loaf pan lightly with aluminum foil. Bake an additional 30 minutes, or until knife inserted in the center comes out clean. Cool to room temperature; chill.

To prepare Herb Sauce: In a blender, combine egg yolks, lemon juice, and salt. With machine at high speed, add oil in a very thin, continuous stream until oil is incorporated and sauce thickens. Add watercress; puree. Add wine to taste.

Turn mousse out onto a serving platter, cut in slices and serve with Herb Sauce.

Duck Liver Pâté

Michael Hirschberg, Restaurant Matisse, Santa Rosa

Serves 8 to 10

A White Zinfandel is suggested.

1 pound duck livers
2 cups milk, or enough to cover livers for soaking
6 egg yolks
1¼ cups whipping cream
½ pound butter, melted
3 tablespoons brandy
1½ teaspoons salt
1½ teaspoons freshly ground black pepper
½ teaspoon ground allspice

French bread, gherkins, and Dijon-style mustard for accompaniment

This pâté is so mild and palatable even those who shun the thought of liver will savor it, asserts Chef Michael Hirschberg. Technically, this is not a pâté at all, but rather a timbale since the recipe incorporates eggs and butter. It is the eggs and butter that give the rich, creamy texture, and the mildness of the duck livers that makes it so agreeable.

Soak livers in milk at least 1 hour or overnight.

Preheat oven to 350 degrees. Butter an 8½- by 4-inch glass loaf pan; line with cooking parchment and butter the parchment. Cut and butter a piece of parchment to fit on top of loaf pan; set aside.

Drain livers and discard milk. Trim livers of any fat or extraneous tissue. In a food processor, puree livers thoroughly along with egg yolks. Add cream and process again. Add butter, brandy, and spices. The mixture will be quite liquid.

Fill the prepared loaf pan with the liver mixture, then cover with buttered parchment.

Set the loaf pan in a 9- by 13-inch baking pan and add enough hot water to reach halfway up the sides of the loaf pan. Bake for 60 to 75 minutes, or until the mixture sets and just barely jiggles when shaken.

Chill overnight in the refrigerator.

To unmold, peel off the top paper. Dip the loaf pan in hot water and turn the pan over onto a cutting board or plate. Peel off paper.

Slice, and serve with French bread, gherkins, and Dijon-style mustard.

Carpaccio

Serves 10 to 12

GARLIC OIL:
1 large clove garlic
¼ cup vegetable oil or olive oil
¼ teaspoon salt
   Freshly ground black pepper

3 tablespoons drained capers
3 tablespoons minced fresh parsley

MUSTARD SAUCE:
1 egg yolk, beaten
2 tablespoons Dijon-style mustard
1 teaspoon tarragon vinegar
2 tablespoons Garlic Oil

1 pound uncooked prime grade eye of round, sliced paper thin
1 lemon, cut in wedges

   Whole capers for garnish

If possible, have your butcher slice the meat for you. To produce the same paper-thin cuts at home, the meat must be first partially frozen. Frozen meat, however, tends to "bleed" as it thaws, which would be most unattractive when the carpaccio is served.

To prepare Garlic Oil: Bruise the garlic and place it in a small cup or jar with the oil. Let garlic stand in the oil at least 2 hours. Remove the garlic and add salt and a few grinds of black pepper.

Combine the capers with the minced parsley.

To prepare Mustard Sauce: Place egg yolk in a small bowl and whisk in mustard and vinegar. Add 2 tablespoons of the Garlic Oil, a few drops at a time, whisking until the sauce is the consistency of thin mayonnaise.

For each serving, place 3 or 4 slices of uncooked beef on individual salad plates. Rub each slice with the cut lemon and brush lightly with Garlic Oil. Spoon a line of the parsley-caper mixture across the meat slices, and serve with a dab of Mustard Sauce on the side. Decorate with a few additional capers.

Batter-fried Mushrooms

*Makes 15 to 20
appetizers*

½ cup all-purpose flour
⅛ teaspoon salt
1 egg
⅓ cup flat beer

Oil for deep frying

¾ pound small mushrooms, wiped clean and trimmed
1½ cups dry French bread crumbs
Salt

DIPPING SAUCE:
1 cup mayonnaise (page 69), substituting hearty prepared mustard for the dry mustard
1 tablespoon drained and chopped capers

*Take the extra
time to prepare
homemade
mayonnaise for the
sauce. The subtle
flavor of the
crusted
mushrooms is best
complemented by
a mayonnaise of
the highest quality.*

Mix flour and salt in a small bowl. Whisk in egg and beer until batter is fairly smooth. Let stand at room temperature 1 hour.

In a deep pan or electric fryer, heat oil to 375 degrees. Dip dry mushrooms into batter, then roll in bread crumbs. Fry in small batches about 2 minutes per batch, turning once, until golden brown and crisp. Drain on paper towels. Sprinkle with salt. Serve hot with Dipping Sauce.

For Dipping Sauce: Combine mayonnaise and capers in a small bowl.

NOTE: As a first course, serve on small salad plates garnished with watercress or parsley and accompanied by Dipping Sauce.

To vary, the batter-and-crumb coating can also be used to fry wedges of yellow onion and green pepper, parsley sprigs, green beans, or small eggplant rounds.

2.
Trout
etching, printed à la poupée

Teriyaki Chicken Wings

Serves 8

MARINADE:
½ cup soy sauce
1 tablespoon dry sherry
1 teaspoon honey
4 green onions, minced (including green portion)
1 tablespoon minced fresh ginger root
2 cloves garlic, minced

2 pounds chicken wing drummettes

½ cup cornstarch (optional method)
2 cups peanut oil for frying (optional method)

Combine marinade ingredients, add chicken wings, and marinate at least 2 hours at room temperature, or overnight in the refrigerator.

Drain and discard the marinade. For a softer-textured appetizer, place wings, not touching each other, in a shallow baking pan and bake in a preheated 400 degree oven for 20 minutes, turning once after 15 minutes.

For a crisper texture, place several tablespoons of cornstarch in a plastic bag, add the marinated wings two at a time, and shake until wings are well coated. Shake off excess. Heat peanut oil to 375 degrees. Fry wings a few at a time in oil for about 5 minutes, turning to brown evenly. Drain well on a wire rack or paper towels.

Serve warm or at room temperature.

Potstickers

*Makes about
24 appetizers*

FILLING:
½ pound Chinese (Napa) cabbage, finely shredded
½ teaspoon salt
1 cup (½ pound) lean ground pork
1 green onion, minced (including green portion)
1½ teaspoons minced fresh ginger root
1½ teaspoons soy sauce
1 teaspoon water
½ teaspoon dry sherry
½ teaspoon sesame oil*

DOUGH:
2 cups all-purpose flour
½ cup cold water
¾ cup boiling water

DIPPING SAUCE:
3 tablespoons soy sauce
1 teaspoon rice wine vinegar*
1 teaspoon chili oil†*
¼ teaspoon sesame oil*
¼ teaspoon salt
4 cloves garlic, minced

*The unusual
method for
making the dough
for these
potstickers
partially cooks the
flour before
steaming.*

To prepare Filling: Bring 1 quart water to a boil in a 2-quart saucepan. Add shredded cabbage and salt. Return to a boil, then reduce heat and simmer for 5 minutes. Drain cabbage, rinse in cold water, and squeeze out moisture. With hands, combine cabbage with remaining filling ingredients and refrigerate for at least 30 minutes.

Meanwhile, to prepare Dough: In a food processor, mix 1 cup of the flour with ½ cup cold water. Process until dough forms a sticky ball. Remove dough and set aside. Place remaining 1 cup of flour in the same work bowl, add ¾ cup boiling water, and process until dough ball forms. Add the cold-water dough and process until a soft dough is formed. Place dough on a generously floured surface and knead briefly until smooth. Cover with a damp cloth and let rest 15 minutes.

To prepare Dipping Sauce: Combine all sauce ingredients in a small bowl and set aside.

continued

To assemble: Pinch off a walnut-sized piece of dough and pat into a 3-inch circle, or roll out on a floured surface. Place a generous teaspoon of filling in the center of the pancake. Fold the pancake in a semicircle and press the edges together to seal. Continue until all of the dough and filling are used.

Place a metal colander or steaming rack in a Dutch oven; add boiling water to just below the base of the colander. In batches, arrange the pastries in the colander so they do not touch each other. Cover and steam for 10 minutes, keeping the water at a constant simmer.

Meanwhile, preheat a heavy skillet over medium heat. Carefully transfer steamed potstickers from the colander to the dry, heated skillet and lightly fry until brown on both sides.

Serve hot or warm with Dipping Sauce.

N O T E : Potstickers may be frozen after steaming, but before browning. Freeze individually on trays, then wrap when frozen. Thaw, and brown in skillet.

†To prepare your own chili oil, heat ¼ cup peanut oil until nearly smoking. Cool 5 seconds, then add ¼ cup crushed red pepper and ½ teaspoon salt.

Remove from heat and stir well. Cool and strain before adding to sauce. Keeps indefinitely.

* Available at oriental markets and well-stocked supermarkets.

Stuffed Potato Crisps

Makes 24 slices

6 extra-large Russet potatoes, scrubbed and dried
⅓ to ½ cup melted butter
1 cup (about 3 ounces) freshly grated Parmesan cheese
8 strips bacon, crisply fried and crumbled
Freshly ground black pepper

2 tablespoons snipped fresh chives for garnish

Preheat oven to 425 degrees.

Cut small slits in the potatoes in several places to allow steam to escape during baking. Bake for 1 hour, or until tender; cool. Quarter the potatoes into lengthwise wedges. With a spoon, scrape away most of the potato pulp, leaving a thin layer of pulp attached to the skin. Reserve pulp for another use.

In a shallow baking dish, place the shells skin side down. Drizzle with melted butter. Sprinkle evenly with cheese, bacon, and pepper.

Bake about 15 minutes, or until cheese is melted and golden, and the skins are crisp.

Garnish with snipped chives.

N O T E : Reserved pulp can be baked in a small casserole, topped in the same manner as the skins, and served as a side dish.

Andouille, Chard, and Sun-dried Tomato Frittata

Makes 12 wedges

1 andouille sausage (about 6 ounces), cut in ¼-inch dice*
1 bunch (approximately ¾ pound) fresh chard
¼ cup olive oil
½ pound mushrooms, sliced
½ cup chopped onion
10 sun-dried tomatoes, packed in olive oil, drained and chopped*
6 eggs
¾ cup (about 2¼ ounces) freshly grated Parmesan cheese
2 cloves garlic, minced
½ teaspoon dried basil
¼ teaspoon dried marjoram
1 cup (about 4 ounces) grated mozzarella cheese
¼ cup (about ¾ ounce) freshly grated Parmesan cheese

Spicy andouille sausage is of Cajun origin. Here in the East Bay, some restaurants and specialty food shops fly in fresh andouille from Louisiana, or offer an excellent locally made version.

Preheat oven to 350 degrees. Butter a 9½-inch deep-dish pie pan.

In a large skillet, brown sausage over medium heat. Remove and drain on paper towels. Pour off any fat from skillet.

Remove and discard center stem from chard leaves. Coarsely chop the leaves.

In the same skillet, heat olive oil until a light haze forms. Add chard and cook 1 to 2 minutes, stirring constantly. Add mushrooms and onion and sauté until onion is translucent. Remove skillet from heat and add tomatoes and sausage. Set aside.

In a large bowl, combine eggs, ¾ cup Parmesan, and seasonings. Add sausage-chard mixture and blend. Turn into prepared pie pan and sprinkle with mozzarella and remaining Parmesan cheese.

Bake for 25 minutes, or until set. To serve, cool 10 minutes, then cut in wedges.

*Available at specialty food stores and well-stocked supermarkets.

Koenigsberger Klopse

Makes about 4 dozen meatballs

A dry Gewürztraminer is suggested.

MEATBALLS:

½ cup finely chopped onions
1 tablespoon butter
¾ pound lean ground beef
¼ pound lean ground lamb
2 slices multi-grain bread, crumbed
1 egg
2 tablespoons finely chopped fresh parsley
1 tablespoon chopped drained capers
1½ teaspoons anchovy paste
½ teaspoon finely grated lemon peel
½ teaspoon salt
¼ teaspoon freshly ground black pepper

POACHING LIQUID:

2 quarts water
1 medium onion, peeled and studded with 8 cloves
1 bay leaf
1 teaspoon salt

SAUCE:

¼ cup butter
¼ cup all-purpose flour
3 tablespoons fresh lemon juice
2 egg yolks

To prepare Meatballs: In a small skillet, sauté onion in butter for about 5 minutes. Cool. Mix with remaining meatball ingredients. Shape in 1-inch balls.

To prepare Poaching Liquid: Combine ingredients. Boil, uncovered, for 10 minutes. Remove and discard onion.

To poach Meatballs: Reduce heat to medium; add meatballs and poach about 5 minutes. Remove meatballs with a slotted spoon. Strain liquid; cool slightly, and skim and discard fat. Set aside.

continued

To prepare Sauce: In a 2-quart saucepan, combine butter and flour, stirring and cooking until bubbly, but not browned. Add 3 cups of the poaching liquid, stirring constantly. Bring to a boil, stirring until thickened. Reduce heat and add lemon juice. Beat egg yolks. Add ¼ cup of hot sauce to the yolks, then add yolk mixture back to the sauce, stirring vigorously until well blended. Add meatballs and simmer until heated through.

Serve hot with toothpicks or skewers.

NOTE: Suitable as a first course or entrée, this variation of German poached meatballs substitutes lamb for the more typical pork. To prepare as an entrée, make meatballs about 1¼ inches in diameter. Do not add chopped capers; add them whole to the sauce instead. Poach meatballs 7 minutes. Serve over steamed white rice tossed with chopped fresh parsley. Serves 4 to 6.

Koenigsberger Klopse can be prepared a day in advance and reheated when ready to serve.

Dolmas Shulamith

Narsai M. David, Narsai's Restaurant and Market, Kensington

Makes about 50 appetizers

A Grey Riesling is suggested.

DOLMAS:

1½	pounds lean lamb, cut in ½-inch dice
¼	cup butter
⅔	cup raw pearl rice
1	cup chopped onion
¾	cup chopped leeks (including green portion)
½	cup stemmed and chopped fresh parsley
¼	cup minced green bell pepper
2	tablespoons snipped fresh dill
2 to 3	cloves garlic, finely minced
	Salt and freshly ground black pepper
1	jar (16 ounces) grape leaves*

	Lettuce or cabbage leaves
¾	cup water or lamb broth
	Juice of 1 lemon

TOMATO BUTTER SAUCE:

1	small onion, minced
2	cloves garlic, minced
¼	cup butter
1	can (6 ounces) tomato paste
2	tablespoons water

Plain yogurt for garnish

While growing up, Narsai David enjoyed the rich and spicy taste of the Assyrian food his mother prepared. Now his restaurant and market reflect this culinary heritage as well as the influence of France and other countries. Shulamith is his mother's name.

To prepare Dolmas: In a medium skillet, sauté the lamb in butter, stirring occasionally, until cubes are lightly browned. Remove from heat and add rice, onion, leeks, parsley, green pepper, dill weed, garlic, salt and pepper. Stir to combine.

Rinse the grape leaves. Place about 1 tablespoon of filling in each grape leaf and roll up, folding ends in, like an envelope.

Preheat oven to 350 degrees.

Line a shallow baking pan, 9- by 13-inches, with lettuce or cabbage leaves. Arrange the rolled dolmas, seam side down, in the prepared pan. Combine water or lamb broth and lemon juice. Pour over dolmas. Cover the rolls with a layer of lettuce or cabbage leaves. Then cover the entire baking pan tightly with aluminum foil. Bake for 75 to 90 minutes, or until the liquid is absorbed.

Discard the lettuce or cabbage covering and lining.

continued

To prepare Tomato Butter Sauce: In a small skillet, sauté the onion and garlic in butter until onion is soft. Remove from heat and whisk in tomato paste and water.

To serve, spoon yogurt and Tomato Butter Sauce over dolmas, or pass the sauce separately. Serve dolmas hot.

*Available at specialty food stores and well-stocked supermarkets.

Italian Fried Cheese with Tomato Sauce

Serves 6

1 cup fine dry bread crumbs
¼ teaspoon dried thyme
¼ teaspoon salt
⅛ teaspoon freshly ground black pepper
1 pound piece mozzarella cheese
3 eggs, beaten
⅓ cup all-purpose flour

TOMATO SAUCE:

1 tablespoon olive oil
6 to 8 ripe tomatoes (about 2½ pounds), peeled, seeded, and coarsely chopped, or 1 can (28 ounces) Italian plum tomatoes, mashed with juices
2 tablespoons chopped fresh basil, or ½ teaspoon dried
1 tablespoon dried oregano, crumbled
½ teaspoon sugar
¼ teaspoon salt
¼ teaspoon freshly ground black pepper

Vegetable oil for frying

Fresh basil leaves for garnish

Combine bread crumbs, thyme, salt, and pepper on a plate.

Cut cheese in 12 equal pieces, about 2½- by 2½- by ½-inches. Dip each piece in egg, then flour, then egg again, then in crumb mixture. Place on a plate, cover lightly with waxed paper, and refrigerate for at least 1 hour, or overnight.

Meanwhile, to prepare Tomato Sauce: In a 2-quart saucepan, combine olive oil, tomatoes, basil, oregano, sugar, salt, and pepper. Simmer, uncovered, for about 2 hours (1 hour if using canned tomatoes), or until sauce is thick.

In a large skillet, add vegetable oil to a depth of ¼ inch; heat the oil until it begins to ripple in the pan. Fry cheese pieces, not touching each other, until brown, about 2 minutes. Turn and continue to fry until brown on the second side and cheese begins to ooze slightly from the sides. Turn only once. Drain on paper towels.

Serve on warm plates, covered with a generous portion of Tomato Sauce. Garnish with basil leaves.

Tiropeta Petris

Senator Nicholas C. and Mrs. Anna S. Petris, Oakland

Serves 12

A Sauvignon Blanc is suggested.

12 sheets phyllo pastry (see Note)*
1 pound feta cheese, finely crumbled
4 ounces grated dry ricotta or dry Jack cheese
4 ounces grated Kasseri or Romano cheese
1½ cups butter, melted
8 eggs, beaten
3 cups milk

Ground nutmeg or paprika for garnish (optional)

Each year, Anna Petris sends a Christmas card with a recipe. This one, from 1982, is a version of tiropeta she discovered while visiting family in Greece.

Butter a 9- by 13-inch baking pan.

Combine the cheeses in a bowl.

Brush 1 sheet of phyllo completely with melted butter. Place a second sheet of phyllo on top of the first sheet and brush with butter. Sprinkle with about ⅓ cup of the cheeses. With one hand at each short end, lift the 2 sheets at the edges and softly gather the phyllo lengthwise (like tissue paper). Carefully lift the bundle into the prepared pan, bending ends to fit. Repeat with remaining phyllo, pushing tightly together to fit in one layer in the pan. Sprinkle any remaining cheese over the top.

Beat eggs and milk together. Pour as much of the mixture as possible over the casserole. Let stand at least 15 minutes. Add any remaining egg-milk mixture. Sprinkle with nutmeg or paprika, if desired.

Preheat oven to 350 degrees.

Bake immediately or refrigerate, covered, overnight.

Bake 45 to 50 minutes (longer if refrigerated), or until puffed, brown, and sizzling around the edges.

Cool at least 10 minutes before cutting in 12 rectangles.

N O T E : Phyllo must be thawed overnight in the refrigerator before using.

* Phyllo pastry, also called strudel leaves, is available in the freezer case of well-stocked supermarkets, and at specialty food stores.

Lobster Tails in Champagne Sauce

Serves 6

Champagne is suggested.

3 lobster tails (about 8 ounces each)
⅔ cup champagne or sparkling white wine
2 green onions, minced (including green portion)
¼ teaspoon salt
¼ cup whipping cream
¼ cup butter, cut in pieces

2 green onions, slivered, for garnish

Rinse lobster tails. Arrange tails side by side in a small skillet, meat side down. Add champagne, minced green onions, and salt. Bring to a boil, then reduce heat and simmer, covered, for 15 minutes. Remove lobster tails with tongs and set aside to cool slightly. Add cream to the skillet and return to a boil. Boil vigorously until liquid is reduced to approximately ½ cup. Stir occasionally.

Meanwhile, remove lobster meat from shells and cut in medallions about ⅓ inch thick. Arrange in an attractive fashion on individual plates.

When sauce is reduced, whisk in butter, one piece at a time.

To serve, spoon sauce over lobster medallions and garnish with slivers of green onion. Serve immediately.

Mussels with Cream and Tarragon

Joseph Phelps, Joseph Phelps Vineyards, St. Helena

Serves 3 to 4

Joseph Phelps suggests a barrel-fermented California Chardonnay.

12 to 16   mussels (small preferred), scrubbed and debearded
¼   cup white wine
3   tablespoons finely chopped shallots
1   tablespoon fresh tarragon (optional, and may be omitted if not available)
3   tablespoons butter
    Fish stock or bottled clam juice
½ to ¾   cup whipping cream, or a mixture of whipping cream and crème fraîche (page 167)
    Salt and ground white pepper

Finely chopped tangerine or orange peel for garnish
Chopped fresh Italian parsley for garnish

At a New York restaurant, Joseph Phelps, a California vintner and proprietor of the acclaimed Oakville Grocery, was treated to an appetizer not listed on the menu— cold mussels in mustard sauce. At home in St. Helena, he tried to re-create the New York dish only to discover most mustards were too strongly flavored for California mussels. This recipe is Mr. Phelps's unique solution.

Place mussels in a large sauté pan with wine. Cover and steam for 4 to 5 minutes until mussels begin to open. Using tongs, remove mussels as they open and place in a bowl to collect residual liquids. Discard any mussels which fail to open after a reasonable time.

Strain liquid remaining in sauté pan into a bowl and reserve. Using the same pan, sauté shallots and tarragon in butter until shallots are translucent. Combine reserved steaming liquids in a measuring cup. If liquids equal less than ¾ cup, add fish stock or clam juice to make up the difference. Add the liquid to the shallots, raise heat to medium-high, and reduce to one-half volume. Raise to high heat, add cream (use ½ cup if using 12 mussels), and stir. As reduction approaches desired consistency, return mussels to sauté pan for 2 to 3 minutes, ladling sauce over the open shells. Season with salt and ground white pepper.

Serve in soup bowls, garnished with a very light sprinkling of tangerine or orange peel and chopped Italian parsley.

Fettuccine with Smoked Poussin

Joseph Phelps, Joseph Phelps Vineyards, St. Helena

Serves 4

Joseph Phelps suggests a Napa Valley Sauvignon Blanc.

4 ounces dried fettuccine
3 tablespoons finely chopped shallots (about 2 large cloves)
3 tablespoons butter
½ cup dry white wine, or ¼ to ⅜ cup dry Amontillado or similar sherry
½ to ¾ cup whipping cream
½ to ¾ cup shredded lean white and dark meat of smoked poussin (see Note)*
¼ cup thinly sliced chanterelles or shiitake mushrooms (see Note)
¼ cup grated Italian Fontina, Monterey Jack, or other mild cheese

Slivers of sweet red bell pepper, or sliced ripe cherry tomatoes for garnish
1 tablespoon chopped fresh Italian parsley for garnish

Cook fettuccine in boiling, salted water until just tender; drain. While pasta is cooking, sauté shallots in butter in a medium saucepan until translucent. Add white wine and increase heat. When liquid is reduced by half, add whipping cream, stirring constantly until ingredients reach a low boil. Stir in shredded poussin, sliced mushrooms, and grated cheese.

When cheese melts and sauce is well blended, turn off heat and toss with freshly cooked pasta.

Serve in warm bowls garnished with slivers of red pepper or cherry tomatoes, and chopped Italian parsley.

NOTE: Poussins are very young birds, usually weighing approximately 1 pound.

If chanterelles or shiitake mushrooms are not available, do not substitute domestic mushrooms, as it is difficult to control the consistency of the sauce as they release their water.

*Available at poultry markets and some specialty food stores.

CHAPTER TWO

Soups

Chilled Cream of Lettuce and Pea Soup

Serves 6

1 large potato, peeled and sliced
1 onion, sliced
3 cups chicken stock
1 large head iceberg lettuce, cut in chunks
1½ to 2 cups fresh peas, or 1 package (10 ounces) frozen peas
2 tablespoons snipped fresh chives
1 cup half-and-half
   Juice of 1 large lemon (about ¼ cup)
   Salt and freshly ground black pepper

Lemon slices or snipped fresh chives for garnish

Cold soups are refreshing as a first course during the warm summer months. Since they can be made ahead, they free the cook from last minute preparation. An unexpected blend of iceberg lettuce and peas infuses this cold cream soup with a delicate and unusual flavor.

In a large saucepan, simmer potato and onion in stock until just tender, about 5 minutes. Add lettuce, peas, and chives and simmer, covered, until lettuce is just tender and still green, 3 to 4 minutes. Cool. Blend in half-and-half, lemon juice, salt, and pepper. In a food processor or blender, puree until smooth (in batches, if necessary). Chill until ready to serve. Adjust seasonings.

Serve ice cold, garnished with a thin slice of lemon or snipped fresh chives.

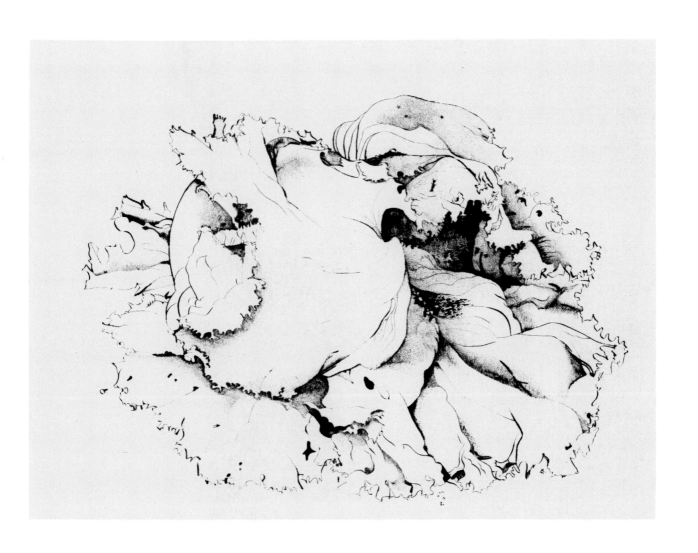

3.
Lea's Lettuce
drypoint

Chilled Cucumber Soup

Serves 8

2 cups chicken stock
3 cucumbers, peeled, seeded, and sliced
1 tablespoon chopped onion
1 teaspoon snipped fresh dill, or ½ teaspoon dried
　Salt and freshly ground black pepper
2 cups plain yogurt
½ cup finely chopped walnuts

　Thin slices of unpeeled cucumber and snipped fresh dill for garnish

In a 4-quart saucepan, combine stock, cucumbers, and onion. Bring to a boil; reduce heat and simmer until cucumbers are just tender, about 5 to 7 minutes. Cool.

In a food processor or blender, puree soup, dill, salt, and pepper until smooth (in batches, if necessary). Add yogurt and walnuts. Chill and adjust seasonings.

Serve cold, garnished with paper-thin slices of cucumber and snipped fresh dill.

Carrot Soup

Serves 8 to 10

3 tablespoons butter
2 pounds carrots, chopped
2 large onions, chopped
1 potato, peeled and chopped
1 bay leaf
6 cups chicken stock
Salt and ground white pepper

Minced fresh parsley or mint for garnish
Sour cream for garnish

In a Dutch oven or large saucepan, melt butter and cook carrots and onions over low heat, covered, about 8 minutes. Add potato, bay leaf, and stock. Simmer, covered, 40 minutes, stirring occasionally. Discard bay leaf. In a food processor or blender, puree soup (in batches, if necessary). Return to pan and season with salt and pepper.

Serve hot. Garnish each portion with minced parsley or mint, and a spoonful of sour cream.

Zucchini Soup

Serves 6 to 8

2 onions, chopped
½ cup butter
5 to 6 small zucchini, sliced
1 teaspoon salt
3 cups chicken stock (more may be necessary to thin soup)
Juice of one-half lemon (about 2 tablespoons)
Salt and freshly ground black pepper

Lemon slices for garnish

In a 4- to 6-quart saucepan, sauté onions in butter until translucent. Add zucchini and 1 teaspoon salt and sauté 1 minute. Add chicken stock and simmer, covered, 15 minutes. In a food processor or blender, puree until smooth (in batches, if necessary). Add more stock if soup is too thick. Season with lemon juice, salt, and pepper.

Serve hot or cold, with a lemon slice on the bottom of each bowl.

Tomato and Basil Soup

Serves 4 to 6

1 large onion, coarsely chopped
1 carrot, grated
¼ cup butter
5 medium ripe tomatoes (about 1½ pounds), peeled and quartered
¼ cup finely chopped fresh basil leaves (about ½ cup packed whole leaves)
1 teaspoon salt
½ teaspoon freshly ground black pepper
¾ teaspoon sugar
2 cups chicken stock

Tomatoes and basil are frequently paired in cooking, and are best enjoyed in the summer months when both are abundant. Basil, while still on the stem, can be stored in the refrigerator for several days if set in a glass of water and covered with a plastic bag. Never refrigerate tomatoes as chilling prevents them from fully ripening.

In a 2-quart saucepan, sauté onion and carrot in butter until onion is soft. Stir in tomatoes, basil, salt, pepper, and sugar. Cover and simmer 15 minutes. Puree in a blender until smooth. Return the puree to the saucepan, add chicken stock, and reheat.

Tomato, Corn, and Okra Soup

Mark Charles Miller, former Chef and Owner, Fourth Street Grill, Berkeley

Serves 6

    1 large white onion, thinly sliced
    4 large cloves garlic, finely minced
    ½ cup virgin olive oil
    6 large, vine-ripened tomatoes, cut in large cubes
    ½ pound fresh okra, stems removed, cut in ½-inch rounds
    6 cups rich chicken stock
    Salt, freshly ground black pepper, and Tabasco sauce
2 to 3 ears Silver Queen or other fresh corn, kernels cut from cob

Finely chopped fresh parsley for garnish

The combination of the seasonal flavors and textures of tomatoes, corn, and okra, all traditionally American vegetables, makes this soup special.

In a 6- to 8-quart saucepan, cook onion and garlic in oil over low heat for 15 minutes. Do not brown onion or garlic. Add the tomatoes, okra, and stock. Cook 15 to 20 minutes. Season with salt, pepper, and Tabasco. Cook 5 minutes; add corn. Cook 3 to 4 minutes more.

Serve garnished with chopped parsley.

Russian Cabbage Soup

Serves 6

A hearty Burgundy is suggested.

SOUP:

5 cups chicken stock
4 celery stalks, thinly sliced
1 large potato, cut in ¼-inch dice (peeling optional)
1 large onion, coarsely chopped
1 large carrot, thinly sliced
4 fresh parsley sprigs

CABBAGE ROLLS:

4 to 5 large cabbage leaves
1 slice bread, crumbed
2 tablespoons water
¼ pound ground veal or lamb
1 egg, beaten
½ teaspoon dried marjoram, crumbled
½ teaspoon dried thyme, crumbled
   Freshly ground black pepper

1 ripe tomato, peeled, seeded, and chopped
½ cup (about 1½ ounces) freshly grated Parmesan cheese

To prepare Soup: Bring stock, celery, potato, onion, carrot, and parsley to a boil. Reduce heat and simmer 20 minutes. While soup simmers, prepare Cabbage Rolls.

Preheat oven to 350 degrees.

To prepare Cabbage Rolls: Cook cabbage leaves in boiling, salted water until limp, about 5 minutes. Drain, rinse, and dry the leaves. Trim away the thick rib from each leaf, and cut the leaves in quarters.

Mix bread crumbs and water; let stand 5 minutes. Combine crumbs, ground meat, egg, and seasonings. Place 1 teaspoon stuffing mixture in the middle of each cabbage leaf quarter. Fold ends in to form an envelope. Place cabbage rolls, seam side down, in a large, deep baking dish. Cover with soup and chopped tomato. Bake 10 minutes. Sprinkle with cheese and broil for 3 minutes, or until cheese is lightly browned.

Serve in large, shallow soup bowls, with the cabbage rolls evenly divided among the servings.

Vegetable Cheddar Chowder

Serves 6 to 8

10 slices bacon, chopped
2 medium onions, coarsely chopped
3 large carrots, coarsely chopped
3 medium potatoes, peeled and diced
2½ cups chicken stock
1 cup milk
3 cups (about 12 ounces) grated Cheddar cheese
3 tablespoons all-purpose flour
Salt and freshly ground black pepper

Chopped fresh parsley for garnish

In a 4-quart saucepan, cook bacon until crisp. Remove bacon and set aside. Drain off all but 2 tablespoons drippings. Sauté onions in drippings until translucent. Add bacon, carrots, potatoes, and stock. Bring to a boil, reduce heat, cover, and simmer 15 minutes, or until potatoes are tender. Stir in milk. Toss together cheese and flour until cheese is coated. Add to soup and stir until cheese melts. Season with salt and pepper.

Garnish each serving with chopped parsley.

Artichoke Soup with Mushrooms and Shrimp

Serves 6 to 8

 2 cans (8½ ounces each) water-packed artichoke hearts, drained
 ½ cup thinly sliced mushrooms
 2 tablespoons finely chopped onion
 3 tablespoons butter
 2 tablespoons all-purpose flour
 2 cups chicken stock
2½ cups half-and-half
 ¼ cup white wine
 ½ teaspoon salt
 1 cup (about ½ pound) tiny cooked shrimp

Chop artichoke hearts. Set aside.

In a 2-quart saucepan, sauté mushrooms and onion in butter for 5 minutes. Stir in flour and cook over medium heat 2 or 3 minutes. Add stock slowly, stirring until thickened. Stir in cream, wine, and salt. Reduce heat and cook until soup thickens slightly. Add shrimp and artichokes; cook 1 to 2 minutes more, or until soup is heated through.

Cream of Mushroom Soup

Serves 8

A dry Riesling is suggested.

¼ cup chopped onion
3 tablespoons butter
3 tablespoons all-purpose flour
6 cups chicken stock
   Salt and freshly ground black pepper
3 tablespoons butter
¾ pound mushrooms, sliced
1 teaspoon fresh lemon juice
   Salt
½ to ¾ cup whipping cream
2 egg yolks

Lightly toasted sliced almonds for garnish†
Chopped fresh parsley for garnish

Select firm mushrooms with round caps completely connected to the stem, and with no gills showing. As mushrooms age, caps and stems separate.

In a 6- to 8-quart saucepan, gently sauté onion in 3 tablespoons butter over medium heat until translucent. Add flour and stir 2 to 3 minutes. Do not brown. While onion is cooking, bring chicken stock to a boil. Remove onion from heat, whisk in boiling stock, and blend thoroughly. Season with salt and pepper. Simmer, partially covered, for 25 minutes.

In a large skillet, melt 3 tablespoons butter. Add mushrooms, lemon juice, and salt. Cover and cook slowly 5 minutes. Add mushrooms and their liquid to soup base; simmer 10 minutes. Beat cream and egg yolks together. Remove 2 tablespoons hot soup to a small bowl; stir in egg yolks and cream. Add 2 more tablespoons soup and stir. Pour egg mixture into soup, stirring constantly; heat gently, but do not boil.

Serve garnished with almonds and parsley.

†Toast almonds in a 325 degree oven 5 to 10 minutes, or until lightly browned. Cool.

Red Onion Soup

Serves 6

¼ cup butter
1½ pounds (about 6 to 8 cups) red onions, thinly sliced
1 cup thinly sliced celery
1 teaspoon salt
¼ teaspoon ground white pepper
¼ teaspoon ground nutmeg
2 cups chicken stock
2 cups half-and-half

Snipped fresh chives for garnish

In a 4-quart saucepan, melt butter and cook onions and celery over very low heat, covered, until soft, about 30 minutes. Add salt, pepper, nutmeg, and stock. Bring to a boil, reduce heat, and simmer, uncovered, about 15 minutes, or until vegetables are very tender. In a food processor or blender, puree soup (in batches, if necessary).

Return soup to saucepan and add half-and-half. Simmer, stirring frequently, 10 minutes.

CHAPTER THREE

Salads

Salad Miramonte

Serves 4 to 6

DRESSING:

- ¾ cup vegetable oil
- 3 tablespoons fresh lemon juice
- 2 cloves garlic, bruised
- Salt and freshly ground black pepper

- 1 to 2 heads romaine lettuce, torn in bite-sized pieces
- 4 slices bacon, crisply fried and crumbled
- 10 ripe cherry tomatoes, stemmed and halved
- 1 cup (4 ounces) grated Swiss cheese
- ⅓ cup (about 1 ounce) freshly grated Parmesan cheese

- ⅔ cup toasted slivered almonds†
- 1 cup French bread croutons†

In a small bowl, combine dressing ingredients. Allow flavors to blend at room temperature for at least 3 hours. Discard garlic cloves.

At serving time, toss the salad ingredients in a large bowl with the dressing. Add almonds and croutons and toss again.

†Toast slivered almonds in a 325 degree oven for 10 minutes, or until lightly browned. Cool.

To make croutons, sauté 1 cup French bread cubes (¾-inch cubes) in 2 tablespoons butter with 1 clove minced garlic until crisp. Spread on paper towels to cool.

Gorgonzola and Walnut Salad

Serves 6 to 8

DRESSING:

1 tablespoon Dijon-style mustard
3 tablespoons white wine vinegar
1 tablespoon fresh lemon juice
½ cup walnut oil
¼ teaspoon salt
¼ teaspoon freshly ground black pepper

1 head romaine lettuce, torn in bite-sized pieces
½ pound Gorgonzola or other blue-veined cheese, crumbled
1 cup coarsely chopped walnuts
1 Red Delicious apple

Put all dressing ingredients in a jar. Cover securely and shake until slightly thickened, creamy, and well combined. Set aside.

In a salad bowl, place lettuce, cheese, and walnuts. Slice the unpeeled apple into the salad. Add enough dressing to just coat the leaves. Toss and serve.

NOTE: Gorgonzola is a semisoft Italian blue cheese.

Tossed Green Salad with Potatoes and Croutons

Serves 8

DRESSING:

½ cup vegetable oil
Juice of 1 large lemon (about ¼ cup)
1 egg
½ teaspoon Worcestershire sauce
1 to 2 cloves garlic, minced
1 teaspoon salt
⅛ teaspoon freshly ground black pepper

1½ pounds baking potatoes (Russet) or new potatoes
1 to 2 cups Croutons (recipe follows)
1 head romaine lettuce, torn in bite-sized pieces
¼ cup chopped green onions (including green portion)
½ cup (1½ ounces) freshly grated Parmesan cheese

Croutons are small cubes of bread sautéed in oil or toasted in the oven. Homemade croutons are simple to prepare and always taste better than store-bought.

Combine dressing ingredients and set aside.

Boil potatoes in their jackets until just tender when pierced with the tip of a sharp knife. Drain and let rest until cool enough to handle, then peel and cut in 1- to 1½-inch dice. Pour dressing over potatoes while they are still warm. Stir to coat, and refrigerate, covered, overnight or longer. The potatoes will absorb most of the dressing.

Prepare Croutons at least 3 hours in advance of assembling the salad.

At serving time, place potato mixture in a large bowl. Add romaine, onions, and cheese; toss well. Add Croutons and toss again.

CROUTONS:

2 cups cubed French bread, crusts removed
⅓ to ½ cup olive oil
1 large clove garlic, bruised

On a cookie sheet, bake the bread cubes for 30 minutes in a 200 degree oven. Place in jar with olive oil and garlic; cover and shake to coat. Rotate jar every hour or so for at least 3 hours to ensure even coverage of the bread cubes. Discard garlic clove. Croutons will keep at room temperature for weeks.

Coleslaw

Serves 8

DRESSING:

DRESSING:
¾ cup mayonnaise (page 69)
¼ cup sour cream
Juice of 1 large lemon (about ¼ cup)
¼ cup sugar
½ teaspoon salt

1 medium cabbage, shredded
2 carrots, cut in julienne
1 green bell pepper, cored, seeded, and cut in julienne
5 green onions, minced (including green portion)
½ cup dry-roasted peanuts

In the 1700s, Dutch settlers were firmly established on the banks of the Hudson River. From their kitchens came such specialties as oliebollen *(later called dumplings),* koekje *(cookies),* pannekoeken *(now called pancakes), and* cool sla *(literally cabbage salad, but corrupted in spelling and pronunciation to* coleslaw*).*

Mix dressing ingredients together thoroughly.

Combine all slaw ingredients in a large bowl. Pour dressing over salad and toss well to coat. Cover and refrigerate several hours. Drain off most of the dressing before serving.

Serve chilled.

NOTE: The dressing is also delicious served over cold blanched asparagus.

Caesar Spinach Salad with Croutons

Serves 4 to 6

DRESSING:

1 egg
Juice of 1 large lemon (about ¼ cup)
2 cloves garlic
1 teaspoon Worcestershire sauce
½ teaspoon salt
½ teaspoon freshly ground black pepper
½ cup olive oil

2 bunches (about 2 pounds) fresh spinach, washed, trimmed, dried, and torn in bite-sized pieces
1 red onion, thinly sliced in rings

Croutons (page 50)
½ cup (about 1½ ounces) freshly grated Romano cheese

Sometime during the 1920s in his Tijuana, Mexico, restaurant, Caesar Cardini first served the toss of romaine lettuce, browned croutons, and tangy dressing that now bears his name. It was an instant hit. Today, Cardini's culinary namesake is as popular as ever. In 1984 Tijuana held its first Caesar Salad celebration. In this variation, the familiar Caesar dressing coats dark green spinach leaves and red onion rings.

In a food processor or blender combine egg, lemon juice, garlic, Worcestershire sauce, salt, and pepper. Process to mince garlic. With machine at high speed, add oil in a very thin, continuous stream until oil is incorporated and dressing thickens. Refrigerate if not using immediately.

When ready to serve, combine the spinach leaves and red onion in a large bowl. Pour dressing over and toss well to coat. Add Croutons and grated cheese and toss again.

4.
Torpedo Onions
color pencil

Spinach Salad with Sweet and Sour Dressing

Serves 8 to 10

DRESSING:

1¼ cups vegetable oil

½ to ¾ cup confectioners' sugar

¼ cup apple cider vinegar

1 tablespoon fresh lemon juice

1½ teaspoons dry mustard

1½ teaspoons paprika

½ teaspoon salt

½ teaspoon ground ginger

2 pounds (about 2 bunches) fresh spinach, washed, trimmed, dried, and torn in bite-sized pieces

CHOOSE SEVERAL OF THE FOLLOWING:

½ pound bacon, crisply fried and crumbled

½ cup golden raisins

1½ cups Jerusalem artichokes, peeled and sliced (see Note)

⅓ cup thinly sliced green onions (including green portion)

2 tablespoons toasted sesame seeds†

3 red apples, cored and cut into bite-sized chunks

½ cup dry-roasted peanuts

Combine dressing ingredients and set aside.

At serving time, place spinach leaves in a large bowl. Add and toss several of the suggested salad ingredients. Toss with dressing and serve.

NOTE: Also called sunchokes or sun roots, Jerusalem artichokes are a tuber or root vegetable.

†Toast sesame seeds in a small skillet over medium heat for about 10 minutes, or until golden, shaking pan frequently. Cool.

Mixed Vegetable Salad

Serves 6

1 pound green beans, trimmed, cut in 2-inch lengths, and cooked until just tender

4 carrots, sliced, and cooked until just tender

1 large onion, sliced

MARINADE:

1⅓ cups vegetable oil

⅔ cup apple cider vinegar

1 teaspoon salt

½ teaspoon freshly ground black pepper

DRESSING:

2 large ripe tomatoes, peeled, seeded, chopped, and drained

1 cup mayonnaise (page 69)

Romaine lettuce leaves for garnish

6 slices bacon, crisply fried and crumbled, for garnish

It is no longer necessary to "string" beans. New strains have been developed without the filament that once ran the length of the bean.

Combine cooked green beans and carrots in a large bowl with sliced onion. Set aside to cool while preparing marinade.

Combine marinade ingredients and pour over vegetables. Refrigerate at least 2 hours or overnight.

At serving time, drain and discard the marinade or reserve for another use. In a bowl, combine tomatoes and mayonnaise for dressing. Arrange the vegetables on a serving platter or in a bowl lined with lettuce leaves; sprinkle with bacon. Pass dressing separately.

Gazpacho Salad

Serves 6 to 8

DRESSING:

½ cup vegetable oil (or ¼ cup olive oil and ¼ cup vegetable oil)
Juice of 1 lime
1 large clove garlic, minced
1 tablespoon finely chopped white onion
1 to 2 teaspoons finely chopped cilantro leaves
¾ teaspoon salt
¼ teaspoon ground cayenne pepper
¼ teaspoon ground cumin
Freshly ground black pepper

1 large cucumber (peeled, if desired), sliced and quartered
1 small green bell pepper, cored, seeded, and cut in thin strips
3 medium ripe tomatoes, cut in chunks
1 large ripe avocado, peeled and cut in chunks
1½ cups (about 6 ounces) grated Monterey Jack cheese
1 can (4 ounces) sliced black olives, drained

Crushed tortilla chips for garnish

Gazpacho, the cold Spanish salad-soup, incorporates chopped fresh tomatoes, cucumbers, peppers, onion, garlic, and a variety of condiments; the mixture is often thickened with bread crumbs. Similar in flavor and equally fresh is this gazpacho salad, garnished with crushed tortilla chips.

Combine dressing ingredients.

Not more than 1 hour before serving, prepare salad ingredients. Just before serving, toss with dressing. Pass crushed tortilla chips for garnish.

Tomato Summer Salad

Serves 6 to 8

6 ripe tomatoes, each cut in 8 wedges
½ cup loosely packed fresh mint leaves, finely chopped
1 red onion, finely chopped
2 tablespoons vegetable oil
1 tablespoon white wine vinegar
2 cloves garlic, minced
1 teaspoon sugar
½ teaspoon salt

Place tomato wedges in bowl. Combine remaining ingredients and pour over tomatoes. Toss to coat. Chill, covered, several hours before serving.

Crunchy Pea Salad

Serves 6 to 8

2 cups shelled raw fresh peas (about 2 pounds unshelled)
1 cup finely chopped celery (including leafy tops, if desired)
1 cup salted dry-roasted peanuts
1 can (8 ounces) sliced water chestnuts, drained
½ cup sour cream
1 teaspoon Beau Monde seasoning
1 tablespoon soy sauce

In a salad bowl, toss together peas, celery, peanuts, and water chestnuts. Combine sour cream, Beau Monde, and soy sauce. Toss with salad ingredients and refrigerate, covered, several hours or overnight.

NOTE: Do not substitute frozen peas in this recipe. Thawed peas lack the crunch that makes this salad interesting.

Green Bean, Walnut, and Feta Salad

Serves 6

DRESSING:

¾ cup olive oil

½ cup loosely packed fresh mint leaves, finely chopped

¼ cup white wine vinegar

¾ teaspoon salt

½ teaspoon minced garlic

¼ teaspoon freshly ground black pepper

1½ pounds green beans, trimmed, halved, blanched, and patted dry

1 cup chopped toasted walnuts†

1 red onion, cut in rings and rings halved

1 cup crumbled feta cheese

½ cup peeled, seeded, diced cucumber

Imported feta is generally made from sheep's milk, aged sixty days, and stored in brine. The Bulgarian varieties tend to be the creamiest, followed by those made in Greece, Corsica, and Denmark. Romanian is usually the driest. Domestic varieties use cow's milk, but otherwise are made in the same way as imported feta.

Combine dressing ingredients.

In a serving bowl, combine beans with walnuts, onion ring halves, cheese, and cucumber. Pour dressing over salad; toss to coat thoroughly.

†Toast walnuts in a 300 degree oven for 10 minutes. Cool.

Greek Salad

Serves 4 to 6

DRESSING:
¼ cup olive oil
2 tablespoons fresh lemon juice
2 medium cloves garlic, minced
½ teaspoon dried tarragon or oregano
¼ teaspoon salt
⅛ teaspoon freshly ground black pepper
Mashed anchovy to taste (optional)

2 large ripe tomatoes, cut in ½-inch cubes
3 ounces Greek olives with pits
1 large cucumber, peeled and cut in ½-inch cubes
1 small green bell pepper, cut in julienne
3 ounces feta cheese, crumbled

Combine dressing ingredients.

Combine salad ingredients in a bowl. Toss with dressing and serve at room temperature.

Celery Root, Endive, and Watercress Salad

Mary Risley, Director of Tante Marie's Cooking School, San Francisco

Serves 8

DRESSING:

2 large shallots, minced
½ cup olive oil
2 tablespoons white wine vinegar
3 tablespoons mayonnaise (page 69)
1 tablespoon Dijon-style mustard
½ teaspoon salt
¼ teaspoon freshly ground black pepper

1 celery root (about 1 pound), peeled and cut in julienne
1 pound endive, cut in 1-inch pieces
2 bunches watercress, coarse stems removed and sprigs separated into bite-sized pieces

Celery root, or celeriac, is not the root of common celery, but a crop grown specifically for its large, brown-skinned, bulbous root. It can be eaten raw or cooked. This salad is best served in February when the freshest celery root and endive are available. Mary Risley likes the combination of textures and serves this salad after an entrée of lamb or roast chicken to "cleanse the palate and aid digestion."

Combine dressing ingredients and set aside until ready to serve.

Toss celery root, endive, and watercress in a bowl and refrigerate.

To serve, toss dressing with mixed vegetables.

Asparagus, Snow Pea, and Mushroom Salad

Serves 8 to 12

DRESSING:

¾ cup rice wine vinegar
½ cup soy sauce
¼ cup vegetable oil
2 slices (1 inch each) fresh ginger root
2 tablespoons sugar
1 large clove garlic, crushed
½ teaspoon freshly ground black pepper

2 pounds fresh asparagus, peeled
1 pound snow peas, stemmed and strings removed
1 pound enoki mushrooms (do not substitute)*

½ cup grated daikon radish for garnish*

The crunchy white enoki resembles a plump strand of spaghetti with a tiny button cap. Clusters of long-stemmed enokis are sold prepackaged at markets offering oriental foods. These mushrooms are best eaten raw, as they toughen when cooked.

Combine dressing ingredients in a small bowl and set aside.

Preheat oven to 350 degrees. Wrap asparagus securely in aluminum foil. Place on oven rack and bake 30 minutes. Remove from oven, open foil, and cool.

Meanwhile, blanch the snow peas 1 to 2 minutes in 1 cup boiling water. Drain and refresh in cold water. Pat dry. Combine cooked asparagus, snow peas, and raw mushrooms in a 9- by 13-inch non-metal baking pan.

Pour dressing ingredients over vegetables. Cover and refrigerate 1 hour (marinating longer will discolor the mushrooms). Drain well before serving, and discard the ginger and garlic.

For an attractive presentation, fan the asparagus on a serving dish. Arrange snow peas and mushrooms between fan ribs and cluster the grated daikon at the center.

*Available at oriental or specialty produce markets and well-stocked supermarkets.

Turkish Salad

2 medium onions, cut in ¼-inch dice
¼ cup olive oil
2 green bell peppers, cored, seeded, and cut in ¼-inch dice
1 sweet red bell pepper, cored, seeded, and cut in ¼-inch dice
1 large ripe tomato, finely chopped
1 jar (approximately 7 ounces) pimiento-stuffed green olives, drained and finely chopped
½ teaspoon salt
½ teaspoon freshly ground black pepper
½ teaspoon ground cumin
2 tablespoons tomato paste
⅛ to ¼ teaspoon cayenne pepper
¼ teaspoon paprika
1 bay leaf

2 tablespoons minced fresh parsley for garnish

This spicy Middle Eastern salad is traditionally a part of Mezza, a full course of appetizers served prior to the main course, which is frequently lamb. Mezza typically includes yogurt, hummus (garbanzo beans and sesame seed paste), tahini (sesame seed paste), eggplant, olives, pickles, fresh vegetables, and warm pita bread.

In a 10-inch skillet, sauté the onions in olive oil until soft and golden. Add the peppers and simmer, covered, 5 minutes. Add tomato, olives, salt, pepper, cumin, tomato paste, cayenne, paprika, and bay leaf. Simmer, covered, about 15 minutes, stirring occasionally.

Let salad cool to room temperature. Discard bay leaf. Sprinkle salad with parsley.

Tabbouleh

Serves 8 to 10

DRESSING:
½ cup olive oil
6 tablespoons fresh lemon juice
¼ cup loosely packed chopped fresh mint leaves
¼ cup loosely packed chopped fresh parsley
3 chopped green onions (including some green portion)
½ teaspoon minced garlic
¾ teaspoon ground cumin
¾ teaspoon salt
¼ teaspoon freshly ground black pepper

1 cup medium bulgur wheat
½ cup boiling water
½ cup pine nuts
2 medium ripe tomatoes, seeded and finely chopped

Romaine lettuce and whole fresh mint leaves for garnish

In California, this cold Middle Eastern salad is popular for picnics or other casual meals. A fine or medium grind of bulgur is recommended for tabbouleh.

Combine dressing ingredients and set aside.

Add boiling water to bulgur and stir to moisten evenly. Immediately stir in dressing, pine nuts, and tomatoes. Set aside for at least 8 hours, or refrigerate overnight to allow bulgur to soften and absorb dressing.

To serve, line a serving bowl with romaine lettuce and fill with tabbouleh. Garnish with mint leaves.

NOTE: Tabbouleh keeps well for several days in the refrigerator.

Marinated Radish Salad

Serves 6 to 8

DRESSING:
- ½ cup vegetable oil
- Juice of 1 large lemon (about ¼ cup)
- 1 teaspoon Dijon-style mustard
- ½ teaspoon dried dill weed
- ½ teaspoon salt
- ½ teaspoon freshly ground black pepper

- 6 ounces Swiss cheese, chopped into pea-sized pieces
- 3 bunches radishes, sliced, and drained on paper towels (about 4 cups)
- 4 green onions, minced (including green portion)

While radishes have always been cultivated and enjoyed in the Orient and India, they were shunned by the British several centuries ago because they were thought to cause disease. Despite this less than promising start, the popularity of the radish has spread throughout Europe and most temperate zones.

Combine the dressing ingredients.

In a medium bowl, combine the cheese, radishes, and green onions. Pour dressing over the salad. Cover and chill several hours or overnight.

Curried Rice Salad

Serves 4 to 6

DRESSING:
½ cup olive oil
⅓ cup red wine vinegar
1 tablespoon fresh lemon juice
1 clove garlic, minced
1 tablespoon sugar
½ teaspoon curry powder
Salt and freshly ground black pepper

3 cups chilled cooked rice (1 cup rice cooked in 2 cups boiling water)
1 green bell pepper, cored, seeded, and slivered
2 tablespoons drained pimientos, cut in strips or diced
2 tablespoons raisins
2 tablespoons chopped fresh parsley
1 green onion, minced (including green portion)

Salad greens and red or green pepper rings for garnish

Combine dressing ingredients and set aside.

Mix together salad ingredients. Chill thoroughly.

Just before serving, dress and toss salad. Garnish with salad greens and pepper rings.

Orange Slices with Pomegranate

Serves 6

Fruit Salad Dressing (page 67)

6 seedless oranges
1 pomegranate

Fresh mint leaves for garnish

To some, the angular, leather-skinned pomegranate, "apple with many seeds," is more seed than flesh. However, for lovers of the fruit, the sweetness of the juicy pulp amply compensates for the work of getting to it. The seeds have a glistening red color, and when ground are used to make grenadine syrup. California is the major domestic supplier.

Prepare Fruit Salad Dressing.

Slice the ends off the oranges, then remove peel and membrane. Slice crosswise into ¼-inch-thick rounds (or thick enough so they will hold their shape). Arrange on individual salad plates or serving platter.

Remove seeds from pomegranate and sprinkle the seeds sparingly over orange slices. Drizzle with Fruit Salad Dressing. Decorate with mint leaves.

Fruit Salad Dressing

Makes 1½ cups

½ cup sugar
1 teaspoon dry mustard
1 teaspoon salt
⅓ cup raspberry wine vinegar*
1 cup grapeseed oil*
2 tablespoons minced red onion
2 teaspoons toasted sesame seeds†
1 teaspoon poppy seeds

Sliced fruits for salad, such as nectarines, melon, peaches, grapes, strawberries, oranges

Generally, grapeseed oil can be used interchangeably with other good-quality cooking oils. It is light in taste and texture and has a high smoke point. For this recipe, use only grapeseed oil, as it imparts a special fruity flavor.

In a food processor or blender, combine sugar, mustard, and salt and blend a few seconds. Add vinegar and blend again. With machine on, slowly add oil in a continuous stream until incorporated. By hand, stir in minced onion, sesame seeds, and poppy seeds.

One quart of fruit will require about 3 to 4 tablespoons of dressing. Spoon over mixed fruit salad and toss well before serving.

N O T E : This dressing is also recommended for Orange Slices with Pomegranate (page 66).

†Toast sesame seeds in a small skillet over medium heat for about 10 minutes, or until golden, shaking pan frequently. Cool.

*Available at specialty food stores and well-stocked supermarkets.

Vinaigrette

Makes about
³⁄₄ cup

½ cup peanut oil (do not substitute)
Juice of 1 large lemon (about ¼ cup)
1 teaspoon red wine vinegar
1 teaspoon dry mustard
1 teaspoon salt
1 teaspoon freshly ground black pepper

In a blender or food processor, combine all ingredients.

Serve with a tossed green salad or use as a marinade for steamed vegetables.

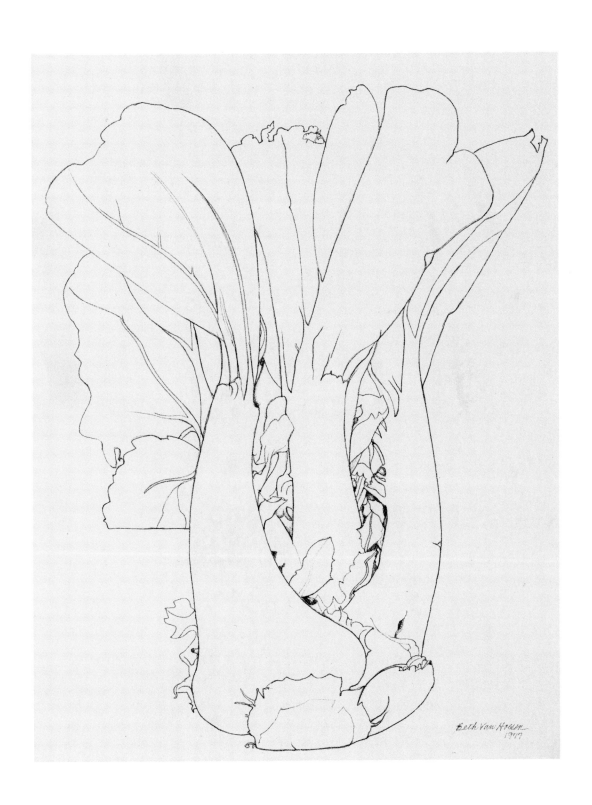

5.
Bok Choy
graphite

Mayonnaise

Makes 1 to 1½ cups

2 eggs
Juice of ½ large lemon (about 2 tablespoons)
1 tablespoon red wine vinegar or balsamic vinegar*
1 teaspoon salt
½ teaspoon dry mustard
¾ to 1½ cups vegetable oil or olive oil

Mayonnaise was perhaps named in commemoration of the French victory over Spain in 1756 at Mahon, capital of the Spanish island of Minorca.

In a blender, combine eggs, lemon juice, vinegar, mustard, and salt. With machine at high speed, add oil in a very thin, continuous stream until oil is incorporated and dressing thickens. Check for desired consistency after ¾ cup of oil has been added. For a thinner dressing, add up to ¾ cup more oil. Store in refrigerator.

N O T E : To vary, experiment with a variety of oils, flavored vinegars, and mustards. Mayonnaise will keep several days covered in the refrigerator.

*Available at specialty food stores and well-stocked supermarkets.

Creamy Garlic Dressing

Makes about
1½ cups

2 cloves garlic
2 teaspoons salt
¾ cup vegetable oil or olive oil
⅓ cup apple cider vinegar
½ cup whipping cream
⅛ teaspoon ground white pepper

In a blender or food processor, puree garlic with salt. Add oil and vinegar and blend until creamy. Add whipping cream and pepper. Blend again until creamy.

This dressing can be stored in the refrigerator for at least 1 week. Bring to room temperature before serving.

N O T E : This dressing would be perfect with a simple salad of romaine lettuce and Croutons (page 50).

Cheddar Cheese Dressing

Makes about
2 cups

1 large green onion (including some green portion)
2 eggs
¼ cup white wine vinegar
Juice of 1 large lemon (about ¼ cup)
1½ teaspoons salt
1 teaspoon dry mustard
1 teaspoon Worcestershire sauce
1 teaspoon prepared white horseradish
2 cups vegetable oil
1 cup (about 4 ounces) grated Cheddar cheese

In a food processor, finely chop green onion. Add eggs, vinegar, lemon juice, and seasonings; blend well. With machine on, add oil in a very thin, continuous stream until oil is incorporated and dressing is creamy. By hand, stir in cheese. Store in refrigerator.

Serve with a tossed green salad or chilled steamed vegetables.

Green Goddess Salad Dressing

Makes 1 quart

1 can (2 ounces) anchovy fillets
¼ cup packed fresh parsley sprigs
¼ cup snipped fresh chives
1 green onion, coarsely chopped (including green portion)
1 clove garlic, coarsely chopped
⅓ cup tarragon vinegar
1 cup sour cream
2 cups mayonnaise (page 69)

In 1915, "The Green Goddess," a play by William Archer, was being performed in San Francisco. Inspired by the play, the chef at the Palace Hotel created the now-famous salad dressing.

Rinse anchovies and pat dry. In a food processor or blender, puree anchovies, parsley, chives, green onion, garlic, and vinegar for 30 seconds. Add sour cream and mayonnaise and mix thoroughly.

The dressing will keep in refrigerator for at least 1 month.

CHAPTER FOUR

Light Entrées

Scampi Bread

O. J. Dettner, Civic Volunteer, San Francisco

Serves 6 to 8

A Fumé Blanc or White Zinfandel is suggested.

1 pound butter, softened
½ cup chopped fresh parsley
2 tablespoons ground almonds
1½ tablespoons minced garlic
1 tablespoon chopped shallots
1 tablespoon Pernod (see Note)
1½ teaspoons salt
1 teaspoon ground white pepper
¾ cup white wine
2 pounds large raw shrimp, shelled
1 large loaf round sourdough bread, 2 standard loaves French bread, or 6 to 8 individual sourdough rolls

Red leaf lettuce and lemon wedges for garnish

O. J. Dettner and Cyril Magnin combined their civic and culinary talents to create Scampi Bread for a recent March of Dimes Gourmet Gala. O. J. suggests serving it as a first course or as a light meal after a football game or skiing.

In a food processor, combine butter, parsley, almonds, garlic, shallots, Pernod, salt, pepper, and white wine until blended to a smooth green butter and wine is incorporated. Set aside.

Cut the top third off the loaf of bread; set top aside for lid. Scoop out the soft crumbs, leaving a firm shell. Reserve crumbs. Paint the interior of the bread shell, including the lid, with the green garlic butter.

Cut 6 shrimp in half lengthwise. Set aside. Arrange half of the remaining shrimp in the bottom of the bread shell. Coat the shrimp thickly with garlic butter. Top with remaining whole shrimp, then remaining butter.

Preheat oven to 400 degrees.

In a clean bowl of the food processor, place the reserved soft bread crumbs and process until fine crumbs are formed. Sprinkle over the top layer of shrimp. Arrange reserved shrimp halves on top.

Place the loaf on a cookie sheet and bake for about 20 to 30 minutes. After 10 minutes, cover the loaf with its buttered lid and bake until loaf is crusty and crisp, but not too brown. Shrimp should be opaque throughout. Slice into desired number of pieces or wedges. Serve hot as a light entrée, an appetizer, or first course. Set each piece on red leaf lettuce and garnish with a lemon wedge.

NOTE: This dish can be assembled a day ahead, refrigerated overnight, and baked just before serving.

Pernod is an anise-flavored aperitif.

Tailgate Tortillas

Makes 4
sandwiches

GUACAMOLE:
1 large or 2 small ripe avocados
2 tablespoons fresh lemon juice
3 tablespoons diced green chiles
3 tablespoons thinly sliced green onions (including green portion)
1 small clove garlic, minced

4 flour tortillas (8-inch size), at room temperature
½ cooked chicken breast, shredded
3 slices bacon, crisply fried and crumbled
1½ cups (about 6 ounces) grated Monterey Jack cheese
3 tablespoons roasted, shelled sunflower seeds
1 cup shredded romaine or iceberg lettuce

The word
guacamole, *derived*
from the Nahuatl
Indians' (of
Southern Mexico
and Central
America) word for
avocado and
sauce, can apply to
either mashed
avocados and
seasonings or to
salads featuring
avocados.

Peel and mash avocado with lemon juice, chiles, green onion, and garlic.

Lightly moisten both sides of tortillas with water. Divide the guacamole evenly among the 4 tortillas and spread to within ½ inch of the edges. Sprinkle each tortilla with shredded chicken, bacon, cheese, sunflower seeds, and lettuce. Roll up. Serve chilled or at room temperature.

NOTE: This recipe can easily be doubled or tripled. If made ahead, wrap tortillas individually in plastic wrap. Slice at serving time.

Cracker Bread Sandwiches with Four Fillings

Each spread fills 1 cracker and makes about 10 small sandwiches

1 package large Armenian cracker bread (Lahvosh), softened

Lahvosh and pita bread can be found throughout the Middle East. Generally the difference between the two breads is determined by the baker's decision as to how thick he wishes to roll the dough. It can be paper thin, as in cracker bread, or thicker, like pita. Often Lahvosh and pita are sold covered with sesame seeds or lightly covered with olive oil and zarter, a wild herb similar to oregano.

Soften cracker bread by holding it under a soft spray of water until moistened. Turn cracker over and moisten the other side. Cover with damp towels and let sit for at least 1 hour, or until soft and pliable. Check the cracker periodically. If there are any dry spots, sprinkle with water and cover again.

Prepare the filling spread(s) of your choice, thinning with a little milk, if necessary, to make more spreadable. Each filling makes enough to fill one large cracker.

When crackers are softened, cover with filling to edges. Leave far edge bare as filling spreads as cracker is rolled.

To serve, slice cracker crosswise with a sharp (preferably serrated) knife to desired thickness (2 to 3 inches for sandwich, 1 to 2 inches for appetizer).

Make up to 2 hours ahead, or wrap tightly in plastic wrap and store overnight in refrigerator.

SPICED CREAM CHEESE FILLING:
Spread
8 ounces cream cheese, softened and whipped
1 teaspoon Worcestershire sauce
1 tablespoon chopped fresh parsley
1 small clove garlic, minced
⅛ teaspoon cayenne pepper
⅛ teaspoon curry powder
⅛ teaspoon ground ginger
⅛ teaspoon ground nutmeg

Topping
¼ pound thinly sliced cooked turkey or roast beef
1 medium ripe tomato, thinly sliced
1 cup loosely packed fresh parsley sprigs
¼ basket clover or alfalfa sprouts (about 1 ounce)

continued

Combine spread ingredients in a small bowl. Cover softened cracker with spread as directed. Evenly distribute turkey or roast beef. Top with tomato, parsley sprigs, and sprouts. Roll up tightly, jelly-roll fashion. Cover with damp towels until ready to serve.

ALMOND-CHEESE FILLING:
Spread
1¼ cups coarsely chopped toasted blanched almonds†
8 ounces cream cheese, softened and whipped
⅓ cup mayonnaise (page 69)
8 slices bacon, crisply fried and crumbled
1 tablespoon chopped green onion
1 tablespoon snipped fresh dill
⅛ teaspoon freshly ground black pepper

Combine spread ingredients in a small bowl. Cover softened cracker with spread as directed. Roll up tightly, jelly-roll fashion. Cover with damp towels until ready to serve.

SMOKED SALMON FILLING:
Spread
8 ounces cream cheese, softened and whipped
¼ cup plain yogurt
1 tablespoon fresh lemon juice
¼ cup chopped green onion (including green portion)
2 tablespoons snipped fresh dill

Topping
½ to ¾ pound thinly sliced smoked salmon
2 tablespoons chopped drained capers

Combine spread ingredients in a small bowl. Cover softened cracker with spread as directed. Top with slices of smoked salmon. Distribute capers over the top. Roll up tightly, jelly-roll fashion. Cover with damp towels until ready to serve.

continued

CURRIED EGG FILLING:
Spread
9 hard-cooked eggs, chopped
⅔ cup mayonnaise (page 69)
¾ cup minced green onion (including green portion)
1½ tablespoons Dijon-style mustard
1 teaspoon curry powder

Topping
¾ cup chopped dry-roasted peanuts
Salt and freshly ground black pepper
¼ basket clover or alfalfa sprouts (about 1 ounce)

Combine spread ingredients in a small bowl. Cover softened cracker with spread as directed. Sprinkle with peanuts, salt, and pepper. Distribute sprouts over top. Roll up tightly, jelly-roll fashion. Cover with damp towels until ready to serve.

†Toast blanched almonds in a 325 degree oven for 5 to 10 minutes, or until lightly browned. Cool.

Sausage-Spinach Baguettes

*Makes 12
baguettes*

PASTRY:

2½ cups all-purpose flour
1 cup chilled butter
1 cup small-curd cottage cheese

FILLING:

1 pound mild Italian sausage, link (casings removed) or bulk
1 bunch fresh spinach, washed, trimmed, blanched, and squeezed dry, or
  1 package (10 ounces) frozen chopped spinach, thawed and squeezed dry
1 clove garlic, minced
3 green onions, thinly sliced (including green portion)
3 sprigs fresh parsley
1 egg

2 egg yolks, lightly beaten

To prepare Pastry: In a food processor or by hand, cut butter into flour until crumbly. Add cottage cheese and mix until dough forms a ball. Knead dough lightly. Divide dough into 2 balls. Roll out 1 ball into a 14- by 18-inch rectangle (about ⅛ inch thick). Cut rectangle in half lengthwise, then divide each half into thirds. Repeat with second half of dough. You should have 12 rectangles. Cover lightly and set aside while preparing filling.

To prepare Filling: Sauté meat until it is cooked through and crumbly. Drain off fat and set the meat aside. In a food processor, chop the spinach with the garlic, onion, and parsley. Do not puree. Add meat to spinach with 1 egg. Blend until just mixed.

Preheat oven to 350 degrees. Butter 2 cookie sheets.

Divide the filling into 12 equal parts. Spoon the filling along the long edge of each pastry rectangle. Gently roll up dough to form a baguette. Place baguettes, seam side down, on prepared cookie sheets. Brush with beaten egg yolks and bake 20 to 25 minutes, or until lightly browned. Cool on racks.

Serve Sausage-Spinach Baguettes warm or at room temperature as a snack.

NOTE: To serve as an appetizer, cut crosswise into 1-inch slices.

Enchiladas Verdes

Serves 6

GREEN SAUCE:

2 cups tomatillos, husked, or 1 can (15¼ ounces) tomatillos, including liquid*
1 medium onion, chopped
¼ cup vegetable oil
1 clove garlic, minced
½ teaspoon salt
½ cup diced green chiles
1 cup (or more) chicken stock

Oil for frying tortillas
12 corn tortillas
6 cups (about 1½ pounds) grated Monterey Jack or Swiss cheese
2 cups sour cream

Resembling a green tomato with a grey-brown paper husk, the tomatillo is a tart Mexican vegetable used in many sauces. When selecting fresh tomatillos, choose smaller ones as they have more flavor.

To prepare Green Sauce: In a blender or food processor, puree tomatillos. Set aside. In a 10-inch skillet, sauté the onion in ¼ cup oil over medium heat for about 5 minutes, or until onion is soft and golden. Add garlic and sauté for an additional minute, stirring. Add reserved tomatillo puree, salt, chiles, and chicken stock and simmer, uncovered, 5 to 10 minutes. Add more stock if mixture becomes too thick (it should remain watery).

Preheat oven to 350 degrees.

Pour enough of the green sauce into the bottom of a 9- by 13-inch baking pan to just barely coat the surface. Set aside.

Pour ½ inch of oil in another skillet and heat to almost smoking. Dip tortillas, one at a time, into hot oil for about 10 seconds, or until they are just limp; drain, then dip into the green sauce to coat. Fill each tortilla with about ½ cup of the grated cheese and roll up. Place side by side in baking pan, seam side down. Pour remaining green sauce over the enchiladas, then spread with the sour cream. Bake for 15 to 20 minutes, or until the cheese is melted and bubbling.

NOTE: These enchiladas freeze well, tightly wrapped, before sour cream is added. Thaw completely, then add sour cream and bake as directed. Rolled tortillas will be less likely to crack if their leathery or bumpy side is on the inside of the roll.

*Available at Latin American markets and well-stocked supermarkets.

Corn Enchiladas

Serves 4

*A Burgundy is
suggested.*

CORN FILLING:
- 1 medium onion, cut in ¼-inch dice
- 1 tablespoon butter
- 1½ cups fresh corn kernels (about 4 ears)
- ¼ teaspoon ground cumin
- 2 tablespoons water
- 2 Anaheim or poblano chiles, seeded and chopped, or 2 canned green chiles, seeded and chopped
- ½ cup sour cream
- ½ cup (about 2 ounces) grated Monterey Jack cheese
- ¼ teaspoon freshly ground black pepper

- 8 corn tortillas
- ¼ cup vegetable oil
- 1 can (10 ounces) red enchilada sauce
- 1 cup (about 4 ounces) grated Monterey Jack cheese

Sour cream, chopped cilantro, and lime wedges for garnish

To prepare Corn Filling: In a 2-quart saucepan, cook onion in butter over medium heat until soft. Add corn, cumin, water, and chiles. Cover and simmer 5 minutes. Uncover and continue simmering until liquid has evaporated. Remove from heat and stir in sour cream, cheese, and pepper. Stir until cheese melts. Set aside.

Preheat oven to 375 degrees.

Fry tortillas, one at a time, in hot oil until just limp, 10 to 15 seconds on each side. Blot the tortillas with paper towels.

Pour ⅓ cup of enchilada sauce in the bottom of a 9- by 13-inch casserole. Tilt the casserole to coat the bottom. Spoon slightly less than ⅓ cup of corn filling down the middle of each tortilla. Roll up and place, seam side down, in casserole. Pour remaining enchilada sauce over the top; sprinkle with grated cheese.

Bake the enchiladas, uncovered, for 20 minutes or until the cheese is melted and bubbling.

Serve topped with sour cream, chopped cilantro, and a lime wedge to squeeze over the top.

Zucchini-Tomato Quiche

Serves 4 to 6

A rosé is suggested.

PASTRY:

1½ cups all-purpose flour
½ teaspoon salt
¼ cup chilled butter
¼ cup vegetable shortening
¼ cup ice water

FILLING:

2 zucchini (about 1 pound), thinly sliced
½ teaspoon salt
2 ripe tomatoes, peeled, seeded, and cut in eighths
1 medium onion, minced
1 teaspoon minced garlic
1 tablespoon butter
½ cup (about 1½ ounces) freshly grated Parmesan cheese
½ teaspoon salt
¼ teaspoon dried oregano, crumbled
⅛ teaspoon freshly ground black pepper
2 eggs, beaten
1 cup whipping cream
⅛ teaspoon cayenne pepper
1 cup (about 4 ounces) grated Gruyère cheese
¾ cup (about 3 ounces) grated Cheddar cheese

To prepare Pastry: In a food processor or by hand, combine flour and salt. Cut in butter and shortening until crumbly. Add ice water and mix until dough forms a ball. Flatten into a disk, wrap in waxed paper, and chill 30 minutes.

To prepare Filling: Sprinkle the zucchini with ½ teaspoon salt. Place zucchini in a single layer on paper towels and let stand 30 minutes to draw out moisture. Pat dry. Drain tomato wedges on paper towels for 30 minutes.

Preheat oven to 425 degrees.

continued

Roll out chilled dough on a lightly floured surface to fit a 9½-inch deep-dish pie pan. Pat into pan, flute edges, and prick the sides and bottom with a fork. Cover the rim with foil to prevent overbrowning; partially bake 8 to 10 minutes. Remove shell from oven and discard foil.

Reduce oven temperature to 350 degrees.

Meanwhile, in a small skillet, sauté onion and garlic in butter until translucent, stirring frequently. Set aside to cool.

Combine Parmesan cheese, salt, oregano, and pepper in a bowl. Stir in zucchini, tomatoes, and onion mixture. In a separate bowl, beat eggs, cream, and cayenne together.

To assemble: Sprinkle Gruyère cheese over the bottom of the partially baked shell. Cover with half the vegetables, then sprinkle with half the Parmesan mixture. Repeat. Pour egg mixture over all and top with Cheddar cheese. Bake for 50 minutes, or until filling has set and Cheddar cheese is melted and golden.

Apple, Cheese, and Sausage Quiche

Serves 4 to 6

A Fumé Blanc is suggested.

PASTRY:

1½ cups all-purpose flour
½ teaspoon salt
¼ cup chilled butter
¼ cup vegetable shortening
¼ cup ice water

FILLING:

½ cup mayonnaise (page 69)
½ cup milk
2 tablespoons all-purpose flour
2 eggs
2 to 3 green apples, peeled, cored, and sliced
1 cup (4 ounces) grated Swiss cheese
1 cup (4 ounces) grated Monterey Jack cheese
8 ounces link sausage, thinly sliced, fried until nearly cooked, and drained of fat

To prepare Pastry: In a food processor or by hand, combine flour and salt. Cut in butter and shortening until crumbly. Add ice water and mix until dough forms a ball. Flatten into disk, wrap in waxed paper, and chill 30 minutes.

Preheat oven to 425 degrees.

Roll out chilled dough on a lightly floured surface to fit a 9½-inch deep-dish pie pan. Pat into pan, flute edges, and prick the sides and bottom with a fork. Cover the rim with foil to prevent overbrowning; partially bake 8 to 10 minutes. Remove shell from oven and discard foil.

Reduce oven temperature to 350 degrees.

To prepare Filling: Combine mayonnaise, milk, flour, and eggs in a bowl. Stir in apples, cheeses, and sausage. Pour the ingredients into the partially baked shell and arrange the sausage pieces and apples so they are well distributed.

Bake 50 to 60 minutes, or until filling is set and the top is nicely browned. Cool in the pan for 10 minutes before serving.

6.
Hawaiian Bananas
color pencil, graphite

Sausage and Tomato Tart

Serves 4 to 6

PASTRY:

1½ cups all-purpose flour
½ teaspoon salt
¼ cup chilled butter
¼ cup vegetable shortening
¼ cup ice water

2 teaspoons Dijon-style mustard

FILLING:

2 Polish sausages (about ¼ pound each)
3 medium ripe tomatoes, cored and thickly sliced
1 tablespoon chopped fresh basil, or ½ teaspoon dried
1 tablespoon snipped fresh chives
2½ cups (about 10 ounces) grated Monterey Jack cheese
⅔ cup mayonnaise (page 69)

To prepare Pastry: In a food processor or by hand, combine flour and salt. Cut in butter and shortening until crumbly. Add ice water and mix until dough forms a ball. Flatten into a disk, wrap in waxed paper, and chill 30 minutes.

Preheat oven to 425 degrees.

Roll out dough on a lightly floured surface to fit a 9½-inch deep-dish pie pan. Pat into pan, flute edges, and prick the sides and bottom with a fork. Reduce oven temperature to 400 degrees; bake pastry shell 10 to 12 minutes, or until very lightly browned, but not quite done. Remove from oven and spread the bottom of the hot shell with mustard. Bake shell for 3 more minutes. Remove and cool slightly while preparing filling.

Reduce oven temperature to 350 degrees.

To prepare Filling: With a sharp knife, coarsely chop the sausage. In a small skillet, cook the sausage over low heat until some fat is released. Increase heat and sauté until cooked through. Drain on paper towels and cool. Sprinkle sausage over cooked pastry. Cover with tomato slices. Combine herbs, cheese, and mayonnaise and distribute over tomatoes. Using the back of a spoon, gently spread the cheese mixture to the edges and fill the surface gaps.

Bake 35 minutes until cheese is thoroughly melted. Cool at least 5 minutes before cutting into wedges. Serve hot or at room temperature.

NOTE: To vary, substitute ¼ cup chopped fresh parsley and 2 tablespoons chopped fresh dill for the chives and basil.

Gougère with Mushrooms and Canadian Bacon

Serves 4 to 6

A Pinot Noir is suggested.

FILLING:

1 cup chopped onion
¼ cup butter
½ pound mushrooms, thickly sliced
2 tablespoons all-purpose flour
1 teaspoon salt
½ teaspoon dried oregano, crumbled
¼ teaspoon freshly ground black pepper
¾ cup chicken stock
2 large ripe tomatoes, peeled, seeded, and cut in ½-inch strips
1 pound Canadian bacon, cut in narrow strips (or other cooked meats, such as roast beef, chicken, turkey, or ham)

PÂTE À CHOUX:

1 cup water
½ cup butter, cut in small pieces
¼ teaspoon dried oregano, crumbled
¼ teaspoon salt
⅛ teaspoon ground white pepper
1 cup all-purpose flour
4 eggs
1 cup (about 4 ounces) grated Gruyère cheese

2 tablespoons grated Gruyère cheese for garnish

Gougère, from France's Burgundy region, is a cheese pastry typically made with Gruyère. The dough is formed into a ring which puffs and turns golden as it bakes.

To prepare Filling: In a 12-inch skillet, sauté the onions in butter over medium-high heat until soft. Reduce heat and add mushrooms; continue to cook, stirring occasionally, for 10 minutes, or until most of the moisture has evaporated. Sprinkle with flour, salt, oregano, and pepper. Stir until flour is absorbed. Slowly add stock, stirring briskly. Raise heat and bring the mixture to a boil, stirring constantly. Stir in tomatoes and Canadian bacon. Simmer about 5 minutes, or until the sauce is very thick. Set aside.

continued

Preheat oven to 400 degrees. Butter a 9½-inch deep-dish pie pan or a shallow casserole.

To prepare Pâte à Choux: In a small saucepan, bring water to a boil. Add butter, oregano, salt, and pepper, stirring until butter melts. Add flour all at once and stir vigorously until the mixture pulls away from the sides of the pan and forms a ball. Remove pan from heat.

Beat in eggs one at a time with a wooden spoon, making certain egg is well incorporated after each addition. Stir in 1 cup grated cheese.

Spoon the pâte à choux in a ring around the slanted side of the prepared pan. The ring may be uneven. Sprinkle the ring with 2 tablespoons grated cheese.

Using a slotted spoon, fill the center of the ring with the mushroom mixture.

Bake 40 to 45 minutes, or until gougère is puffed and golden and the filling is hot.

Serve at once.

Pizza with Two Toppings

Jamie Davies, Schramsberg Vineyards, Calistoga

Makes two 12-inch pizzas, or four 8-inch pizzas

Jamie Davies suggests a sparkling Cuvée de Pinot.

Professional-looking (and tasting) pizza is possible to prepare at home in a regular oven if you use a pizza stone, or unglazed, high-fired quarry tiles, and a wooden baker's peel. The porous stone or tiles ensure a crisp crust by absorbing moisture from the dough. The peel is the safest and easiest way to transfer the ready-to-bake pizza to the hot oven.

PIZZA DOUGH:

1	envelope dry yeast
1½	cups lukewarm water (110 to 115 degrees)
2	tablespoons olive oil
3½ to 4	cups unbleached all-purpose flour or bread flour
1	teaspoon salt
1	teaspoon sugar

Rice flour or cornmeal

In a small bowl, combine yeast, water, and oil. In a large mixing bowl, combine 3½ cups flour, salt, and sugar. Add the yeast mixture and stir with a wooden spoon to blend; add additional flour as needed to make a soft dough. Turn out onto a lightly floured surface and knead 8 to 10 minutes, or until smooth and elastic. Add additional flour if dough seems sticky. Shape into a ball and place in a lightly oiled bowl, turning to coat all sides with oil. Cover bowl with a clean dish towel or plastic wrap and let rise in a warm, draft-free place until doubled in bulk, about 1 hour. Punch down; divide in half for 2 large pizzas, in quarters for 4 individual pizzas (see Note).

Place the pizza stone* or tiles on the center oven rack. Preheat oven to 500 degrees.

While shaping each pizza, cover unused dough to keep dough from drying out. Dust hands with rice flour or all-purpose flour to prevent dough from sticking to hands. Depending on size desired, shape half the dough into a 12-inch circle, or one-fourth of the dough into an 8-inch circle. Dust a wooden baker's peel* with a generous amount of rice flour or cornmeal. Lay the dough on the peel; let rest for 10 to 15 minutes. Cover dough with one of the two toppings given below.

After checking that the pizza glides easily on the rice flour or cornmeal by jerking the peel slightly, slide the pizza off of the peel onto the preheated stone in the oven (the stone is hot, so don't take it out of the oven at this point). Bake 14 minutes, or until crust is golden brown. When baked, pizza will release from stone with a gentle tug. Slide pizza back onto the peel and slice in wedges. If making more than one pizza, bake remaining pizzas in the same way.

Serve pizza hot or at room temperature.

continued

With this easy recipe for pizza dough are two toppings. Pizza Margherita is the familiar tomato sauce and cheese version. To vary, experiment with several cheeses (or without any cheese), fresh vegetables and herbs, shellfish, or meat. The second topping, Jamie's Topping, is in the new style of California pizzas, using ripe tomatoes, sweet red bell peppers, onions, Fontina cheese, and fresh rosemary. Jamie Davies owns Schramsberg Vineyards with her husband, Jack. Schramsberg is known for its fine sparkling wines.

PIZZA MARGHERITA TOPPING:

1 can (28 ounces) Italian plum tomatoes in juice
1 to 2 tablespoons minced garlic
¼ cup olive oil
¼ cup tomato paste
1 tablespoon chopped fresh oregano or basil, or 1 teaspoon dried
Salt and freshly ground black pepper

1 cup (about 4 ounces) grated mozzarella cheese

In a food processor or blender, chop the tomatoes with their juice, or pour tomatoes in a bowl and crush with a wooden spoon or your fingers.

In a 2-quart saucepan, lightly sauté garlic in oil. Add tomatoes, tomato paste, and seasonings. Bring to a boil; reduce heat and simmer 15 to 20 minutes, stirring occasionally. Approximately 1 cup sauce covers a 12-inch pizza. Makes about 3 cups sauce.

To assemble, lightly cover the dough with tomato sauce, leaving a 1-inch rim uncovered. Sprinkle with 1 cup mozzarella cheese for a 12-inch pizza or ½ cup for an 8-inch pizza.

JAMIE'S PIZZA TOPPING:

6 large ripe tomatoes, peeled, seeded, and chopped
3 cloves garlic, finely chopped
6 tablespoons olive oil
3 large onions, thinly sliced
2 large sweet red bell peppers, cored, seeded, and chopped
1 cup (about 3 ounces) freshly grated Parmesan cheese
1 pound Fontina or goat cheese
1 tablespoon finely chopped fresh rosemary, or 2 teaspoons chopped dried
Freshly ground black pepper

Freshly grated Parmesan cheese for garnish (optional)
Whole fresh basil leaves for garnish

In a sauté pan, cook tomatoes and garlic in 1 tablespoon oil until moisture is reduced and a thick mixture results. Reserve.

In the same pan, gently sauté onions in 3 tablespoons oil until golden (do not brown). Reserve.

continued

In the same pan, sauté red peppers in 2 tablespoons oil until just tender. Reserve.

To assemble, brush each of four 8-inch circles of dough lightly with olive oil. Sprinkle each with ¼ cup Parmesan cheese. Add thin slices of Fontina cheese or crumbled goat cheese. Spread on tomato mixture and sprinkle with rosemary. Top with sautéed onions and red peppers and a generous grinding of black pepper. Add a dusting of Parmesan cheese, if desired. After baking, garnish with fresh basil.

N O T E : The pizza dough can be prepared with a food processor, an electric mixer with a dough hook, or by hand. The dough can be refrigerated or frozen after rising. Punch down; shape into 2 or 4 balls. Flatten and wrap in plastic wrap. To use, thaw completely, then shape, top, and bake. Pizza Margherita sauce doubles well, can be prepared ahead, and frozen in 1-cup containers.

*Pizza stones and wooden baker's peels are available at many cookware stores and by mail through gourmet products catalogs. Unglazed quarry tile is sold through floor tile suppliers.

Mediterranean Chicken Salad

Marilyn Rinzler, Poulet, Berkeley

Serves 6

A French Colombard is suggested.

2 medium zucchini, halved lengthwise, and sliced ¼ inch thick
1 medium red onion, thinly sliced
1 pound (about 8 small) unpeeled red potatoes, scrubbed, boiled until tender, cooled, and thinly sliced
2 cucumbers, peeled, seeded, and sliced
4 small ripe tomatoes, diced
1 pound (about 2 large whole breasts) chicken meat, cooked, skinned, boned, and sliced
¼ cup chopped fresh parsley
1½ teaspoons minced garlic
1½ teaspoons crushed red pepper
1½ teaspoons salt
½ teaspoon freshly ground black pepper
½ cup mayonnaise (page 69)

A truly good chicken salad is prepared so that the dressing does not overpower the mild flavor of the chicken. In this colorful recipe from Poulet, a charcuterie specializing in chicken, the simple mayonnaise dressing adds piquancy without compromising the delicate taste of the chicken and vegetables.

Combine all ingredients in a 3-quart mixing bowl. Chill the salad at least 1 hour and toss again just before serving.

Chicken Canton

Serves 4 to 6

A Dry Semillon is suggested.

MARINADE:
1 tablespoon soy sauce
2 tablespoons vegetable oil
1 clove garlic, minced
½ teaspoon grated lemon peel

2 whole chicken breasts, halved, skinned, boned, and cut in ½-inch-wide strips

SALAD:
4 cups torn spinach leaves (about 1 bunch)
4 cups thinly sliced Chinese (Napa) cabbage
¼ cup vegetable oil
4 teaspoons fresh lemon juice
2 teaspoons soy sauce
¼ teaspoon grated lemon peel
¼ teaspoon salt
2 tablespoons toasted sesame seeds†

Combine marinade ingredients; pour over chicken and marinate 3 hours. In a medium skillet, sauté chicken strips in marinade over medium-high heat, stirring frequently, 4 to 5 minutes. Chicken should be cooked through but not dry. Chill chicken with cooking juices.

To serve, toss spinach and cabbage with remaining salad ingredients until leaves are evenly coated. Add chicken with cooking juices, toss again, and serve at once.

†Toast sesame seeds in a small skillet over medium heat for about 10 minutes, or until golden, shaking pan frequently. Cool.

Oriental Chicken Salad

Serves 8 to 10

A White Zinfandel is suggested.

DRESSING:
½ cup vegetable oil
½ cup rice wine vinegar*
½ cup soy sauce
½ teaspoon freshly grated ginger root
½ teaspoon ground white pepper
  Juice of 1 large lemon (about ¼ cup)

2 whole chicken breasts
1 package (8 ounces) wonton skins (round, if available)*
  Oil for frying

2 heads ruffled leaf lettuce
3 green onions, thinly sliced (including green portion)
¼ cup slivered almonds
1 ripe tomato, cut in small dice

Familiar to Western tastes as the peppery ingredient in gingerbread and ginger snaps, ginger has flavored the cooking of China and India since pre-Roman times. Hundreds of varieties exist, exhibiting a range of physical characteristics and intensity of flavors. Dried ground ginger does not substitute well for fresh. Store ginger root in the freezer. When needed, grate it, peel and all, while still frozen.

In a small bowl, combine dressing ingredients. Set aside.

Simmer chicken breasts in water about 30 minutes, or until cooked through. Cool, skin, bone, and cut into small cubes. Add chicken cubes to dressing and marinate at least 30 minutes.

Fry unfolded wonton skins in hot oil, several at a time, until crisp. Drain on paper towels. Set aside.

When ready to serve, tear lettuce into bite-sized pieces and place in a serving bowl. Add all other ingredients except the wonton skins and toss well to coat lettuce.

Crumble approximately 2 dozen of the wonton skins and toss with the salad. Use any remaining ones to line the bowl decoratively.

*Available at oriental markets and well-stocked supermarkets.

Pacific Coast Chicken

Serves 6

1½ cups diagonally sliced asparagus
6 ounces mushrooms, sliced
¼ cup chopped onion
¼ cup butter
¼ cup all-purpose flour
1 teaspoon salt
½ teaspoon curry powder
¼ teaspoon freshly ground black pepper
½ cup chicken stock
12 ounces half-and-half
6 chicken thighs, poached in water, skinned, boned, and cut in bite-sized pieces
¾ cup (about 3 ounces) grated Cheddar cheese

1 can (3 ounces) crisp chow mein noodles or boiled, soft Chinese noodles for accompaniment

Blanch asparagus in boiling water 1 to 2 minutes. Drain, then plunge into cold water to stop the cooking process. Drain again, and set aside.

In a large skillet, sauté mushrooms and onions in butter until soft. Stir in flour, salt, curry powder, and pepper, and continue cooking for 1 more minute. Slowly add stock and half-and-half, stirring constantly to prevent lumps from forming. Cook gently until thickened. Add chicken pieces and blanched asparagus and heat through.

Place the mixture in a 2-quart casserole, scatter the cheese over the top, and broil just until cheese melts.

Serve on a bed of Chinese noodles, either crisp or soft.

CHAPTER FIVE

Pasta

Lemon Cream Sauce for Pasta

Serves 6

*A dry Chenin
Blanc is suggested.*

Grated peel and juice of 2 large lemons (about ½ cup juice)
1 teaspoon salt
1 tablespoon olive oil
1 pound dried fettuccine
1 cup whipping cream
½ cup (1½ ounces) freshly grated Parmesan cheese
Freshly ground black pepper

Set lemon peel aside. Bring 3 quarts water to a rapid boil; add lemon juice, salt, and olive oil. Drop in fettuccine; boil until just tender. Drain. Return the pasta to the pot and add cream, cheese, lemon peel, and a few grindings of black pepper. Toss gently until the cheese has melted.
   Serve at once.

Parsley-Thyme Sauce for Pasta

Serves 4 to 6

A Grey Riesling is suggested.

1 package (12 ounces) pasta (corkscrew or shell works best)
1 bunch (3 to 4 ounces) fresh parsley, stems removed
1 tablespoon fresh thyme leaves, or 1 teaspoon dried
3 green onions, cut in pieces (including green portion)
½ cup butter, cut in pieces
  Grated peel of 1 lemon
  Salt and freshly ground black pepper

Cook pasta in boiling, salted water until just tender.

While pasta cooks, thoroughly mince the parsley, thyme, and green onions in a food processor.

Drain the cooked pasta. Return to the pot and toss with butter until butter begins to melt. Add the minced herbs, onions, and lemon peel. Continue tossing until the butter has completely melted. Season with salt and pepper, if desired.

Serve immediately.

Pimiento Pasta

Lisa Dollar Buehler, Buehler Vineyards Winery, St. Helena

Serves 6

*Lisa Buehler
suggests a Pinot
Blanc or White
Zinfandel.*

*To accompany her
pasta, Lisa Buehler
suggests a butter
and cream
reduction seasoned
with freshly grated
ginger and served
over diced, cooked
seafood. Finish
with golden caviar
and chopped fresh
cilantro. The
Salmon and
Scallop Sauce
(page 101) is also
a superb match.*

1 jar (4 ounces) chopped pimientos, seeds and loose skin removed
1 whole egg plus 1 egg yolk
2 cups unbleached all-purpose flour
½ teaspoon salt
½ cup additional flour for dusting dough during rolling

In a food processor with a metal blade, puree pimientos with whole egg and yolk for about 1 minute. Add flour and salt and process until a dough ball forms. Wrap in plastic wrap and allow to sit for 1 hour. With a sharp knife, cut dough in 8 equal pieces. Using a pasta maker, run the first piece of dough through the #1 setting several times, folding the piece in half after each run. Dust with flour if dough strips are sticky. Keep remaining dough covered. Roll the dough through the next 4 settings. Lay the strip of pasta on a tea towel. Proceed in same fashion with the remaining dough. Allow the strips to rest for 15 to 30 minutes (do not let edges dry out). Cut each strip of pasta into fettuccine and toss with a little additional flour.

Cook the pasta in boiling, salted water 2 to 3 minutes. Drain and toss with sauce of your choice.

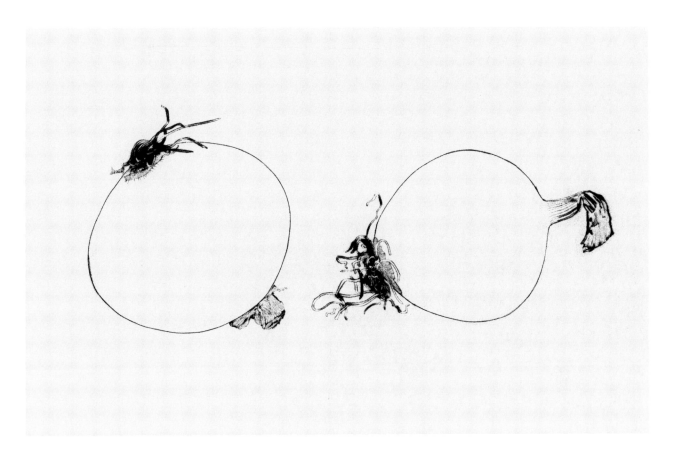

7.
Sweet Spanish Yellow
mixed intaglio

Spinach Fettuccine with Salmon and Scallops

Phillip Lacock, California Cafe Bar and Grill, Walnut Creek

Serves 2 as a main course or 4 to 6 as a first course

A White Zinfandel is suggested.

Chef Phillip Lacock particularly likes this recipe because of the mild seafood flavors and the appealing combination of colors.

PASTA:

1½ cups all-purpose flour
¼ teaspoon salt
1 whole egg
2 egg yolks
¼ cup cooked spinach, squeezed dry

SAUCE:

2 cups whipping cream
½ cup diced salmon
½ cup scallops, cut in bite-sized pieces
1 small sweet red bell pepper, cored, seeded, and cut in julienne
½ cup small snow peas, trimmed and strings removed
⅔ cup freshly grated Parmesan cheese

Salt and freshly ground black pepper
Freshly grated Parmesan cheese for garnish

To prepare Pasta: In a food processor with a metal blade, process the flour and salt for several seconds. Then add the whole egg, egg yolks, and spinach. Process until a dough ball forms. If a dough ball does not form, warm water may be added, 1 tablespoon at a time. If too sticky, flour may be added, 1 tablespoon at a time. Knead the dough ball on a floured surface for several minutes until it forms a smooth ball. With a sharp knife, cut dough in 4 equal pieces. Using a pasta maker, run the first piece of dough through the #1 setting several times, folding the piece in half after each run. Dust with flour if dough strips are sticky. Keep remaining dough covered to prevent drying. Roll the dough through the next four settings. Proceed with the remaining dough. Cut each strip of pasta into fettuccine. After cutting, toss fettuccine with a little additional flour.

Bring 3 quarts of water and 1 tablespoon salt to a boil.

Meanwhile, to prepare Sauce: In a sauté pan, bring the cream to a gentle boil and reduce to 1½ cups. Add salmon, scallops, bell pepper, and snow peas and continue to boil gently about 5 minutes until fish pieces are cooked. Remove from heat and add Parmesan cheese; mix well (sauce will be thin).

Place fettuccine in rapidly boiling water and cook until just tender, about 1 minute. Drain and toss with sauce.

Add salt and pepper and additional Parmesan cheese as desired.

Spinach-Gorgonzola Sauce for Pasta

Arel Wente, Wente Bros. Winery, Livermore

Serves 2 as a main course

A Sauvignon Blanc or Cabernet Sauvignon is suggested.

8 ounces dried fettuccine or fusilli
2 tablespoons butter
4 ounces Gorgonzola cheese, crumbled
1 bunch fresh spinach, cooked, drained, and pureed, or 1 package (10 ounces) frozen spinach, thawed, squeezed dry, and pureed
1 tablespoon beef extract paste, such as Bovril, undiluted
¼ cup Wente Bros. Sparkling Brut
1 clove garlic, minced
Freshly ground black pepper
½ to ¾ cup whipping cream

Freshly grated Parmesan cheese for garnish

Spinach, because of the variety of ways it can be prepared and its nutritional value, is one of Arel Wente's favorite ingredients. Guests at Arel's home are frequently treated to a delicious meal featuring a spinach dish and a carefully selected wine.

Bring 3 quarts water plus 1 tablespoon salt to a boil.

Meanwhile, in a 2-quart saucepan, melt butter and cheese over low heat. Stir to blend. Add spinach, beef extract, and wine. Simmer about 5 minutes. Add garlic and pepper. Gradually stir in cream to form a soft, but not runny, sauce. Simmer 3 to 4 minutes.

Cook pasta in the boiling salted water until just tender; drain. Pour sauce over the pasta and garnish with freshly grated Parmesan cheese.

N O T E : To serve as a first course, divide into 4 to 6 portions and serve on individual plates.

Eggplant Lasagna

Serves 8 to 10

A Charbono is suggested.

¼ cup olive oil
1 large onion, finely chopped
2 large cloves garlic, minced
1 eggplant (about 2 pounds), peeled and cut in ¼- to ½-inch dice
½ pound mushrooms, sliced
1½ pounds ripe tomatoes, peeled and chopped (including juices)
8 ounces tomato paste
½ cup red wine
2 carrots, grated
¼ cup minced fresh parsley
1 tablespoon fresh oregano, or 1 teaspoon dried, crumbled
2 tablespoons chopped fresh basil, or 2 teaspoons dried leaves
1 teaspoon salt
¼ teaspoon freshly ground black pepper
8 ounces dried lasagna noodles
1 pound ricotta cheese
1 pound mozzarella cheese, thinly sliced
1½ cups (about 5 ounces) freshly grated Romano or Parmesan cheese (reserve 3 tablespoons for garnish)

In a large skillet, heat olive oil over medium-low heat. Sauté onion, garlic, eggplant, and mushrooms for 15 minutes, stirring until soft. Stir in tomatoes, tomato paste, wine, carrots, and seasonings. Simmer, covered, for 30 minutes.

Preheat oven to 350 degrees.

Toward the end of the sauce's cooking time, cook lasagna noodles in boiling, salted water until just tender; drain.

In a 9- by 13-inch baking dish (or larger), layer eggplant sauce, noodles, and the three cheeses. Repeat layers, ending with the sauce. Sprinkle with reserved Romano or Parmesan.

Bake, uncovered, 30 to 45 minutes, or until cheese is melted and lasagna is heated through. Remove from oven and let stand for 15 minutes before cutting into squares.

Grilled Summer Vegetable Pasta

Alice Waters, Chez Panisse, Berkeley

Serves 2

A Zinfandel is suggested.

2 salt-packed anchovies, filleted and rinsed
  Virgin olive oil
3 bell peppers: yellow, green, red
6 to 8 small Japanese eggplants
  Salt and freshly ground black pepper
8 ripe plum tomatoes
1 young red onion
1 or 2 cloves garlic, finely minced
  Tagliatelle for 2 (about 6 ounces uncooked pasta)
  A few fresh basil leaves, cut in a chiffonade (fine strips)

One summer day in Provence, Alice Waters and some friends decided it was simply too hot to cook in the kitchen. They made an outside grill and sat down to this enticing summer meal.

Pound the anchovy fillets in a mortar with a little olive oil to make a smooth paste.

Make a charcoal fire.

While the charcoal is still flaming, grill the peppers so that the skin is black and blistered all around. Let them cool and peel away the charred skin. Cut in half lengthwise and remove the seeds and stem. Use a paring knife or a towel to remove any little bits of black on the exterior, then cut the peppers into wide strips.

Cut the unpeeled eggplants in lengthwise slices about ¼ inch thick. Brush the slices with olive oil and season with salt and pepper. Grill them over the hot fire a few minutes on each side so that they are lightly browned. Cut the plum tomatoes in half and season with salt and pepper. Grill them, skin side down, until they get a little color and begin to soften.

Slice the onion in rings. Brush with olive oil, season with salt and pepper, and grill them until browned and tender.

Combine the anchovy paste, tomato halves, garlic, and a tablespoon of oil in a sauté pan. Cook gently a few minutes until the tomatoes release their juices and form a sauce. Add the grilled vegetables and continue to simmer a few minutes more.

Meanwhile, cook the pasta in boiling, salted water until just tender. Drain and add to the vegetables. Season with pepper and toss the noodles well in the juices. Serve garnished with all the vegetables and the chiffonade of basil.

Veal and Canadian Bacon with Pasta

Serves 4 to 6

A Merlot is suggested.

1 pound ground veal
¼ cup olive oil
½ teaspoon salt
¼ teaspoon freshly ground black pepper
½ pound small mushrooms, halved
½ pound Canadian bacon, cut in ½-inch dice
1 large red onion, minced
1 large ripe tomato, coarsely chopped
1 cup chopped fresh parsley
½ cup butter
1 pound dried spaghetti or fettuccine
¼ cup butter

Freshly grated Parmesan cheese for garnish

In a large skillet, lightly brown veal in olive oil over medium heat, breaking up chunks with a spoon. Season with salt and pepper. Stir in mushrooms, Canadian bacon, onion, tomato, parsley, and ½ cup butter. Sauté, stirring occasionally, until vegetables are soft. Reduce heat; simmer, uncovered, for about 10 to 15 minutes.

Meanwhile, cook the pasta in boiling, salted water until just tender. Drain well. Return to cooking pot and add ¼ cup butter; season with additional salt and pepper, if desired. Toss until butter has melted.

To serve, top pasta with hot veal sauce. Pass Parmesan cheese to sprinkle over top.

N O T E : To vary, substitute ground turkey for the veal, or prosciutto for the Canadian bacon.

Spaghettini with Hot Italian Sausage

Elizabeth Martini, Louis M. Martini Winery, St. Helena

Serves 4 to 6

The Martinis suggest their Cabernet or Merlot.

1 pound hot Italian sausage in casings
2 tablespoons olive oil
2 cloves garlic, finely minced
1 can (28 ounces) Italian plum tomatoes, drained and chopped
1 cup finely chopped fresh parsley
1 sprig fresh oregano, or 1 teaspoon dried
   Salt and freshly ground black pepper
1 pound dried spaghettini
½ pound snow peas, strings removed, and peas chilled in ice water
½ pound tender, young zucchini, thinly sliced
3 sweet red bell peppers, cored, seeded, and thinly sliced
2 tablespoons olive oil
¼ cup chopped fresh basil

Chopped fresh parsley and freshly grated Parmesan cheese for garnish
French bread for accompaniment

This recipe was developed in honor of the fiftieth anniversary of the Louis M. Martini Winery.

In a medium skillet, boil sausage in water to cover until cooked through, about 30 minutes. Set aside until cool enough to handle. Remove casings and slice thinly. Discard cooking liquid.

In the same skillet, brown sausage in 2 tablespoons hot oil over medium-high heat. Remove sausage. Discard all but 2 tablespoons fat from skillet. Add garlic and sauté until translucent. Do not brown. Add tomatoes, parsley, oregano, salt, and pepper. Cover and simmer gently 15 minutes, stirring occasionally. If necessary, add a little water to keep moist. Add sausage, cover, and keep warm.

Cook the spaghettini in boiling, salted water until just tender; drain.

Meanwhile, drain the snow peas and dry on paper towels. In a large skillet, sauté the zucchini and red bell peppers in remaining 2 tablespoons oil over medium-high heat 1 to 2 minutes. Add the snow peas and sauté until they turn bright green, but are still tender-crisp. Add the vegetables to the sauce and toss thoroughly with the pasta and basil in a very large bowl.

To serve, sprinkle with parsley and Parmesan cheese. Pass additional Parmesan cheese and serve with French bread.

Seafood Spaghetti

Serves 6 to 8

A dry Chenin Blanc or a Dry Semillon is suggested.

1 large onion, minced
2 cloves garlic, minced
3 tablespoons olive oil
¼ cup dry white wine
1½ tablespoons chopped fresh basil, or 1½ teaspoons dried
1 tablespoon minced fresh marjoram leaves, or 1 teaspoon dried
2½ cups peeled and chopped ripe tomatoes, including juice
1 pound dried spaghetti
1½ pounds small clams in their shells
1 pound scallops, cut in bite-sized pieces
½ pound large raw shrimp, shelled, deveined, and butterflied
Salt and freshly ground black pepper

In a 4-quart saucepan, sauté onion and garlic in oil over medium-high heat until lightly colored, but not brown. Stir in wine, basil, and marjoram, and cook 1 minute. Reduce heat, add tomatoes, and simmer, covered, for about 10 minutes.

Meanwhile, cook spaghetti in boiling, salted water until just tender; drain.

Add clams to tomato mixture and cook until shells open (about 5 minutes). Discard any shells which fail to open. Add scallops and shrimp. Cover and cook 2 to 3 minutes, or until scallops are opaque and shrimp are pink. Season with salt and pepper.

Toss the tomato-seafood sauce with the spaghetti.

Pasta with Shrimp Butter

Elizabeth Martini, Louis M. Martini Winery, St. Helena

Serves 4

Elizabeth Martini suggests a crisp Chardonnay.

The Martinis are particularly interested in pairing wines with food. Elizabeth Martini finds pasta to be especially versatile and complemented by both red and white wines.

SHRIMP BUTTER:
1 pound medium raw shrimp in their shells
½ cup white wine
½ pound butter, clarified

PASTA:
½ pound dried egg or spinach pasta (fettuccine or other ribbon pasta works well)
1 medium clove garlic, minced
Freshly grated Parmesan cheese
1 medium clove garlic, minced

Chopped fresh parsley or fresh basil for garnish

To prepare Shrimp Butter: Clean shrimp, saving shells. Set shrimp aside for later use. In a food processor, process shells and wine until shells are finely chopped. In a medium skillet, cook shell mixture with butter over low heat for 15 minutes, stirring frequently. Strain through cheesecloth into a bowl, squeezing out all the juices. Discard the shells.

Cook pasta in boiling, salted water until just tender; drain. In a large skillet, melt half the Shrimp Butter over low heat. Add 1 clove minced garlic and sauté for 1 minute. Add cooked pasta, and toss until well coated. Place in a serving bowl and sprinkle with Parmesan cheese.

In the same skillet, sauté 1 clove minced garlic in remaining Shrimp Butter over low heat for 1 minute. Add the reserved shrimp and sauté 1 to 2 minutes, or until they turn pink and are just cooked through. Pour over pasta and toss. Serve immediately.

Garnish with chopped parsley or basil.

NOTE: The Shrimp Butter can be made up to 1 day in advance and refrigerated until needed.

Pasta Primavera Salad

Serves 8 to 10

A Burgundy is suggested.

DRESSING:
⅔ cup olive oil
Juice of 1 large lemon (about ¼ cup)
¼ cup wine vinegar
2 teaspoons salt
½ teaspoon freshly ground black pepper
3 cloves garlic, minced
2 tablespoons chopped fresh basil leaves
2 tablespoons Dijon-style mustard

1 package (12 ounces) large shell macaroni
1 pound mushrooms, thinly sliced
1 pint whole ripe cherry tomatoes, stemmed
1 can (6 ounces) pitted whole black olives, drained
1 bunch green onions (about 6), thinly sliced (including green portion)
1 pound snow peas, trimmed and strings removed
4 carrots, thinly sliced
1 bunch broccoli, cut in flowerets
1 head cauliflower, cut in flowerets

Salt and freshly ground black pepper

Red leaf lettuce leaves

Also known as Chinese pea pods and sugar peas, snow peas are very young pea pods that are so tender the whole pod can be eaten. Cook snow peas just until bright green and still crunchy. Mature snow peas should have their stringy filament removed.

In a small bowl, combine dressing ingredients and set aside.

Cook pasta in boiling, salted water until just tender; drain.

In a large mixing bowl, combine pasta, mushrooms, tomatoes, olives, green onions, and snow peas. Refrigerate while blanching remaining vegetables.

Drop carrots and broccoli into briskly boiling water for 2 to 3 minutes. Drain, and plunge immediately into cold water to stop the cooking process. Drain well. Blanch the cauliflower in briskly boiling water for 3 to 5 minutes. Drain and plunge into cold water; drain well. Carrot slices, broccoli, and cauliflower should all be tender-crisp. Toss vegetables with the chilled pasta mixture.

Pour dressing over the salad and toss. Chill until ready to serve. Season with salt and pepper as desired.

Serve on a bed of red leaf lettuce leaves.

Vermicelli Salad

Serves 8 to 10

A Dry Semillon is suggested.

1 pound dried vermicelli, broken in pieces
Juice of 3 large lemons (about ¾ cup)
1½ pounds tiny cooked shrimp
1½ cups chopped celery
6 green onions, thinly sliced (including green portion)
3 hard-cooked eggs, chopped
1 jar (4 ounces) pimientos, drained and chopped
2 cups mayonnaise (page 69)
2 tablespoons snipped fresh dill
Salt and freshly ground black pepper

Paprika, chopped fresh parsley, and 1 sliced hard-cooked egg for garnish

Cook vermicelli in boiling, salted water until just tender. Drain well and toss with lemon juice.

Combine remaining ingredients, except garnishes, and toss well with the vermicelli. Refrigerate overnight. Adjust seasonings, if necessary.

To serve, garnish with paprika, parsley, and egg.

Smoked Salmon Pasta Salad

Elaine C. Bell, Elaine Bell Catering Company, Sonoma

Serves 6

*Elaine Bell
suggests a
Sauvignon Blanc.*

8 ounces small shell pasta
8 ounces smoked salmon, cut in ½-inch-wide strips
1 cucumber, peeled, seeded, sliced, and cut in quarters
1 small white boiling onion, sliced in thin rings
4 green onions, thinly sliced (including green portion)
2 tablespoons drained capers
1 tablespoon fresh dill, or 1 teaspoon dried
¾ cup sour cream
¼ cup mayonnaise (page 69)
2 tablespoons fresh lemon juice
Salt and freshly ground black pepper

*This salad is one
of many Elaine
Bell creates for the
Oakville Grocery.
In the summer she
serves it with
mixed greens, and
in the winter with
hot tomato soup.*

Cook pasta in boiling, salted water until just tender. Drain and cool.

Combine all ingredients in a large bowl and cover tightly with plastic wrap. Refrigerate 1 to 2 days.

At serving time, taste for seasoning and add additional salt and pepper as desired.

N O T E : This recipe doubles or triples well. Cooked scallops and prawns can be substituted for the salmon.

Chinese Noodle Salad

Serves 6 to 8

DRESSING:

½ cup peanut oil

2 tablespoons sesame oil*

¾ cup soy sauce

¾ cup rice wine vinegar*

½ cup sugar

1 pound package uncooked Chinese soft noodles*

1 tablespoon sesame oil*

TOPPINGS (CHOOSE SEVERAL OR
ALL OF THE FOLLOWING):

½ cup cooked tiny shrimp

½ cup cooked ham, cut in julienne

½ cup cooked chicken, cut in julienne

½ cup thinly sliced cucumber

1 sweet red bell pepper, cored, seeded, and cut in julienne

½ cup cooked green beans, cut in julienne

½ cup blanched broccoli flowerets

3 tablespoons toasted sesame seeds†

1 can (8 ounces) sliced water chestnuts, drained

1 cup shelled green peas, cooked

2 green onions, thinly sliced (including green portion)

½ pound blanched snow peas, strings removed

Combine dressing ingredients in a small bowl.

Cook noodles according to package directions. Drain and rinse well in cold water. Let noodles sit for 5 minutes in cold water to which 1 tablespoon of sesame oil has been added. Stir, then drain.

To serve, heap noodles in the center of a serving platter, surround with desired toppings, and pass dressing separately. Guests assemble their own salads.

NOTE: The number of servings will vary according to the number of toppings selected.

†Toast sesame seeds in a small skillet over medium heat for about 10 minutes, or until golden, shaking the pan frequently. Cool.

*Available at oriental markets and well-stocked supermarkets.

CHAPTER SIX

Vegetables

Vegetable Terrine

Serves 8

CUSTARD:

3 eggs
¼ cup whipping cream

MUSHROOM LAYER:

½ pound mushrooms, coarsely chopped
2 tablespoons butter
¼ teaspoon salt
⅛ teaspoon ground white pepper

CARROT LAYER:

½ pound carrots (about 2 large), sliced
1 tablespoon butter
1 tablespoon sugar
¼ teaspoon salt
⅛ teaspoon ground white pepper

BROCCOLI LAYER:

¾ to 1 pound broccoli, flowerets removed and reserved for garnish
¼ teaspoon salt
⅛ teaspoon ground white pepper

JERUSALEM ARTICHOKE LAYER:

¾ pound Jerusalem artichokes (see Note)
¼ teaspoon salt
⅛ teaspoon ground white pepper

Originally, terrine referred to the earthenware dish used to prepare a baked meat dish, as well as the food it contained. Now the term includes all types of baked loaves, whether vegetable, fish, or meat.

Butter a 1½-quart non-metal loaf pan.

To prepare Custard: Combine eggs and whipping cream and beat until they are well blended. Set aside.

To prepare Mushroom Layer: In a 10-inch skillet, sauté mushrooms in butter until mushrooms are soft and the moisture released by the mushrooms evaporates, about 8 to 10 minutes. Stir in salt and pepper. Puree mushrooms in a food processor or blender. Add ¼ cup of the custard mixture and blend. Pour the puree into the prepared loaf pan and smooth with a rubber spatula.

To prepare Carrot Layer: In the same skillet, combine carrots, butter, sugar, salt, and pepper. Simmer, covered, until moisture evaporates, about 10 to 15 minutes. Puree carrots in a food processor. Add ¼ cup custard mixture and blend. Pour the puree over the mushroom layer and smooth.

continued

To prepare Broccoli Layer: Peel broccoli stems with a vegetable peeler to remove the tough, fibrous parts. Slice stems and leaves. Place broccoli in the same skillet. Add just enough water to cover, and cook with salt and pepper for 5 to 10 minutes, or until just tender. Drain. Puree, add ¼ cup custard mixture, and blend. Pour broccoli mixture over carrot layer and smooth.

To prepare Jerusalem Artichoke Layer: Peel the Jerusalem artichokes as well as possible and cut in chunks. Boil chunks in covered skillet with just enough water to cover, and cook with salt and pepper for 5 to 7 minutes. Drain. Puree, add remaining custard mixture, and blend. Pour over broccoli layer and smooth.

Preheat oven to 325 degrees.

Cut a piece of waxed paper to cover the top of the loaf pan; butter one side. Set buttered waxed paper, buttered side down, over the Jerusalem artichoke puree. Cover tightly with aluminum foil, then set in a 9- by 13-inch baking pan. Add enough hot water to reach halfway up the sides of the loaf pan.

Bake 40 to 50 minutes, or until terrine is set and has pulled away slightly from the sides of the loaf pan. Cool at least 15 minutes before unmolding. Remove foil and waxed paper from top.

While terrine is cooling, blanch reserved broccoli flowerets in ½ cup boiling water 2 to 3 minutes. Drain, then refresh under cold water.

Gently invert terrine onto a serving platter.

To serve, slice terrine in ¾-inch slices. Arrange the reserved broccoli flowerets around the terrine.

NOTE: Also called sunchokes or sun roots, Jerusalem artichokes are a tuber or root vegetable.

This terrine is equally good served hot, chilled, or reheated. The terrine can also be made in ½-cup individual buttered molds. Any vegetable can be substituted for those in the recipe as long as the color contrast between each layer is maintained.

Artichokes with Crumb Topping

Serves 8

4 to 6 large artichokes
1 teaspoon salt

WHITE SAUCE:
3 tablespoons butter
3 tablespoons all-purpose flour
1½ cups milk
½ teaspoon salt

½ cup mayonnaise (page 69)
¾ cup (about 3 ounces) grated Cheddar cheese
¾ cup fresh bread crumbs combined with 2 tablespoons melted butter

Artichokes, primarily the Green Globe variety, are grown in Castroville, just south of San Francisco. California is the world's largest supplier of this vegetable.

Wash artichokes and trim off stems. Place in a large kettle, add boiling water to cover and 1 teaspoon salt. Boil gently, covered, about 45 minutes, or until artichokes are very tender when the bottom is pierced with the tip of a knife. Drain and cool.

With a stainless steel spoon, scrape the meat off each leaf. Discard the remainder of the leaf. When the tender, purple-tipped cone of light-colored leaves is reached, coarsely chop the bottom portions and discard the tops. Discard the choke (thistle) and coarsely chop the heart. Set artichoke meat aside. There should be 3 to 4 cups.

In a small skillet, melt butter and blend in flour until smooth. Cook several minutes over medium heat. Gradually add milk, stirring constantly to prevent lumps from forming. Cook, stirring until thickened, about 5 minutes. Add salt. Mix white sauce with artichoke meat, then add mayonnaise and cheese.

Preheat oven to 350 degrees.

Turn the mixture into a shallow 1-quart baking dish. Sprinkle with buttered bread crumbs. Bake 35 to 40 minutes, or until bread crumbs are lightly browned and artichoke mixture is bubbling.

Serve hot.

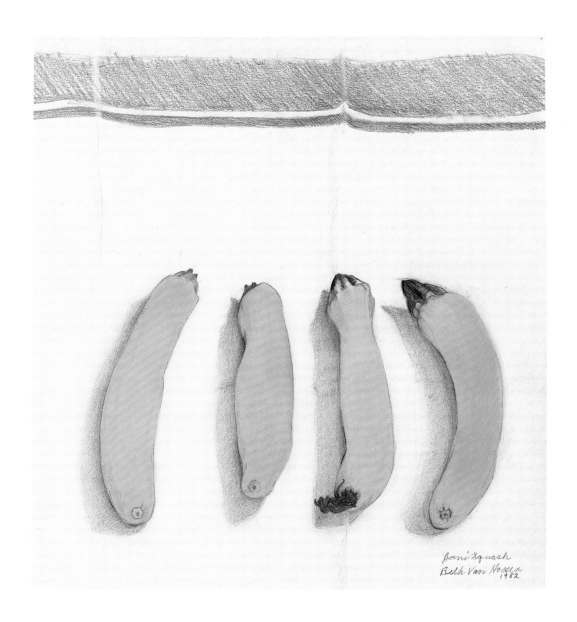

8.
Jan's Squash
color pencil

Artichokes Florentine

Makes 18 to 24 pieces

18 to 24 small mushrooms (each about 1 inch in diameter)
　　2 tablespoons butter
　¼ cup butter
　　1 small clove garlic, minced
　　1 tablespoon all-purpose flour
　½ cup milk
　　2 bunches fresh spinach, washed, trimmed, chopped, blanched, and squeezed dry, or 2 packages (10 ounces each) frozen chopped spinach, thawed and squeezed dry
　½ teaspoon salt
　⅛ teaspoon ground nutmeg
　　3 cans (8 ounces each) water-packed artichoke bottoms, drained

SAUCE:
　½ cup sour cream
　½ cup mayonnaise (page 69)
　　2 tablespoons fresh lemon juice

Separate mushroom caps and stems. Chop stems and set aside. In a medium skillet, sauté caps on both sides in 2 tablespoons butter until lightly browned. Remove with a slotted spoon and set aside. Melt ¼ cup butter in the same skillet. Lightly sauté chopped stems and minced garlic 1 to 2 minutes. Sprinkle with flour and stir well to incorporate. Slowly add milk, stirring constantly, until sauce thickens. Stir in spinach, salt, and nutmeg.

Lay artichoke bottoms in a 9- by 13-inch baking dish. Fill each bottom with the spinach mixture, mounding slightly.

Preheat oven to 375 degrees.

To prepare Sauce: Combine all sauce ingredients in a bowl, stirring until smooth. Spoon about 1 tablespoon sauce over each spinach mound and top with a mushroom cap.

Bake for 15 minutes, or until heated through.

Norwegian Asparagus

Serves 6 to 8

2 pounds asparagus
Salt and freshly ground black pepper
½ cup lime marmalade
1 tablespoon rum
1 tablespoon butter
2 strips orange peel

½ cup (about 2 ounces) toasted slivered almonds for garnish†

Asparagus, herald of spring, has a very short season—April to June. Choose stalks that are bright green and firm, with closed tips. As the stalks are extremely perishable, store them wrapped in a moist paper towel in the refrigerator and use as soon as possible.

Preheat oven to 350 degrees.

Trim asparagus and peel the bottom of the stalks if they are woody. Place the asparagus on a large sheet of aluminum foil; sprinkle with salt and pepper. Wrap the asparagus securely with the foil and bake for 30 minutes.

In a small saucepan, combine marmalade, rum, butter, and orange peel. Heat until marmalade melts and the sauce is hot. Discard the orange peel.

Transfer the cooked asparagus to a serving plate. Pour the sauce over the asparagus. Top with toasted almonds and serve hot.

†Toast almonds in a 325 degree oven for 5 to 10 minutes, or until lightly browned. Cool.

Sautéed Red Bell Peppers

Victoria Wise, Pig-by-the-Tail Charcuterie, Berkeley

Serves 8

3 pounds sweet red bell peppers (about 8 large), cored, seeded, and sliced in ½-inch strips

12 cloves garlic, peeled and coarsely chopped

1 tablespoon chopped fresh oregano, or 1 teaspoon dried

½ teaspoon salt

¼ teaspoon freshly ground black pepper

½ cup olive oil

2 tablespoons capers, rinsed and squeezed dry

Early Spanish explorers were seeking the peppercorn berry when they came upon this native American vegetable. They gave it the name of what they had originally hoped to find. The bell pepper, named for its shape, is a large sweet variety, green when young and bright red when mature. Red bell peppers, once only seasonally available, can now be found nearly all year in California markets. For this recipe, Victoria Wise suggests selecting red peppers with unwrinkled skins.

In a skillet, sauté peppers, garlic, oregano, salt, and pepper in oil over medium heat, stirring occasionally, for 20 to 30 minutes, or until peppers are cooked through but still hold their shape. Remove from heat and stir in capers.

Serve hot, cold, or at room temperature.

Broccoli California

Serves 4 to 6

1 small bunch broccoli (about 1 pound)
2 tablespoons butter
2 tablespoons all-purpose flour
½ cup milk
2 tablespoons sherry
½ cup mayonnaise (page 69)
3 eggs, well beaten
¼ to ½ cup grated onion (about ½ of a small onion)
½ teaspoon salt
¼ teaspoon freshly ground black pepper
3 tablespoons freshly grated Romano or Asiago cheese
Paprika

Broccoli, a relative of the cabbage family, has enjoyed cyclical popularity in America. It was grown prior to the Revolution, faded into obscurity during the days of protein-rich diets in the eighteenth and nineteenth centuries, and once again regained a place on the American dining table in the 1920s, where it has remained ever since.

Wash, trim, and separate broccoli into flowerets and stems. Steam broccoli 5 to 7 minutes, or until tender when pierced with the tip of a knife. Plunge into cold water to refresh. Drain and chop finely. Set aside.

Preheat oven to 350 degrees. Butter a 1-quart straight-sided baking dish.

In a small saucepan, melt butter; stir in flour until smooth. Cook over medium heat several minutes, but do not brown. Slowly whisk in milk and bring mixture to a boil, stirring constantly. Remove from heat and briskly stir in sherry, mayonnaise, and eggs. Fold in broccoli, onion, salt, and pepper. Turn mixture into prepared baking dish. Sprinkle with cheese and paprika.

Bake about 30 minutes, or until set.

Broccoli with Orange Sauce

Paul Mayer, Paul Mayer Cooking School, San Francisco

Serves 6

1½ pounds broccoli
¼ cup butter, melted
¼ cup freshly grated Parmesan cheese

ORANGE SAUCE:
3 tablespoons butter
3 tablespoons all-purpose flour
¼ teaspoon salt
⅛ teaspoon cayenne pepper
¼ teaspoon celery salt
1 cup milk
¼ cup whipping cream
3 tablespoons fresh orange juice
1 tablespoon fresh lemon juice
1 tablespoon grated orange peel
1 teaspoon grated lemon peel

¼ cup sliced almonds for garnish

Wash and peel broccoli and cut into lengthwise strips with flowerets attached to each piece of stalk. Cook in boiling water to cover about 7 minutes, or until just tender. Drain and rinse in cold water to stop the cooking process. Drain again. Dip each broccoli stalk in melted butter, then place in a 9- by 13-inch baking dish. Sprinkle broccoli with Parmesan cheese.

Preheat oven to 425 degrees.

To prepare the Orange Sauce: In a small saucepan, melt butter over low heat. Remove from heat and stir in flour. Season with salt, cayenne, and celery salt. Return to heat and slowly add milk, stirring constantly, until a thick sauce forms. Add whipping cream, orange and lemon juices, and peels; stir until creamy. Pour over broccoli and sprinkle with almonds.

Bake the broccoli about 10 minutes, until sauce is bubbling and almonds are lightly toasted.

Beer-glazed Carrots

Serves 4 to 6

2 pounds carrots, halved lengthwise, and cut in 2- to 3-inch pieces
1 teaspoon grated lemon peel
¼ teaspoon salt
¼ teaspoon freshly ground black pepper
1 tablespoon sugar
3 tablespoons butter, cut in pieces
1 cup beef stock
1 cup beer
6 large mushroom caps (optional)

1 tablespoon chopped fresh parsley for garnish

Place carrots in a 10-inch skillet and sprinkle with lemon peel, salt, pepper, and sugar. Dot with butter. Add stock and beer. Top with mushroom caps, if desired. Bring to a boil, reduce heat, and simmer, uncovered, for about 40 minutes, or until liquid is thick and syrupy. Stir occasionally. If necessary, remove carrots (and mushrooms) with a slotted spoon when tender and continue to boil liquid until syrupy. Return carrots to the skillet and coat with syrup.

To serve, sprinkle with parsley. Top each serving with a mushroom, if desired.

Winter Vegetable Bake

Serves 6

1 head cauliflower (about 2½ pounds), cut in flowerets
⅓ cup butter
½ pound mushrooms, thickly sliced
½ green bell pepper, cored, seeded, and cut in ¼-inch dice
¼ cup all-purpose flour
2 cups milk
1 teaspoon salt
Dash cayenne pepper
1 cup (about 4 ounces) grated sharp Cheddar cheese
1 jar (2 ounces) diced pimientos, drained

Paprika for garnish

"Cauliflower,"
said Mark Twain,
"is nothing but a
cabbage with a
college education."

Preheat oven to 350 degrees.

Cook cauliflower in boiling water until barely tender, about 3 to 6 minutes. Drain well. Set aside.

In a 2-quart saucepan, melt butter over medium heat. Add mushrooms and green pepper. Blend in flour and cook, stirring, 2 to 3 minutes. Gradually add milk, stirring constantly, until a thick sauce forms. Mix in salt and cayenne.

Place half the cauliflowerets in a 1½-quart casserole. Cover with half the cheese, half the pimientos, and half the mushroom-cream sauce. Repeat layers, ending with sauce. Sprinkle with paprika.

Bake, uncovered, for 30 minutes.

Creamed Chard

Judy Rodgers, former Chef, The Union Hotel, Benicia

Serves 4

1 pound fresh, young white-ribbed Swiss chard, washed
2 tablespoons butter
½ cup finely chopped white onion
1½ tablespoons Dijon-style mustard
1 teaspoon minced garlic
¼ cup sour cream
¼ to ½ teaspoon salt
⅛ teaspoon ground white pepper

Chard, or white beet, is at its peak during July. Its name is derived from the French word for thistle, and although a member of the beet family, chard is prized for its leaves rather than its root.

Remove the ribs from the chard, separating green from white portions and removing stringy filaments (as for celery). Discard blemished pieces. Coarsely chop white ribs. If mature or at all leathery, blanch the green portions of the chard in salted water 1 to 2 minutes, or until leaves just begin to wilt. Drain and coarsely chop.

In a medium stainless steel skillet, sauté the ribs in butter 2 to 3 minutes. Add onion. Reduce heat to low and cook 10 minutes or until onion is soft, but not browned. Add chopped greens, mustard, garlic, and sour cream. Taste for seasoning; add salt and pepper, if desired.

Gently cook, covered, 5 minutes, or until flavors are blended and chard is tender.

Corn Pudding

Serves 6

4 large ears fresh corn, or 2 packages (10 ounces each) frozen corn kernels
¼ cup butter
3 eggs
½ cup whipping cream
½ teaspoon salt
¼ teaspoon freshly ground black pepper

Preheat oven to 350 degrees.

Husk fresh corn and cook for 5 minutes in boiling water to cover. Drain and cool just enough to handle. With a sharp knife, remove kernels from cobs. There should be 3 to 4 cups. Place kernels in a bowl and toss with butter. If using frozen corn, cook according to package directions, drain well, and toss with butter. Add eggs, cream, salt, and pepper, and beat vigorously with a spoon until well blended. Pour mixture into a 1-quart casserole and bake, uncovered, for 45 minutes, or until golden brown on top.

Jerusalem Artichokes with Cream Sauce

Paul Mayer, Paul Mayer Cooking School, San Francisco

Serves 4

1 pound Jerusalem artichokes (see Note)
½ cup chopped onion
2 tablespoons chopped fresh parsley
1 clove garlic, minced
2 tablespoons butter
2 tablespoons olive oil

SAUCE (OPTIONAL):
2 tablespoons butter
1 tablespoon all-purpose flour
Salt and freshly ground black pepper
½ cup milk
½ cup whipping cream
1 chicken bouillon cube, crumbled

Chopped fresh parsley for garnish

Jerusalem artichokes are native to America, not the Holy Land as their name implies. When cooked, their flavor is reminiscent of the globe artichoke, but when served raw is similar to water chestnuts. Jerusalem artichokes are best if used promptly, as their texture deteriorates quickly once harvested.

Scrub artichokes under running water to remove any trace of sand or dirt. Peeling is optional. Drain, dry, and cut in ½-inch cubes. Set aside. In a small bowl, combine onion, parsley, and garlic and mix well.

In a 2-quart saucepan, sauté onion mixture in 2 tablespoons butter and olive oil over medium heat, stirring frequently, until onions are translucent. Add artichoke cubes, stir well, and cover pot. Cook over low heat for 25 minutes, or until artichokes are tender, but not mushy.

To prepare optional Sauce: In a small skillet or saucepan, melt 2 tablespoons butter. Stir in flour and cook several minutes, stirring. Season with salt and pepper. Remove from heat and stir in milk, cream, and the crumbled bouillon cube. Return to medium heat and cook, stirring, until sauce boils. Pour sauce over artichokes and cook an additional 5 minutes.

Serve plain or with sauce. Garnish with chopped parsley.

NOTE: Also called sunchokes or sun roots, Jerusalem artichokes are a tuber or root vegetable.

Clam-stuffed Mushrooms

Serves 4

8 large (2½ inches in diameter) mushrooms
1 small onion, minced
2 tablespoons butter
½ cup fresh white bread crumbs (about 1 slice bread, crusts removed)
1 can (7½ ounces) minced clams, drained
1 tablespoon minced fresh parsley
3 tablespoons dry vermouth
1 clove garlic, minced
¼ teaspoon dried tarragon, crumbled
1 egg yolk
3 tablespoons whipping cream
2 tablespoons butter
3 tablespoons freshly grated Parmesan cheese

Preheat oven to 350 degrees.

Pull stems from mushrooms. Set caps aside and mince stems. In a small skillet, sauté the minced stems and onion in 2 tablespoons butter over medium heat until onion is translucent. Add the bread crumbs, clams, parsley, vermouth, garlic, and tarragon and cook 3 minutes longer, stirring to combine. Beat egg yolk with cream and stir into the mushroom mixture.

Melt 2 tablespoons butter in an 8- by 8-inch baking pan, or a pan large enough to hold mushrooms in a single layer. Tilt pan to coat bottom, add mushroom caps, and coat with butter. Arrange caps with gills facing up and mound with the stuffing. Sprinkle with grated Parmesan cheese. Bake 15 minutes.

Serve hot.

Baked Curried Onions

Serves 6

1 pound pearl onions or small white boiling onions
3 tablespoons butter
2 tablespoons all-purpose flour
½ cup beef stock
½ cup milk
½ teaspoon curry powder
½ teaspoon salt
¼ teaspoon cayenne pepper
¼ teaspoon paprika
¼ teaspoon freshly ground black pepper
¼ cup (about 1 ounce) grated sharp Cheddar cheese

The smallest in the onion hierarchy, white pearl onions are marble-sized. Boiling onions range from one to three inches in diameter and are yellow, red, or white.

In a 2-quart saucepan, parboil the onions in boiling water to cover, 3 to 5 minutes (less for pearl onions). Drain and set aside to cool while preparing sauce.

In a small saucepan, heat butter until foamy. Stir in flour. Cook several minutes over low heat, stirring constantly. Gradually add stock and milk, stirring constantly until thickened. Add spices and cheese and stir until cheese has melted. Remove from heat and set aside.

Preheat oven to 300 degrees.

Cut root and stem ends off each onion. Slip off skins. Place onions in a 1-quart casserole. Pour sauce over onions. Cover and bake for 45 minutes, or until onions are tender.

Scalloped Potatoes Gruyère

Serves 8 to 10

8 large potatoes (about 4 pounds), unpeeled
1 cup (about 4 ounces) grated Gruyère cheese
½ cup chopped fresh parsley
½ cup thinly sliced green onions (including green portion)
1 pound bacon, crisply fried and crumbled
¼ to ½ teaspoon cayenne pepper
1 cup beef stock
3 tablespoons butter

½ cup (about 2 ounces) Gruyère cheese for topping

Preheat oven to 350 degrees. Butter a 9- by 13-inch baking dish.

Scrub potatoes and cut in ¼-inch-thick slices and set aside. Combine 1 cup cheese, parsley, green onions, bacon, and cayenne.

Arrange about one-third of the potato slices in the bottom of the prepared pan. Sprinkle with half the cheese mixture. Layer another one-third of the potatoes and sprinkle with remaining cheese mixture. Top with remaining potatoes and pour stock over all. Dot with butter.

Bake for 1 hour. Sprinkle with ½ cup grated cheese and return to oven until cheese melts, about 5 minutes.

Reheats well.

Spinach Strudel

Serves 8

¾ pound mushrooms, thinly sliced
4 green onions, minced (including green portion)
3 tablespoons butter

WHITE SAUCE:
2 tablespoons butter
2 tablespoons all-purpose flour
¾ cup milk
½ cup whipping cream
⅛ teaspoon ground nutmeg
⅛ teaspoon freshly ground black pepper

3 bunches fresh spinach (about 3 pounds), washed, trimmed, chopped, blanched, and squeezed dry, or 3 packages (10 ounces each) frozen chopped spinach, thawed and squeezed dry

6 leaves phyllo pastry (see Note)*
¾ cup melted butter
1 cup fine dry bread crumbs (2 slices day-old bread)

In a medium skillet, sauté the mushrooms and green onions in butter over medium-high heat, stirring, until mushrooms are soft, about 5 minutes. Remove mushrooms and onions with a slotted spoon and set aside.

To prepare White Sauce: In the same skillet, over medium heat, melt 2 tablespoons butter. Add flour and cook 1 to 2 minutes, stirring until lightly browned. Add milk slowly, stirring constantly to prevent lumps from forming. Mix in cream, nutmeg, and pepper; continue stirring until sauce is thick and smooth. Stir in chopped spinach. Set mixture aside.

To ready Phyllo: Cover the 6 phyllo leaves with a slightly dampened towel to prevent pastry from drying out. Return the remaining phyllo to the freezer for another use.

To assemble Strudel: Place one leaf of phyllo on a sheet of waxed paper. Brush the leaf completely with melted butter and sprinkle with some of the bread crumbs. Repeat with remaining 5 phyllo leaves, stacking. Arrange the spinach mixture lengthwise along the stack, about 3 inches from one long edge of the phyllo, stopping an inch from each short edge. Place the mushrooms on the spinach. Using the waxed paper as an aid, roll the phyllo around the spinach, jelly-roll fashion.

continued

Place the roll, seam side down, on an ungreased cookie sheet (it will fit diagonally whole, or cut in two pieces arranged side by side). Remove the waxed paper and paint the top and sides of the strudel with melted butter.

If assembled in advance, cover the roll with waxed paper and a lightly dampened towel until ready to bake.

Preheat oven to 375 degrees.

Bake the strudel, uncovered, about 25 minutes, or until phyllo is golden brown.

With a very sharp knife, slice the strudel diagonally in 4-inch-wide pieces.

N O T E : Phyllo must be thawed overnight in the refrigerator before using.

*Phyllo pastry, also called strudel leaves, is available in the freezer case of well-stocked supermarkets and at specialty food stores.

Summer Sauté

Serves 6 to 8

1 large onion, thinly sliced
¼ cup olive oil
2 cloves garlic, minced
2 pounds mixed squash (thinly sliced zucchini, patty pan, and crookneck squash)
1 green bell pepper, cored, seeded, and sliced in thin strips
1 sweet red bell pepper, cored, seeded, and sliced in thin strips
2 large ripe tomatoes, diced
1½ teaspoons salt
½ teaspoon freshly ground black pepper
1 teaspoon dried oregano, crumbled

As many varieties of squash are available most of the year, summer and winter designations are actually misnomers. The summer varieties (crookneck, zucchini, patty pan) have thin, edible skins, can be eaten raw or cooked, and are most flavorful when young and small. Even their blossoms are edible. However, winter squash (chayote, acorn, butternut) are like their relative the pumpkin and have hard shells, mature seeds, and bright orange flesh.

In a large skillet, sauté onion in oil over medium-high heat until golden. Add garlic and reduce heat to low. Cook another 2 minutes. Add squash and peppers. Cook 5 minutes, stirring occasionally. Add tomatoes and seasonings. Stir and cook 5 minutes more. When done, squash should give gentle resistance when pierced with the tip of a knife. Be careful not to overcook.

Serve at once.

NOTE: For visual appeal, try cutting the crookneck squash in half lengthwise, patty pan in wedges, and zucchini in julienne or thin slices. Adjust the cooking time by sautéing the larger pieces first.

9.
Brussels Sprouts
ink

Stuffed Zucchini

Serves 6 to 8

½ cup raw long-grain rice
1 cup water
6 to 8 medium zucchini
1 cup pine nuts
1 ripe tomato, peeled, seeded, and chopped
6 tablespoons chopped fresh basil, or 2 tablespoons dried
1½ teaspoons salt
1 teaspoon freshly ground black pepper
¼ cup olive oil

BASTING SAUCE:
¼ cup olive oil
¼ cup dry white wine
¼ cup chicken stock

In a small saucepan, add the rice to 1 cup boiling water and cook, covered, over low heat, for 20 minutes. Cool.

Preheat oven to 350 degrees.

Trim ends from zucchini, then cut each zucchini in halves or thirds, crosswise. Stand on end and scoop out centers with a small spoon (a melon baller also works well) leaving a ¼-inch rim and about ½ inch of the bottom intact. Reserve the centers for another use.

Combine the cooled rice, pine nuts, tomato, basil, salt, pepper, and olive oil. Stuff each section of the zucchini with some of this mixture.

Stand stuffed zucchini sections upright in a baking dish just large enough to hold them side by side.

Combine Basting Sauce ingredients.

Bake zucchini 30 to 40 minutes, basting 2 to 3 times, until sides of the zucchini are soft, but still hold their shape.

NOTE: Stuffed Zucchini can be prepared up to a day in advance and stored in the refrigerator. Bring to room temperature before baking.

Bourbon Yams with Pecan Topping

Serves 10 to 12

5 to 6 pounds yams or sweet potatoes
3 eggs
¼ cup granulated sugar
½ cup butter, melted
½ cup whipping cream
2 tablespoons bourbon
1 teaspoon vanilla extract

PECAN TOPPING:
½ cup butter, melted
1 cup chopped pecans
1 cup brown sugar
1 cup all-purpose flour

Whole pecans for garnish

Preheat oven to 375 degrees. Butter a shallow 2-quart casserole.

Bake the yams on an oven rack for 45 minutes, or until soft. Halve and scoop out pulp. Mash pulp, then add eggs, granulated sugar, butter, cream, bourbon, and vanilla. Stir well to combine. Pour into prepared casserole.

Reduce oven temperature to 350 degrees.

To prepare Pecan Topping: Combine all ingredients except whole pecans and sprinkle over yams. Decorate top with whole pecans.

Bake, uncovered, 40 minutes, or until heated through and top is lightly browned.

Baked Garden Vegetables

Serves 6 to 8

1 large potato (about 8 ounces), cut in 1-inch dice (peeling is optional)
1 small zucchini, cut in 1-inch dice
1 small eggplant, cut in 1-inch dice (peeling is optional)
2 green bell peppers, cored, seeded, and cut in 1-inch dice
2 medium carrots, sliced
1 small onion, cut in 1-inch dice
½ cup shelled green peas
2 tablespoons chopped fresh parsley
1½ teaspoons salt
¾ teaspoon freshly ground black pepper
4 medium ripe tomatoes, sliced
1 cup cooked rice (white or brown)
2 tablespoons red wine vinegar
1 cup (about 4 ounces) grated Cheddar cheese

Preheat oven to 350 degrees. Lightly butter a 9- by 13-inch (or larger) shallow baking dish.

In a large bowl, mix together the diced potato, zucchini, eggplant, peppers, carrots, onion, peas, parsley, salt, and pepper.

Arrange half the tomato slices in the bottom of the prepared pan. Cover with half the vegetable mixture. Spread cooked rice over the top. Add remaining vegetables and top with the remaining tomato slices. Sprinkle with vinegar.

Cover pan lightly with aluminum foil and bake 1 hour and 45 minutes. Remove foil, sprinkle with cheese, and return to the oven, uncovered, until cheese has melted.

Serve hot.

NOTE: As the sole accompaniment to grilled chicken or meat, or as a meatless meal served alone, this vegetable-rich casserole can be assembled early in the day, refrigerated, and baked when needed.

Pesto Sauce for Vegetables or Pasta

Makes about 1 cup

1 cup packed fresh basil leaves
½ teaspoon salt
⅛ teaspoon freshly ground black pepper
1 large clove garlic
2 tablespoons chopped fresh parsley
2 tablespoons chopped walnuts
¼ cup olive oil
½ cup (about 1½ ounces) freshly grated Parmesan or Romano cheese

In a food processor or blender, puree basil leaves, salt, pepper, garlic, parsley, and walnuts, scraping down sides of work bowl as necessary. With machine on, add olive oil in a very thin stream until incorporated. Stir in cheese by hand.

Serve pesto over hot steamed vegetables such as zucchini or green beans, or over hot cooked pasta.

NOTE: Pesto may be frozen before cheese is added, or stored in the refrigerator with a thin film of olive oil poured over the top to prevent discoloration. Bring pesto to room temperature by gently warming over low heat to keep cheese from becoming leathery. California walnuts are substituted in this recipe for the pine nuts of the traditional Italian version.

Pistachio Butter Sauce for Vegetables or Steamed Fish

The California Pistachio Commission, Fresno

Makes about 1 cup

¼ cup finely chopped green onion (including green portion)
2 tablespoons water
1 tablespoon vinegar
⅛ teaspoon freshly ground black pepper
¾ cup chilled butter, cut in pieces
⅓ cup coarsely chopped pistachios
1 tablespoon minced fresh parsley
1½ teaspoons fresh lime juice

Most of the pistachios grown in California, the world's second largest producer after Iran, are sold without the red dye. The skin, which stains the outer shell, is removed during the mechanical harvesting process before the staining can occur. Elsewhere, pistachios are hand-harvested and the skin isn't removed in time to avoid staining. To make the stain appear uniform, the pistachios are dyed.

In a small saucepan, combine onion, water, vinegar, and pepper. Bring to a boil over medium heat. Simmer gently until liquid is reduced by half. Add about ¼ cup of the butter to the sauce. Beat vigorously with a whisk over medium heat. Continue whisking in butter, one piece at a time, until just melted. Add pistachios, parsley, and lime juice. Beat again until creamy.

Serve over steamed vegetables such as green beans, celery, Brussels sprouts, or zucchini, or steamed white fish such as red snapper, halibut, or swordfish.

Tomato-Herb Sauce for Green Beans or Zucchini

*Makes about
2 cups*

1 onion, chopped
1 clove garlic, minced
3 tablespoons olive oil
1 tablespoon butter
2 ripe tomatoes, peeled, seeded, and chopped
1 tablespoon chopped celery
1 tablespoon chopped fresh parsley
1 teaspoon herb vinegar
¾ teaspoon chopped fresh rosemary, or ¼ teaspoon chopped dried
½ teaspoon salt
¼ teaspoon freshly ground black pepper

*This sauce is
especially good
during the
summer, when
tomatoes are at
their peak of
flavor, fresh herbs
are readily
available, and
fresh-picked green
beans and zucchini
can be rushed from
garden to cooking
pot.*

In a small skillet, sauté onion and garlic in oil and butter until onion is translucent. Add remaining ingredients and bring to a boil. Reduce heat and simmer, uncovered, for 10 minutes.

Spoon sauce over hot steamed green beans or zucchini.

CHAPTER SEVEN

Rice, Grains, and Breads

Parsley Rice with Almonds and Jack Cheese

Serves 10 to 12

1 quart chicken stock
2 cups raw long-grain white rice
1 teaspoon salt
½ cup thinly sliced green onions (including green portion)
½ cup sliced almonds
¼ cup butter
½ cup chopped fresh parsley
2 cups sour cream
1 pound grated Monterey Jack cheese

A Scotsman named David Jacks, living in Monterey County, California, developed a method for making a soft cheese originally prepared by Spanish missionaries in Northern California. Jacks began marketing his dairy's version in 1882. To this day, the cheese bears Jacks's name as well as the name of the county where his dairy was located.

In a 2-quart saucepan, bring the chicken stock to a boil. Stir in rice and salt. Cover and reduce heat to low. Cook about 20 minutes, or until rice has absorbed liquid.

Preheat oven to 350 degrees.

In a small skillet, sauté onions and almonds in butter over medium heat, stirring occasionally, until onions are soft and almonds are slightly toasted, about 5 minutes.

Fold parsley into rice, then add sour cream and onion-almond mixture.

Spread half the rice mixture into a 9- by 13-inch baking pan. Sprinkle half the grated cheese over the rice mixture. Repeat with remaining rice and top with cheese.

Bake 30 minutes, or until golden on top and cheese is melted.

Moroccan Rice

Serves 6

  1 small onion, finely chopped
  2 tablespoons butter
  2 tablespoons vegetable oil
  1 cup raw long-grain white rice
  ½ cup raw bulgur wheat
2½ cups chicken stock
  ¼ cup dried currants
  ½ teaspoon ground allspice
    Salt and freshly ground black pepper

  1 cup plain yogurt for accompaniment
  ½ cup toasted almonds or pine nuts for garnish†

In a 10-inch skillet, sauté onion in butter and oil over medium heat until golden. Add rice and bulgur and stir to coat grains. Stir in stock, currants, allspice, salt, and pepper. Bring to a boil, reduce heat to low, cover, and cook 15 to 20 minutes, or until liquid is absorbed.

Accompany each serving with yogurt and a sprinkling of toasted nuts.

†Toast almonds in a 325 degree oven for 5 to 10 minutes, or until lightly browned. Toast pine nuts in 1 tablespoon olive oil in a small skillet, stirring frequently, until lightly browned.

Pine Nut Pilaf

Serves 6

1 cup raw long-grain white rice
1 small onion, finely chopped
½ cup pine nuts or blanched slivered almonds
1 tablespoon butter
2 tablespoons olive oil
2½ cups chicken stock
½ teaspoon grated lemon peel
¼ teaspoon salt
2 tablespoons minced fresh parsley

Delicate pine nuts are costly because it is difficult to extract the nut in its shell from the surrounding cone, and then to remove the small soft nut from its hard shell.

In a medium skillet, lightly brown the rice, onion, and nuts in butter and oil over moderate heat. Stir often to ensure an even color. Add stock, lemon peel, and salt.

Cook, covered, over low heat, about 20 minutes, or until rice has absorbed liquid.

Toss with parsley.

Rice Pilaf with Minced Vegetables

Serves 4 to 6

2 cups water
1 cup raw long-grain white rice
½ teaspoon salt
¼ teaspoon ground white pepper
2 stalks celery, very finely minced
1 large carrot, very finely minced
2 tablespoons snipped fresh chives
¼ cup butter

Mincing the vegetables is the key to success with this recipe. The carrots and celery are never fully cooked, only lightly steamed when folded into the hot rice. Minced finely, the vegetable pieces will be small enough to require only the briefest exposure to heat to lose their raw texture.

In a 1-quart saucepan, bring water to a boil; add rice, salt, and pepper, and cook for 20 minutes, or until rice has absorbed liquid. While rice cooks, combine the celery, carrot, and chives, and mince again.

In a 10-inch skillet, sauté the cooked rice in butter over medium heat until golden, breaking up lumps with a spatula or spoon. Remove the rice from the heat and fold in the minced vegetables.

Serve at once.

NOTE: The rice can be sautéed right after cooking or cooked in advance and chilled until needed.

Monterey Brown Rice

Serves 6 to 8

2 cups water
1 cup raw brown rice
⅓ cup roasted, salted, shelled sunflower seeds
¼ pound mushrooms, sliced
4 green onions, thinly sliced (including green portion)
2 tablespoons butter
1½ cups (about 6 ounces) grated Monterey Jack cheese
2 tablespoons butter
2 tablespoons all-purpose flour
¾ cup milk
½ cup (about 2 ounces) grated Swiss or Jarlsberg cheese
2 bunches fresh spinach, washed, trimmed, chopped, blanched, and squeezed dry, or 2 packages (10 ounces each) frozen chopped spinach, thawed and squeezed dry

Butter a 2½-quart casserole.

In a small saucepan, bring water to a boil. Add brown rice and cook, covered, over very low heat 30 minutes, or until water is absorbed. Remove from heat. Stir in sunflower seeds. Spread in bottom of prepared casserole.

Preheat oven to 350 degrees.

In a medium skillet, sauté mushrooms and green onions in 2 tablespoons butter, 5 minutes, or until mushrooms are soft and liquid evaporates. Spread evenly over rice layer. Sprinkle with Jack cheese.

In the same skillet, make sauce for the spinach. Melt 2 tablespoons butter and blend in flour. Cook, stirring, until bubbly, 1 to 2 minutes. Slowly add milk, stirring constantly, until mixture is thick and smooth. Remove from heat. Stir in Swiss or Jarlsberg cheese until it melts. Add spinach and combine well.

Spread spinach mixture over mushroom-cheese layer. Cover and bake 30 minutes, or until mixture bubbles.

Serve hot.

NOTE: This casserole can be assembled a day in advance and refrigerated. Bring to room temperature before baking or allow an additional 10 to 15 minutes baking time.

Brown Rice with Pecans

Serves 6 to 8

½ pound mushrooms, sliced
2 green onions, thinly sliced (white part only, green tops reserved for garnish)
1 clove garlic, minced
½ cup butter
1 cup raw brown rice
¼ teaspoon dried marjoram leaves, crumbled
⅛ teaspoon freshly ground black pepper
3 cups chicken stock
3 ounces chopped pecans (about ¾ cup)

Whole pecans and sliced green onion tops for garnish

Preheat oven to 400 degrees.

In a Dutch oven over direct heat, sauté mushrooms, onions, and garlic in butter about 5 minutes, stirring frequently. Stir in rice and sauté an additional 2 to 3 minutes, or until rice sizzles. Add marjoram, pepper, and chicken stock. Bring to a boil, cover, place in the oven, and bake 1 hour, or until liquid is absorbed.

Before serving, add chopped pecans and fluff with a fork until well combined.

Garnish with whole pecans and sliced green onion tops.

Brother Timothy's Turkey Stuffing

Brother Timothy, F.S.C., Cellarmaster, The Christian Brothers, Napa

Makes about 2⅓ quarts

1 pound bulk pork sausage
¼ pound chicken or turkey livers (optional)
   Sausage drippings and butter to equal 1 cup
1 cup chopped onion
½ teaspoon dried rosemary, crumbled
½ teaspoon dried mint flakes
⅛ teaspoon ground nutmeg
½ cup chicken stock, or ½ cup water and 1 chicken bouillon cube
½ cup brandy
1 teaspoon salt
⅛ teaspoon freshly ground black pepper
1 package (10 ounces) frozen chopped spinach, thawed and squeezed dry
3 quarts day-old soft bread crumbs
½ cup toasted blanched almonds†
⅓ cup freshly grated Parmesan cheese

For the past fifty years, Brother Timothy has been supervising The Christian Brothers' vineyards and wine cellar. Although he is most knowledgeable about wines, he also enjoys experimenting with cooking and providing suggestions for The Christian Brothers' kitchen. This curiosity led Brother Timothy to create this savory stuffing recipe.

In a medium skillet, brown the sausage. Cut livers in small pieces and add to skillet when sausage is about half cooked. Continue to sauté until meats are fully cooked. Remove meats with a slotted spoon and set aside.

Preheat oven to 325 degrees.

Measure drippings and add enough butter to measure 1 cup. Return the drippings to the skillet and add the onion, rosemary, mint flakes, and nutmeg. Cook slowly over low heat until onions are soft, but not browned. Add stock, brandy, salt, pepper, spinach, and sausage. Heat to simmering.

Place bread in a large mixing bowl. Pour the sausage mixture over the bread and toss to moisten evenly. Stir in almonds and Parmesan cheese. Place stuffing in a 3-quart casserole and bake, covered, about 1 hour, or place in turkey before roasting and bake inside the bird.

†Toast almonds in a 325 degree oven for 5 to 10 minutes, or until lightly browned.

Refried Beans

Makes about
3 quarts

1 pound dried pinto beans, rinsed and picked over
1 large onion, chopped
2 cloves garlic, minced
¼ cup bacon grease or lard
1 tablespoon salt
1½ teaspoons freshly ground black pepper
1½ teaspoons ground cumin
1 teaspoon chili powder

1½ cups (about 6 ounces) grated Monterey Jack or Swiss cheese for garnish

Place beans in a kettle, cover with water, and soak overnight.

When ready to cook beans, add additional water to cover. Place on stove and bring to a boil. Add chopped onion and garlic and reduce heat to a simmer. Cook on low heat, covered, for 2 hours, stirring about every half hour. Beans should be very tender.

Let beans cool slightly, then place about 2 quarts of the beans, including some of the cooking liquid, in a food processor or blender (in batches if necessary) and process until mixture is thick, but not completely smooth.

In a large skillet, heat the bacon grease until nearly smoking. Add the pureed beans and fry, stirring, until mixture is bubbling. Stir in salt, pepper, cumin, and chili powder. Add remaining whole beans and enough cooking liquid so beans will hold a soft shape, but are not stiff and dry. Continue to fry, mashing the whole beans with the back of a spoon, until desired consistency (some texture makes a more interesting dish). If necessary, thin with additional cooking liquid or water.

To serve, top with grated cheese.

Union Hotel Cream Biscuits

Judy Rodgers, former Chef, The Union Hotel, Benicia

Makes about 30
2-inch squares

4 cups all-purpose flour
2 tablespoons baking powder
1 teaspoon salt
½ cup salted butter
2 cups plus 2 tablespoons whipping cream

Preheat oven to 400 degrees.

Stir together flour, baking powder, and salt. Cut in butter, leaving it in very coarse shards. Pour cream in gradually, stirring, then quickly knead to make a stiff dough. Do not overwork.

Roll out dough ½ inch thick on a lightly floured surface. Cut into squares of desired size.

Place the biscuits on an ungreased cookie sheet on lowest rack of oven and bake 18 minutes.

Serve immediately.

NOTE: Once rolled and cut, the dough will keep in the refrigerator, covered, up to 6 hours before baking.

10.
Pomegranates
mixed intaglio

Onion-Cheese Cornbread

Makes 9 squares

1 medium onion, finely chopped
3 tablespoons butter
⅔ cup (about 2½ ounces) grated sharp Cheddar cheese
½ cup sour cream
1 cup all-purpose flour
2 tablespoons sugar
4 teaspoons baking powder
¾ teaspoon salt
1 cup yellow cornmeal
2 eggs
1 cup milk
¼ cup melted butter or vegetable oil

Cornbread served warm from the oven is redolent of country suppers from America's rural past. As this type of bread does not reheat well, plan to eat it all at one meal.

Preheat oven to 400 degrees. Butter an 8- by 8-inch baking pan.

In a small skillet, sauté onion in butter until soft and barely golden. While onion is still warm, stir in grated cheese until it melts, then sour cream. Set aside.

Combine flour, sugar, baking powder, salt, and cornmeal in a mixing bowl. Make a well in the center and add eggs, milk, and melted butter or oil all at once. Mix with a wooden spoon until ingredients are barely moistened. The batter will be lumpy. Pour batter into prepared pan. Dot top with onion mixture. Swirl onion mixture deep into batter with a knife.

Bake for 20 to 25 minutes, or until the top is golden. Cut in squares and serve promptly.

Cheese Popovers

*Makes 4 large
popovers*

2 tablespoons solid vegetable shortening
⅔ cup all-purpose flour
¼ teaspoon salt
⅓ cup milk
⅓ cup water
2 eggs
¼ cup (about 1 ounce) grated Cheddar cheese

Preheat oven to 375 degrees. Place 1½ teaspoons shortening in the bottom of each of four 6-ounce custard cups. Put prepared cups on a baking sheet and place in the oven while it preheats.

Combine flour and salt. Gradually add milk and water, stirring constantly with a wooden spoon. Beat in eggs until smooth. Fold in cheese.

Fill hot custard cups a little more than half full with batter. Bake 45 minutes, or until puffed and golden. Do not open oven door before 35 minutes or popovers may deflate.

NOTE: This recipe can be doubled or tripled.

Kummelstiks (Caraway Sticks)

Makes 32 sticks

3 medium baking potatoes (about 1¼ pounds), peeled and halved
1 cup butter, melted
2½ cups all-purpose flour
2 tablespoons finely minced onion
½ teaspoon salt
1 egg beaten with 1 tablespoon water
2 tablespoons caraway seeds
1 tablespoon Kosher salt or rock salt, lightly crushed

Boil potatoes in water to cover until very tender. Drain and mash. Blend mashed potatoes with melted butter, flour, onion, and salt. Wrap dough in waxed paper and chill at least 2 hours or overnight.

Preheat oven to 350 degrees. Butter 2 baking sheets.

Divide dough in 32 equal pieces. By hand, roll out each piece, one at a time, on a floured surface, to make a rope 6 to 8 inches long. Brush with egg wash, then sprinkle lightly with caraway seeds and salt. Place on prepared baking sheets and bake 40 to 45 minutes, or until sticks are golden. Remove immediately from baking sheets and cool on wire racks.

Serve hot or at room temperature with cold beer or hot soup.

Orange Crescent Breakfast Rolls

Makes 2 dozen rolls

1 envelope dry yeast
¼ cup warm water (110 to 115 degrees)
¼ cup sugar
1 teaspoon salt
2 eggs
½ cup sour cream
⅓ cup butter, melted
3½ cups all-purpose flour

FILLING:
Grated peel of 2 oranges
¾ cup sugar
2 tablespoons butter, melted

GLAZE:
⅓ cup sugar
¼ cup sour cream
1 tablespoon orange juice
¼ cup butter

In a large bowl, dissolve yeast in ¼ cup warm water. With an electric mixer, stir in sugar, salt, eggs, sour cream, and melted butter. Beat in 2 cups of the flour, in batches, until a soft dough forms. Shape into a smooth ball.

Let dough rise, covered with a damp dish towel, in a warm place until doubled in bulk, about 2 hours. Punch dough down and divide in half.

Butter 2 cookie sheets.

In a small bowl, combine orange peel and ¾ cup sugar. Roll out half the dough in a 12-inch circle, sprinkling with a little flour, if necessary, to prevent sticking. Paint the surface with 1 tablespoon melted butter. Sprinkle with one-half of the sugar-orange peel mixture. Divide the circle in 12 wedges. Starting at the wide end, roll up each wedge to its pointed end. Bend the roll into a crescent and arrange all 12 crescents, seam side down, on a prepared cookie sheet.

continued

Repeat with the remaining dough, filling, and melted butter. Cover the cookie sheets with a clean towel and allow the dough to rise again until doubled, at least 1 hour.

Preheat oven to 350 degrees.

Bake crescents 20 minutes, or until golden brown.

When rolls are almost done, prepare glaze. Combine all glaze ingredients in a small saucepan. Bring the mixture to a boil, stirring constantly. Boil for about 3 minutes.

While crescents are hot, paint with glaze and immediately remove from cookie sheet.

N O T E : Trays of unbaked, rolled crescents can be tightly covered with plastic wrap and stored no longer than overnight in the refrigerator. Bring back to room temperature and allow time for the second rising before baking.

Walnut Crunch Coffee Cake

Serves 6 to 8

CAKE:
1 egg
½ cup brown sugar
½ cup milk
¼ cup vegetable oil
1 cup all-purpose flour
2 teaspoons baking powder
½ teaspoon salt
½ teaspoon ground cinnamon

TOPPING:
⅓ cup chopped walnuts
2 tablespoons granulated sugar
½ teaspoon ground cinnamon

This is the quintessential coffee cake—quick to prepare, light-textured, and fragrant with cinnamon.

Preheat oven to 375 degrees. Butter an 8- by 8-inch baking pan.

To prepare Cake: With an electric mixer, beat egg and brown sugar together. Add milk and oil and mix well. Blend in flour, baking powder, salt, and cinnamon, and beat until well blended, about 2 minutes. Pour batter into prepared pan. Sprinkle with walnuts, sugar, and cinnamon. Bake 20 to 25 minutes, or until a toothpick inserted in the center comes out clean.

Serve warm.

CHAPTER EIGHT

Main Courses

Stroganoff Brochettes

Serves 8

*A Zinfandel is
suggested.*

MARINADE:
1 cup sour cream
2 tablespoons fresh lemon juice
2 teaspoons Worcestershire sauce
2 to 4 cloves garlic, minced
1 teaspoon ground white pepper
1 teaspoon celery salt

3 pounds beef tenderloin, cut in 1½-inch cubes

½ pound bacon
16 small white boiling onions
2 green bell peppers, cored, seeded, and each cut in 8 squares
1 sweet red bell pepper, cored, seeded, and cut in 8 squares
16 whole mushrooms

Rice Pilaf with Minced Vegetables for accompaniment (page 143)

Combine the marinade ingredients; marinate meat overnight in refrigerator.

Partially cook bacon by frying until its fat becomes translucent, but not crisp. Drain on paper towels, cool slightly, and cut each slice in 4 pieces. In a small saucepan, parboil the onions in boiling water to cover, about 5 minutes. Drain, cool, then cut root and stem ends off each onion. Slip off skins. Place meat on skewers, alternating bacon, meat, bacon, vegetables, until all ingredients are used.

Grill on a wire rack set approximately 6 inches over hot coals for about 10 minutes per side, turning once, or until the meat is pink in the center.

Serve with Rice Pilaf.

Marinated Flank Steak

Serves 4 to 6

*A Petite Sirah is
suggested.*

MARINADE:
- 2 tablespoons tomato paste
- 3 to 4 teaspoons soy sauce
- 1 tablespoon vegetable oil
- 1 clove garlic, minced
- 1½ teaspoons dried oregano, crumbled
- 1 teaspoon salt
- ½ teaspoon freshly ground black pepper

- 1 flank steak (about 2 pounds)

Combine marinade ingredients. Beat to thicken. Paint both sides of steak
with marinade. Roll up jelly-roll fashion and wrap in aluminum foil or
plastic wrap. Marinate at least 1 hour.

Unroll meat; broil or grill until pink in center. Slice in thin strips at an
angle to the grain.

NOTE: The marinated steak may be frozen, tightly wrapped; thaw when
ready to cook.

Sweet and Salty Barbecued Beef

Serves 12

A Charbono is suggested.

MARINADE:
½ cup Worcestershire sauce
4 ounces Scotch or bourbon
2 cloves garlic, minced
4 teaspoons granulated sugar
1 teaspoon freshly ground black pepper
¼ teaspoon ground ginger

1 eye of round roast (about 6 pounds)

½ cup salt
½ cup confectioners' sugar

Whiskey adds a sophisticated note to this marinade. Another unusual feature is the salt-and-confectioners' sugar coat applied to the beef before grilling.

Combine marinade ingredients. Marinate beef at room temperature for 2 hours or longer, turning frequently to baste.

Combine salt and confectioners' sugar on a flat plate. Remove meat from marinade and roll in salt mixture until coated. Discard any salt mixture which does not adhere readily.

On a covered barbecue, grill over low charcoal fire until charred on the outside and juicy on the inside, about 40 minutes for rare meat.

Serve in very thin slices and pass the meat juices.

Beef Marengo

Serves 6

A Petite Sirah is
suggested.

2½ pounds boneless top round, fat trimmed, and meat cut in 1-inch cubes
2 tablespoons vegetable oil
2 tablespoons olive oil
1 teaspoon salt
½ teaspoon freshly ground black pepper
2 tablespoons all-purpose flour
2 tablespoons tomato paste
1 cup dry red wine
1 cup beef stock
2 sprigs fresh parsley
1 bay leaf
2 to 3 celery tops tied together with string
1 teaspoon dried thyme
24 small white boiling onions
2 tablespoons butter
½ pound mushrooms, thickly sliced
1 large ripe tomato, peeled, seeded, and diced

In a 4- to 6-quart heavy casserole, sauté meat in oils over medium-high
heat in small batches until brown; remove and set aside. Return all the
browned meat to the casserole and sprinkle with salt, pepper, and flour;
sauté several minutes. Mix in tomato paste, wine, stock, parsley, bay leaf,
celery tops, and thyme. Simmer, uncovered, for 2 hours, or until meat is
fork-tender, stirring occasionally. Cover casserole if contents begin to dry
out. Remove and discard parsley, bay leaf, and celery tops.

Meanwhile, cut both ends from onions. Blanch in boiling water to cover
for 2 minutes. Drain, cool slightly, and slip off paper skins.

In a medium skillet, sauté onions in butter until they begin to brown.
Add mushrooms and brown lightly. Transfer the partially cooked vegetables
to the casserole and simmer together, covered, 30 minutes more. Add
tomato during last 10 minutes of cooking time.

Serve piping hot.

Hearty Beef Casserole

Paul Mayer, Paul Mayer Cooking School, San Francisco

Serves 6 to 8

A hearty Burgundy is suggested.

2 tablespoons butter
½ cup pearl barley
½ cup wheat berries*
¾ cup coarsely chopped onion
2 tablespoons butter
½ pound mushrooms, thickly sliced
¼ cup all-purpose flour
1 cup beef stock
1 cup whipping cream or half and half
Freshly ground black pepper

2 pounds lean stewing beef, cut in ½-inch cubes
⅓ cup fine dry bread crumbs
1 teaspoon paprika
1 teaspoon salt
1 teaspoon sesame seeds
2 tablespoons butter

1 jar (4 ounces) chopped pimientos, drained
1 tablespoon Dijon-style mustard
1 tablespoon Worcestershire sauce
1 teaspoon dried oregano
2 cups beef stock

1 cup salted cashews for garnish

In a 10-inch skillet, melt 2 tablespoons butter over medium heat. Add grains and onion; cook slowly until onion is limp, stirring occasionally to prevent the grains from burning.

Stir in 2 more tablespoons butter and increase heat to medium-high. Add mushrooms and cook, stirring, until soft. Remove skillet from heat and sprinkle mushrooms with flour, stirring until flour is incorporated. Slowly add 1 cup beef stock, cream, and a few grinds of pepper; mix well. Return to heat and bring to a boil, stirring constantly until thickened. Cover and reduce heat to low; simmer 15 minutes.

continued

Preheat oven to 425 degrees.

Dry the beef with paper towels. Combine bread crumbs, paprika, salt, and sesame seeds. Gently roll beef cubes in crumb mixture.

In a second skillet, melt 2 tablespoons butter. When the butter sizzles, add beef cubes in batches and brown on all sides. Turn browned meat into a 3-quart casserole. Add the partially cooked barley-wheat mixture. Stir in pimientos, mustard, Worcestershire, oregano, and remaining 2 cups of beef stock.

Bake, uncovered, about 1½ hours, or until liquid is absorbed and barley and wheat berries are tender. Stir once or twice near the end of the cooking time.

Sprinkle a garnish of cashews over the top of individual servings.

*Available where bulk foods are sold, at health food stores, or well-stocked supermarkets.

Mild Mexican Salsa for Grilled Beef

Makes about 1 quart

3 large ripe tomatoes
4 to 5 fresh poblano chiles, or 1 can (4 ounces) diced green chiles
2 cloves garlic, minced
½ teaspoon salt
1 can (15 ounces) tomato sauce
2 teaspoons olive oil
1 tablespoon red wine vinegar
8 green onions, thinly sliced (including green portion)
1½ tablespoons fresh oregano, or 1½ teaspoons dried
2 tablespoons chopped fresh cilantro

Salsas are relishes made from chopped tomatoes, chiles, and seasonings, usually including fresh cilantro. They are excellent companions to a variety of foods, including beef, pork, chicken, even eggs. Cilantro, also called Mexican or Chinese parsley, is actually the leaf of the coriander plant. It is much stronger in taste than regular parsley and has a unique flavor that adds zest to any dish. Use sparingly!

Peel the tomatoes by placing them directly over the burner coils of an electric stove or directly in the flame of a gas burner. Rotate the tomatoes, one at a time, until the skin is blackened and is peeling away from the tomato flesh. Remove tomatoes from heat and set aside until cool enough to handle. Remove as much of the blackened skin as can be peeled off easily. If using fresh chiles, prepare in the same fashion. (For a milder salsa, remove seeds and veins of the chiles before chopping.) Discard the stems.

By hand, chop the tomatoes and chiles, retaining juices. Combine with the remaining ingredients and mix well.

Refrigerate overnight to blend the flavors.

Serve hot, warm, or cold over grilled beef.

NOTE: The salsa will keep for one week in the refrigerator.

Wine Sauce for Tenderloin of Beef

Makes 1½ cups

A Cabernet Sauvignon is suggested.

2 carrots, cut in chunks
2 stalks celery, cut in chunks
¼ cup coarsely chopped shallots
½ teaspoon dried thyme
¼ teaspoon salt
¼ teaspoon freshly ground black pepper
2 cups dry red wine
1 cup beef stock
Beurre manié (2 tablespoons each butter and all-purpose flour kneaded together by hand)

In a small saucepan combine carrots, celery, shallots, thyme, salt, pepper, and red wine. Bring the mixture to a boil and cook, uncovered, over low heat for 10 minutes. Add stock and simmer 10 minutes more. Strain the sauce and return it to the saucepan. Discard the vegetables.

Over low heat stir in the beurre manié, in several small pieces, stirring well to incorporate. Simmer gently until the sauce has thickened.

Serve hot over roasted, broiled, or barbecued tenderloin of beef.

Veal with Mushrooms and Sour Cream

Serves 4

A Chardonnay is suggested.

1 medium onion, minced
12 large mushrooms, thickly sliced
2 tablespoons butter
4 veal loin chops (about 2 pounds total), each 1 to 1½ inches thick
1 tablespoon butter
½ teaspoon salt
½ teaspoon dried marjoram leaves, crumbled
½ teaspoon paprika
¼ teaspoon freshly ground black pepper
⅔ cup chicken stock
2 strips fresh lemon peel, each 1 inch wide
¾ cup sour cream

Steamed rice or hot cooked pasta for accompaniment

In a skillet large enough to hold the chops in a single layer, cook onion and mushrooms in 2 tablespoons butter until tender, about 10 minutes, stirring frequently. Transfer vegetables to a bowl and set aside.

In the same skillet, fry veal in 1 tablespoon butter over medium heat until golden brown on both sides, turning only once. Sprinkle chops on both sides with salt, marjoram, paprika, and pepper. Spread reserved vegetables over veal and cover with chicken stock. Tuck strips of lemon peel around sides of pan.

Cover the pan, reduce heat to low, and simmer 30 minutes or until veal is very tender. Remove veal chops. With a slotted spoon, remove as much of the vegetables as possible and distribute over veal chops. Keep veal and vegetables warm. Discard lemon peel.

Over high heat, reduce liquid in the skillet by half. Remove skillet from the heat and add sour cream, stirring until sauce is slightly thickened. Pour the sauce over the chops or pass separately.

Serve with steamed white rice or hot cooked pasta.

11.
Mushrooms
mixed intaglio

Roast Veal with Orange Sauce

Sylvia Coeytaux, Caterer and Cooking Instructor, Napa Valley

Serves 6 to 8

A Pinot Noir is suggested.

Finely grated peel of 2 oranges
Grated peel of ½ lemon
1 teaspoon Dijon-style mustard
1 teaspoon dry chicken bouillon (use powdered bouillon or mashed bouillon cube)
3 pounds boned veal shoulder or leg, rolled and tied
½ teaspoon salt
1 tablespoon all-purpose flour
2 tablespoons butter
½ cup white wine
¼ cup Grand Marnier or other orange liqueur
Juice of 2 oranges

ORANGE SAUCE:
1 tablespoon cornstarch
Juice of 2 oranges
¼ cup whipping cream

Fresh parsley sprigs and thinly sliced fresh orange for garnish

While growing up in Switzerland, Sylvia Coeytaux enjoyed veal as an everyday meat. In America, she discovered many people think veal is dry and tasteless; she created this savory recipe to correct that common misconception.

Mix together grated orange and lemon peels, mustard, and chicken bouillon. Spread over veal to coat and let stand at room temperature 2 hours.

Preheat oven to 350 degrees.

Gently scrape coating from meat and pat meat dry with paper towels. Sprinkle veal lightly with salt and flour. In a skillet, brown roast quickly on all sides in butter over medium-high heat. Transfer veal to a shallow baking pan and roast 15 minutes. Remove from oven; add white wine, Grand Marnier, and orange juice. Return to oven and continue roasting 1 hour, basting with pan juices several times. Remove to a carving platter and keep warm.

To prepare Orange Sauce: Combine cornstarch with orange juice; blend until smooth. Pour into hot roasting pan, stirring constantly and scraping up browned bits from the bottom. Bring the mixture to a boil over direct heat. Reduce heat to low and add whipping cream, stirring to make a thin sauce.

To serve, thinly slice the veal and arrange in an overlapping pattern on a serving platter. Surround with parsley and orange slices. Pour some of the Orange Sauce over the meat and pass remainder.

Blanquette de Veau (Veal Stew)

Mary Hafner and Julie Rumsey, Hafner/Rumsey Cooking Classes, Berkeley

Serves 6 to 8

Mary Hafner and Julie Rumsey suggest a full-bodied California Chardonnay or a Beaujolais.

2¼ pounds milk-fed or white veal breast or shoulder, well trimmed and cut in 1½-inch cubes
3 cups chicken stock
1 carrot, quartered
1 onion, halved
1 stalk celery
Bouquet garni (3 sprigs parsley, 1 bay leaf, 1 teaspoon thyme, 10 peppercorns tied together in a square of cheesecloth)
1 teaspoon salt

20 fresh pearl onions
1 tablespoon butter
2 teaspoons fresh lemon juice
20 whole small mushrooms

¼ cup butter
¼ cup all-purpose flour
Salt and freshly ground black pepper
2 egg yolks
1 cup Crème Fraîche (recipe follows)

Chopped fresh parsley for garnish

Every French cook knows how to prepare a blanquette de veau, a simple but elegant veal stew. Having watched friends prepare the dish in France, Mary Hafner and Julie Rumsey decided to create their own version of this classic recipe.

Place veal in an acid-resistant Dutch oven or flameproof casserole with 6 cups of water. Boil for 2 minutes; drain. Rinse veal and Dutch oven well to remove scum. Return veal to Dutch oven with stock, carrot, onion, celery, bouquet garni, and salt. Bring to a boil, cover, and simmer for 1½ hours.

Meanwhile, cut root and stem ends off each onion; score bottoms. Remove peels. In an acid-resistant 2-quart saucepan, parboil the onions for 10 minutes in ½ cup stock taken from the casserole, and 1 tablespoon butter. Remove onions with a slotted spoon and set aside.

To the stock left in the saucepan, add lemon juice and mushrooms and simmer 5 minutes. Remove mushrooms and discard cooking liquid.

When veal is tender, pour contents of Dutch oven into a colander set over a bowl to catch the poaching liquid. Discard bouquet garni and poaching vegetables.

continued

In the Dutch oven, melt ¼ cup butter and stir in flour. Cook, stirring constantly, 1 minute without browning. Whisk in all the reserved poaching liquid and bring to a boil. Reduce heat and simmer 15 minutes. Season with salt and pepper. Combine egg yolks and crème fraîche. Remove 1 cup of the cooked sauce and gradually whisk with the egg mixture. Return the combined sauce to the Dutch oven, stirring constantly to prevent curdling. Cook gently 2 to 3 minutes, or until sauce is the consistency of light gravy. Do not allow sauce to come to a boil. Add reserved veal, onions, and mushrooms and heat through.

Garnish with parsley.

CRÈME FRAÎCHE:

1 tablespoon buttermilk
1 cup whipping cream (not ultrapasteurized)

Combine buttermilk and cream in a small saucepan. Heat until lukewarm and pour into a glass container just large enough to hold the mixture. Leave at room temperature with lid askew 36 to 60 hours until cream thickens to a point where it will hold a soft shape. Use immediately or store in refrigerator up to 4 weeks.

NOTE: Blanquette de Veau can be prepared a day ahead and refrigerated; add the egg yolks and Crème Fraîche just after reheating. To reheat, bring to room temperature and cook over low heat just until meat is warm.

Sweetbreads

Serves 6

A dry Pinot Noir is suggested.

2 pounds veal sweetbreads
1 quart water
1 tablespoon fresh lemon juice
1 teaspoon salt
¼ cup butter
2 small cloves garlic, minced
8 small green onions, minced (including green portion)
½ pound mushrooms, caps removed and sliced, stems chopped
¾ cup beef stock
¼ cup dry red wine, or sherry if a sweeter sauce is preferred
1 tablespoon all-purpose flour
½ to 1 cup whipping cream

Steamed rice for accompaniment

It is not known why the thymus or pancreas of lambs and calves, when so prepared, is called sweetbreads. The dish was considered such a delicacy in the 1700s that it was said one could be bribed with sweetbreads.

Soak sweetbreads 2 hours in ice water, changing water 2 or 3 times. Drain. Place in boiling, acidulated water (1 quart water, 1 tablespoon lemon juice, 1 teaspoon salt) and boil 5 minutes. Drain. Separate into small pieces by removing all connective tissue. In a large skillet, sauté sweetbreads in butter with garlic, green onions, and chopped mushroom stems, stirring constantly, for 3 minutes. Add stock and wine. Cover and simmer until tender, approximately 25 minutes. Blend flour with 2 tablespoons whipping cream. Add to simmering sweetbreads, stirring constantly. Let the sauce thicken. Add additional cream until sauce is of medium-thick consistency. Add sliced mushroom caps just before serving.

Serve over steamed rice.

Roast Pork with Applesauce

Serves 4 to 6

A Gewürztraminer is suggested.

1 boned pork roast (about 3 pounds), rolled and tied
3 cloves garlic, slivered

MARINADE:
⅔ cup vermouth or other dry white wine
Juice of 2 large lemons (about ½ cup)
1 onion, thickly sliced
2 bay leaves
1 tablespoon dried thyme
½ teaspoon salt
½ teaspoon freshly ground black pepper

APPLESAUCE:
12 small tart green apples, peeled, cored, and sliced
2 tablespoons granulated sugar (or more, depending on tartness of apples)
3 tablespoons brown sugar (or more, depending on tartness of apples)
2 tablespoons butter

The simple applesauce that accompanies this pork roast cooks without water. The sugar draws out the apples' natural juices, so no extra liquid needs to be added.

With a sharp knife, cut slits under the fat of the pork roast and insert some slivers of garlic beneath fat. Distribute remaining garlic into gaps and cavities of pork. Place roast in a bowl. Add marinade ingredients, cover bowl with plastic wrap, and refrigerate 24 to 48 hours, turning roast several times.

One hour before roasting, remove pork from marinade and let stand at room temperature. Strain marinade into a small saucepan and set aside.

Preheat oven to 350 degrees.

Place meat on a rack, fat side up, and roast approximately 40 minutes per pound (or until 170 degrees on a meat thermometer). Meat juices should run clear when roast is pierced with the tip of a sharp knife. Do not overcook.

Meanwhile, to prepare Applesauce: Place apple slices in a large saucepan and sprinkle with granulated sugar. Cook, stirring frequently, over very low heat 30 to 60 minutes, or until apples reach desired softness. When done, stir in brown sugar and butter.

When ready to serve, transfer roast to a carving board or platter; slice thinly. Scrape roasting juices and brown bits from bottom of roasting pan into the marinade. Bring marinade to a boil and serve separately with pork and Applesauce.

Teriyaki Pork Tenderloin

Serves 6 to 8

A Merlot is suggested.

MARINADE:
1 cup chicken stock
¼ cup soy sauce
¼ cup honey
2 tablespoons sherry
1 tablespoon fresh lemon juice
1 clove garlic, minced
1 teaspoon ground cinnamon
1 teaspoon salt
2-inch piece of ginger root, unpeeled

2 to 3 pork tenderloins (about 3 pounds total)
¼ cup cornstarch

Combine marinade ingredients. Add the tenderloins and marinate at room temperature for 2 hours. Refrigerate if marinating longer. Return to room temperature before roasting.

Preheat oven to 325 degrees.

Drain the meat, reserving marinade; dust tenderloins with cornstarch. Bake in a shallow roasting pan 1 hour (or until 170 degrees on a meat thermometer), basting frequently with drippings.

Strain the reserved marinade and warm in a small saucepan.

To serve, slice tenderloins thinly on the diagonal. Pass warmed marinade separately.

Pork Chops in Green Peppercorn Sauce

Serves 4

A Gewürztraminer is suggested.

4 loin pork chops, each ¾ inch thick
  Salt and freshly ground black pepper
1 tablespoon dried tarragon
¼ cup butter
¼ cup cognac
2 tablespoons vinegar (white wine or tarragon)
1 cup whipping cream
1 to 2 tablespoons bottled green peppercorns, rinsed, drained, and slightly crushed
  Fresh lemon juice
½ teaspoon dried tarragon

Unlike black peppercorns, soft-textured green peppercorns are quite mild. They add special flavor to sauces such as this cognac-and-cream combination.

Sprinkle pork chops with salt and pepper and rub with 1 tablespoon tarragon. In a 10- to 12-inch skillet, brown chops in butter over medium-high heat on both sides. Reduce heat to medium and cook chops 5 to 7 minutes longer on each side. Remove to a heated platter and keep warm.

Pour off all but a thin film of fat from the skillet. Over high heat, add cognac and vinegar to the skillet, scraping browned bits from the sides and bottom. Reduce liquid to about 2 tablespoons. Add cream, peppercorns, a squeeze of lemon juice, and ½ teaspoon tarragon. Reduce heat and bring sauce to a simmer, stirring frequently. Correct seasonings with salt, pepper, and lemon juice.

Pour sauce over chops and serve at once.

Javanese Grilled Pork

Serves 4

*A Merlot is
suggested.*

MARINADE:
- 1 cup coarsely chopped onion
- ¼ cup soy sauce
- 1 tablespoon fresh lemon juice
- 1 teaspoon ground coriander (optional)
- 1 teaspoon minced garlic
- 2 tablespoons brown sugar
- ½ teaspoon salt
- ½ teaspoon freshly ground black pepper
- ½ teaspoon ground cumin

1½ pounds pork loin or pork shoulder, trimmed and cut in ½-inch cubes

In a food processor or blender, puree marinade ingredients until blended and smooth. Marinate the pork cubes at room temperature about 1 hour. Refrigerate if marinating longer.

Thread pork cubes on 6-inch skewers (see Note), leaving enough room at one end to allow for handling.

Grill over hot coals 5 minutes on each side, or until meat is brown and crisp.

NOTE: Before using, soak wood or bamboo skewers in water to cover for about 10 minutes. This helps prevent skewers from burning.

Apple Brandy Butter

Phillip Lacock, California Cafe Bar and Grill, Walnut Creek

Makes about
1 cup

1 apple, peeled and finely diced
2 tablespoons butter
2 to 4 tablespoons brandy
½ pound unsalted butter, softened
¼ cup sugar
2 teaspoons ground cinnamon
¼ teaspoon ground nutmeg

In a small skillet, gently sauté diced apple in 2 tablespoons butter 3 to 5 minutes. Remove from heat, add brandy, and mix thoroughly. Set aside.

In a small bowl, beat ½ pound butter with a wooden spoon until smooth. Add sugar and spices and blend until creamy. Stir in apple mixture. Add a little hot water if a creamier texture is desired. Refrigerate until ready to serve.

Serve on slices of roast pork or grilled chops.

NOTE: Apple Brandy Butter can be scooped or spooned cold. Return to room temperature to mold, or to roll and slice.

Baked Ham with Whipped Mustard Sauce

Serves 8 to 10

A Pinot Noir is suggested.

1 ready-to-eat boneless ham (4 to 5 pounds)
½ cup red currant jelly
2 tablespoons Dijon-style mustard
⅛ teaspoon ground cloves

WHIPPED MUSTARD SAUCE:
2 egg yolks
3 tablespoons Dijon-style mustard
2 tablespoons apple cider vinegar
1 tablespoon water
4 teaspoons sugar
¾ teaspoon salt
2 tablespoons drained prepared white horseradish
1 tablespoon butter
½ cup whipping cream

Mustard is a blend of white and black mustard seeds and must, an unfermented or partially fermented wine. What distinguishes French Dijon mustard from other types of mustard is the addition of verjuice, an acidic extract made from unripened grapes.

Preheat oven to 325 degrees.

Bake ham in a shallow pan 1 hour; remove from oven. Increase oven temperature to 400 degrees.

Cut ham into ½-inch slices and overlap slices in baking pan.

Combine jelly, 2 tablespoons mustard, and cloves in a small saucepan. Heat, stirring constantly, until jelly melts. Spread over ham. Return to oven and bake an additional 15 to 20 minutes, basting occasionally, until glazed.

Meanwhile, to prepare Whipped Mustard Sauce: In a very small saucepan, beat egg yolks. Add 3 tablespoons mustard, vinegar, water, sugar, and salt. Cook over low heat, stirring constantly, until mixture thickens. Remove from heat. Stir in horseradish and butter. Cool thoroughly.

Whip cream until thick. Fold into mustard sauce. Makes 1½ cups.

When ready to serve, transfer ham to platter. Pass sauce separately.

NOTE: Whipped Mustard Sauce is delicious on other types of cold or hot meat.

Ham in Sour Cream Crust

Serves 8

A Zinfandel is suggested.

CRUST:

2 cups all-purpose flour
½ teaspoon salt
¼ cup butter
1 egg
½ cup sour cream

FILLING:

4 cups (1¼ pounds) very finely chopped baked ham
½ cup minced celery
½ cup (about 2 ounces) grated Gruyère cheese
3 tablespoons minced onion
2 tablespoons minced green bell pepper
2 eggs, beaten

SAUCE:

6 ounces cream cheese, softened
3 tablespoons butter, softened
3 tablespoons prepared white horseradish

To prepare Crust: In a food processor or by hand, combine flour, salt, and butter and process until crumbly. Combine egg and sour cream, add to flour mixture, and mix until dough forms a ball. Flatten the dough ball slightly, wrap in waxed paper, and chill 30 minutes.

To prepare Filling: Combine all filling ingredients in a bowl and set aside.

To prepare Sauce: Blend sauce ingredients in a food processor or with an electric mixer. Set aside.

Preheat oven to 375 degrees.

To assemble: On a lightly floured surface, roll half the dough into a 6- by 14-inch rectangle. Place in the center of an ungreased cookie sheet. Mound filling along the center of the dough.

Roll the remaining dough into a second 6- by 14-inch rectangle. Lay this rectangle over the filling. Moisten the inside edges of the top dough with water, tuck bottom edges of dough up under the top and seal top to bottom all around.

With a sharp knife, slash top in several places to allow steam to escape. Decorate top with shapes made from any leftover dough, lightly brushing underside of cutouts with water before setting in place.

Bake 30 to 35 minutes, or until crust is nicely browned.

To serve, slice crosswise. Pass the sauce separately.

Tomatillo-Pork Burritos

Ofelia and Robert Berber, Mi Rancho, Oakland

*Makes about
2 dozen*

*A Charbono is
suggested.*

2	pounds fresh tomatillos, or 3 cans (13 ounces each) tomatillos, including liquid*
1 to 2	jalapeño chiles (depending on spiciness desired)
8 to 10	cloves garlic, peeled
1	bunch cilantro, leaves only
3	pounds pork loin roast, trimmed of fat and cut in 2-inch cubes
3	tablespoons vegetable oil
1	onion, chopped
1	teaspoon salt
2	dozen large flour tortillas
½	recipe Refried Beans (page 147)
2	cups (about 8 ounces) grated Monterey Jack cheese

*The influence of
Mexican cooking
and culture is very
strong throughout
California. For
thirty years, local
restaurants and
cooks have
enjoyed fresh
tortillas, salsas,
spices, and other
Mexican
ingredients from
Mi Rancho, a
family-run
Mexican market
and Oakland
landmark.*

Remove papery husks from fresh tomatillos and stems from chiles. Combine tomatillos and chiles in a 2-quart saucepan and add water almost to cover. If using canned tomatillos, combine with the chiles without adding additional liquid. Bring to a boil, then reduce heat and simmer until soft, about 10 minutes. Drain, reserve the liquid, and set aside to cool slightly. In a food processor or blender, puree the drained tomatillos and chiles, garlic, and cilantro. Set aside.

In a Dutch oven, brown the pork cubes in oil over medium-high heat, a few at a time. Add reserved tomatillo liquid to barely cover the meat, then add onion. Simmer for 2 hours, covered, or until pork is fork-tender, stirring occasionally and checking to make certain pork has not dried out. Add additional tomatillo liquid or water, if necessary. Remove meat with a slotted spoon; let cool. Shred with fingers. Skim fat from meat-poaching liquid.

In a 2-quart saucepan, combine the shredded meat, the pureed tomatillo-chile sauce, salt, and 1 to 2 cups of the meat-poaching liquid, or enough to make a thin but not watery sauce. Simmer 30 to 40 minutes uncovered. Stir occasionally.

Meanwhile, preheat oven to 350 degrees.

Wrap tortillas in aluminum foil and heat in oven 20 to 30 minutes, or until they are warmed through.

For each burrito, place about 2 tablespoons of Refried Beans in the center of a warm tortilla, then 3 tablespoons of the tomatillo-pork sauce. Top with 2 tablespoons of grated cheese. Roll up and serve warm.

*Available at Latin American markets and well-stocked supermarkets.

Jambalaya

Serves 12

A Burgundy is
suggested.

1½ pounds hot Italian sausage, thickly sliced
12 chicken thighs (or other meaty portion), skinned
2 teaspoons salt
¼ teaspoon cayenne pepper
¾ cup vegetable oil
2 tablespoons brown sugar
3 large onions, chopped
5 stalks celery, chopped
2 large green bell peppers, cored, seeded, and chopped
4 cloves garlic, minced (about 1 tablespoon)
5 cups heated chicken stock
1 tablespoon salt
¼ teaspoon cayenne pepper

4 cups raw long-grain white rice

1 cup chopped fresh parsley
2 bunches green onions, chopped (about 1 cup, including green portion)

2 large ripe tomatoes, chopped, for garnish

Introduced by the
Spaniards,
jambalaya, a Cajun
favorite, is a form
of paella. Its name
comes from
jambon, French for
ham. The mixed
heritage of this rich
and flavorful stew
reflects the Cajun
blend of cultures.
This cuisine has
become
increasingly
popular outside of
its native South.

In a 6-quart cooking pot with cover, or flameproof casserole, sauté sausage over moderate heat. Remove with a slotted spoon and set aside. Brown chicken, a few pieces at a time, in fat remaining in the casserole. Sprinkle chicken pieces with 2 teaspoons salt and ¼ teaspoon cayenne. Remove chicken pieces and set aside. Add oil to pan drippings and heat to nearly smoking. Add brown sugar and caramelize, stirring constantly. Turn off heat and immediately add chopped onions, celery, and green peppers. Stir to sauté vegetables. Add garlic. Return heat to moderate, add stock, 1 tablespoon salt, ¼ teaspoon cayenne, and rice; bring to a boil. Stir well, then add sausage and chicken. Do not stir again.

Cover casserole tightly and cook over low heat 40 to 50 minutes, or until rice has absorbed the liquid.

Fluff rice with a fork. Remove from heat and add parsley and green onions. Just before serving, fluff mixture again. Garnish with chopped tomatoes.

Lamb Merlot

Serves 8 to 10

A Merlot is suggested.

MARINADE:
½ cup soy sauce
½ cup sesame oil*
½ cup olive oil
¼ cup chopped celery leaves
2 cloves garlic, minced
1 tablespoon dried thyme
1 teaspoon dried rosemary
1 teaspoon dry mustard
½ teaspoon dried oregano

1 leg of lamb (5 to 6 pounds)
1 cup Merlot or other full-bodied dry red wine

Combine marinade ingredients and blend well. Pour marinade over the lamb and refrigerate overnight, turning the meat at least once the next morning to coat well.

Preheat oven to 350 degrees.

Drain lamb, reserving marinade, and place on a rack in a roasting pan. Roast 12 to 15 minutes per pound (or until 147 to 150 degrees on a meat thermometer). The lamb should be slightly pink inside.

Let lamb sit at room temperature 15 minutes before carving.

Meanwhile, combine reserved marinade and Merlot in a small saucepan and bring to a boil. Reduce heat and simmer for several minutes to blend flavors. Serve separately.

NOTE: Three boned and trimmed racks of lamb may be substituted for the leg. Roast marinated racks in a 450 degree oven 20 to 25 minutes, basting frequently. A rack usually contains 8 ribs. Three racks serve 10 to 12 generously.

*Available at oriental markets and well-stocked supermarkets.

Olive-stuffed Lamb

Serves 8

*A Pinot Noir is
suggested.*

*Over ninety-eight
percent of all olives
consumed in the
United States are
grown in
California's warm
inland valleys
where the mild
winters and hot,
dry summers allow
them to flourish.*

3 cloves garlic, minced
½ teaspoon dried marjoram
½ teaspoon salt
2 tablespoons fresh lime juice
¼ teaspoon Tabasco sauce
1 leg of lamb, boned, rolled, and tied (5 to 6 pounds boned weight), at
room temperature
24 small pimiento-stuffed green olives
2 strips bacon, each cut in 6 pieces

Preheat oven to 450 degrees.

Mix garlic, marjoram, salt, lime juice, and Tabasco.

Make 12 holes in the meat with a sharp knife, widening each hole with
the handle of a wooden spoon. Into each hole push a stuffed olive, a piece of
bacon, about ½ teaspoon garlic-lime mixture, then another olive.

Place meat fat side up on a rack in a roasting pan. Set in oven and
immediately reduce heat to 350 degrees. Roast 25 to 30 minutes per pound
(or until 147 to 150 degrees on a meat thermometer). The lamb should be
slightly pink inside.

Let lamb sit at room temperature 15 minutes before carving.

Butterflied Leg of Lamb

Serves 8 to 10

A Cabernet Sauvignon is suggested.

MARINADE:

⅔ cup fresh lemon juice
½ cup brown sugar
¼ cup Dijon-style mustard
¼ cup soy sauce
¼ cup olive oil
2 cloves garlic, minced
1 teaspoon salt
½ teaspoon freshly ground black pepper
  ½-inch slice fresh ginger root, unpeeled

1 leg of lamb, boned and butterflied (5 to 6 pounds boned weight)

Combine marinade ingredients and pour over lamb. Marinate at least 2 hours at room temperature, or overnight in refrigerator, turning meat at least once. Drain before cooking, and reserve marinade.

Preheat oven to 450 degrees or prepare coals for barbecuing.

In the oven: Place meat on a rack, fat side up, and roast 20 minutes. Turn meat over and roast 20 minutes more.

On the barbecue: Place grill 4 to 5 inches above coals and grill, fat side down, covered, 15 minutes. Turn meat and grill, covered, about 10 minutes more on the other side. Lamb should still be slightly pink inside.

To serve, cut in slices across the grain. Heat remaining marinade, discard ginger root, and serve with lamb.

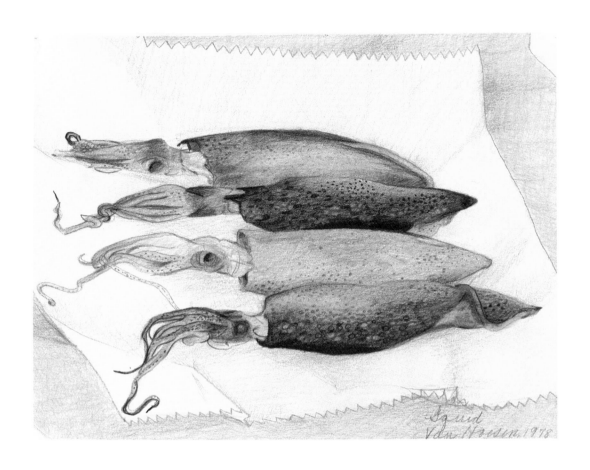

12.
Squid
color pencil, graphite

Barbecued Lamb Steaks with Garlic and Herbs

Susan Johnson, Mange Toute Cooking School, Dallas

Serves 6

A Burgundy is suggested.

6 lamb sirloin steaks, each about 1 inch thick
3 cloves garlic
6 tablespoons olive oil
2 tablespoons fresh thyme
2 tablespoons fresh rosemary
1 tablespoon ground sage

Rub both sides of each steak with a cut clove of garlic, then with oil. Chop the herbs together with 1 clove of garlic. Press herb-garlic mixture onto both sides of each steak.

Refrigerate, covered, at least 1 hour, or overnight.

Grill over very hot coals 2 to 3 minutes per side, or until the lamb is slightly pink in the center.

Persian Lamb Stew with Apricots

Joyce Goldstein, Chef and Owner of Square One, San Francisco

Serves 8

A Gewürztraminer is suggested.

1 pound dried apricots
½ cup raisins (optional)
5 pounds lamb shoulder, cut in 1½-inch cubes
1 cup butter
3 onions, chopped
2 teaspoons ground coriander
2 teaspoons ground cumin
1 teaspoon ground cinnamon
1 teaspoon ground ginger
¼ to ½ teaspoon ground saffron, steeped in 2 tablespoons red wine
¼ teaspoon cayenne pepper
5½ to 6 cups lamb stock or water
Salt and freshly ground black pepper

Couscous (a Moroccan grain) or rice for accompaniment

Joyce Goldstein discovered this classic Persian dish while researching recipes for a Middle Eastern cooking class she was teaching. Its proper name is Mishmishmaya, derived from the Persian word for apricot. First planted in California by Spanish missionaries, almost all of the apricots produced in the United States are now grown here.

Soak apricots and raisins in water to cover. Set aside.

Meanwhile, in a large casserole or Dutch oven, brown lamb cubes in butter over medium-high heat. Set aside. In same pan, sauté onions and spices until onions are soft. Add lamb back to casserole. Cover with stock or water. Reduce heat and simmer, covered, about 30 to 45 minutes.

Drain apricots and raisins, add to stew, and simmer another 30 minutes, or until lamb is tender. Skim excess fat from stew. Season with salt and pepper.

Serve with couscous or rice.

Leg of Lamb with White Beans

Serves 10

*A Zinfandel is
suggested.*

1 pound dried Great Northern beans
2 pounds onions, thinly sliced
¼ cup butter
1 clove garlic, minced
1 tablespoon salt
1 teaspoon dried rosemary leaves
1 teaspoon dried thyme leaves
¼ teaspoon freshly ground black pepper
2 pounds ripe tomatoes, peeled, seeded, and halved, or 2 cans (1 pound each) Italian plum tomatoes, drained

1 leg of lamb (6 to 7 pounds)
2 cloves garlic, cut in slivers

Chopped fresh parsley for garnish

Place beans in a 6-quart kettle. Soak in 6 cups cold water overnight. When ready to cook, add more water, if necessary, to cover beans. Bring to a boil. Reduce heat and simmer 1 hour until the beans are tender, but not mushy.

Drain beans in a colander and set aside. Discard cooking liquid or save for stock.

Preheat oven to 325 degrees.

In a large skillet, sauté onions and minced garlic in butter over medium heat until golden.

In a shallow roasting pan, combine the drained beans, sautéed onions, 2 teaspoons salt, ½ teaspoon rosemary, ½ teaspoon thyme, ¼ teaspoon pepper, and tomatoes. Stir well to combine.

Dry the lamb with paper towels and trim off most of the fat. Make slits in the lamb and insert slivers of garlic. Sprinkle meat with remaining rosemary, thyme, and salt. Set seasoned lamb on top of the bean mixture and roast, uncovered, 2½ to 3 hours (or until 147 to 150 degrees on a meat thermometer).

Let stand at room temperature for 20 minutes before carving. Slice and serve surrounded by bean mixture. Sprinkle with parsley.

Saucisse au Greg (Greek Sausage)

CeCe Dove, CC Dove Fine Foods, Oakland

Makes about 2 pounds

CeCe Dove suggests a Zinfandel.

2 pounds untrimmed shoulder of lamb
¾ pound untrimmed pork butt
½ pound pork fatback
1½ ounces garlic, finely minced (6 to 8 cloves)
2 teaspoons salt
5 teaspoons dried oregano
½ teaspoon freshly ground black pepper
¼ teaspoon crushed red pepper
2½ tablespoons red wine
Hog casings, rinsed and soaked in white vinegar for 10 minutes, rinsed again and soaked in warm water for 1 hour or longer*

For six months, CeCe Dove and her chef experimented with the idea of making a sausage with lamb instead of the traditional pork. This is the recipe CeCe devised.

Trim fat and gristle from lamb. Trim fat from pork. Cube lamb, pork, and fatback and put through medium blade of meat grinder (or have butcher trim and grind meats together). Combine garlic, salt, oregano, pepper, and red pepper; add to meat along with wine and mix well. Chill for several hours or overnight. (Meat mixture must be as cold as possible for stuffing.)

Using the sausage-stuffing attachment to your electric mixer, stuff meat mixture into hog casings. Link the sausage by twisting into desired lengths. Refrigerate, loosely covered, 12 hours. May be grilled, oven roasted, or panfried.

N O T E : To make sausage patties, omit the hog casings, form chilled meat mixture into patties and panfry or grill.

This recipe doubles or triples easily and freezes well.

*Available at meat markets or specialty food stores.

Chicken Rose Marie

Serves 6 to 8

A Sauvignon Blanc is suggested.

4 whole chicken breasts, halved and skinned
1 cup French bread crumbs (preferably fresh)

SAUCE:
Juice of 2 large lemons (about ½ cup)
½ cup olive oil
½ cup water
2 cloves garlic, minced
1 teaspoon dried oregano
¼ cup chopped fresh parsley

Salt and freshly ground black pepper

Fresh parsley sprigs and lemon slices for garnish

Preheat oven to 325 degrees.

Rinse chicken in cold water; shake off excess water. Roll the damp breasts in the bread crumbs; shake off excess crumbs. Place chicken in a shallow 9- by 13-inch baking pan or one large enough to hold the breasts in a single layer.

Combine sauce ingredients. Spoon 1 cup of sauce over breast halves. Sprinkle with salt and pepper.

Bake, uncovered, 30 minutes. Spoon the remaining sauce over chicken and continue to bake for another 30 minutes, or until chicken is lightly browned, but not dried out.

Serve garnished with parsley sprigs and lemon slices.

Chicken and Chives

Susan Johnson, Mange Toute Cooking School, Dallas

Serves 6 to 8

A Sauvignon Blanc is suggested.

4 whole chicken breasts, halved, skinned, and boned
½ cup butter
2 tablespoons snipped fresh chives
1 teaspoon chopped fresh parsley
 Dash of ground nutmeg
4 ounces Monterey Jack cheese
½ cup all-purpose flour
2 eggs, beaten with 2 teaspoons vegetable oil
1 cup dry bread crumbs
6 ounces dry white wine

 Snipped fresh chives for garnish

In French, mange toute *literally means "eat it all," and no one leaves a bite unfinished when Susan Johnson demonstrates the preparation of dishes for her classes. She believes her students must not only be able to see how a dish is prepared and how it should look, but also must taste the results for themselves.*

Place chicken breasts between 2 sheets of waxed paper or plastic wrap and pound them to ¼-inch thickness.

Melt butter and add chives, parsley, and nutmeg. Brush the chicken with the seasoned butter. Cut cheese in 8 equal pieces. Place a finger of cheese on each piece of chicken. Roll up chicken pieces, tucking in sides, and refrigerate 30 minutes.

Preheat oven to 350 degrees.

Roll each chicken packet in flour, then dip in egg mixture. Roll in bread crumbs. Place in a 9- by 13-inch baking pan and bake 20 minutes.

Meanwhile, mix any remaining seasoned butter with the wine. After chicken has baked 20 minutes, pour wine mixture into baking pan (but not over chicken packets). Return to oven and bake an additional 20 to 25 minutes, or until the tops of the chicken are browned.

To serve, pour some of the sauce from pan over the chicken and sprinkle with fresh chives.

Chicken Piccata

Serves 6 to 8

*A dry Chenin
Blanc is suggested.*

4 whole chicken breasts, halved, skinned, and boned
½ cup all-purpose flour
½ teaspoon salt
¼ teaspoon freshly ground black pepper
¼ cup clarified butter
1 tablespoon olive oil
¼ cup dry white wine
2 tablespoons fresh lemon juice
1 teaspoon finely grated lemon peel

¼ cup drained capers
¼ cup minced fresh parsley

Lemon slices for garnish

*Although this dish
is traditionally
made with veal,
chicken is a less
costly but flavorful
alternative.*

Place chicken breasts between 2 sheets of waxed paper or plastic wrap and pound them to ¼-inch thickness. Combine flour, salt, and pepper in a plastic bag. Add breasts and shake to coat. Shake off excess flour.

In a large skillet, heat butter and oil until bubbling. Sauté chicken breasts, a few at a time, 2 to 3 minutes on each side. Drain on paper towels and cover to keep warm.

Pour off all but 2 tablespoons of the fat left in the skillet. Stir in the wine, scraping the bottom to loosen browned bits. Add lemon juice and peel. Return chicken to skillet, and heat until sauce thickens.

Spoon any sauce remaining in the skillet over chicken; sprinkle with capers and parsley, and serve garnished with lemon slices.

Chicken Sonora

Serves 6 to 8

A White Zinfandel is suggested.

SEASONING MIXTURE:
1 large onion, sliced
3 cloves garlic, peeled
1-inch piece of fresh ginger root (do not substitute ground)
1 teaspoon salt
¼ teaspoon cayenne pepper
Juice of 1 lime
¼ cup melted butter

4 whole chicken breasts, boned but not skinned

12 to 16 flour tortillas, buttered on one side, stacked, and wrapped in foil

1 cup sour cream
½ teaspoon salt
½ teaspoon ground cumin
2 teaspoons finely chopped fresh cilantro

VEGETABLE GARNISH:
2 to 3 large ripe tomatoes, halved and thinly sliced
1 to 2 cucumbers, peeled, quartered lengthwise, and thinly sliced
1 large bunch green onions, sliced (including green portion)
1 large ripe avocado, sliced in crescents
2 tablespoons olive oil
Juice of 1 lime
Salt and freshly ground black pepper

Pine Nut Pilaf for accompaniment (page 142)

Preheat oven to 350 degrees.

In a blender, combine seasoning mixture ingredients. Blend until smooth. Rinse and dry chicken breasts. Dip the chicken pieces into the seasoning mixture to coat. Place chicken, skin side up, in a shallow baking pan. Pour any remaining seasoning mixture over the breasts. Bake, uncovered, 45 minutes to 1 hour. Chicken breasts should be nicely browned, but not dried out.

During the last 20 minutes of baking time, place wrapped tortillas in oven alongside the chicken, and heat through.

continued

Meanwhile, combine sour cream, salt, cumin, and cilantro in a serving bowl and refrigerate to allow flavors to blend while chicken is baking.

Arrange the vegetable garnishes on a serving platter and sprinkle with olive oil, lime juice, salt, and pepper.

Just before serving, cut cooked chicken into strips.

To serve: Onto a hot tortilla spoon some chicken, vegetables, and seasoned sour cream. Roll up the tortilla. Do not overfill, or tortilla will tear when rolled.

Serve with a simple rice pilaf.

N O T E : Much of this dish can be prepared ahead, but bake the chicken at the last minute.

Chicken Madeira

Serves 4

A Fumé Blanc is suggested.

2 whole chicken breasts, halved, skinned, and boned
½ cup butter
½ pound mushrooms, quartered
⅓ cup dry vermouth
2 tablespoons Madeira
  Salt and ground white pepper
1 cup (about 4 ounces) grated Fontina or mozzarella cheese

Madeira is an amber-colored dessert wine and the chief export of the Portuguese island of the same name.

Place chicken breasts between 2 sheets of waxed paper or plastic wrap and pound them to ¼-inch thickness. Dry with paper towels.

In a 10-inch skillet, melt ¼ cup butter and sauté mushrooms briefly, about 2 to 3 minutes. Remove mushrooms and set aside.

In the same skillet, melt remaining butter. Sauté the chicken breasts about 2 to 3 minutes on each side, turning only once. Remove chicken and keep warm.

In the same skillet, add vermouth, and cook over medium heat, scraping up browned bits from the bottom of the pan, until vermouth is reduced by half. Return chicken to skillet and top with mushrooms. Pour Madeira over chicken, cover, and simmer 5 minutes. Remove chicken to a flameproof, shallow baking dish. Spoon sauce over all, and sprinkle with salt and pepper. Place several mushrooms on each piece, then sprinkle with cheese. Place under the broiler to melt cheese (watch carefully as cheese will brown quickly). Remove from heat just as cheese turns golden.

Serve immediately, spooning sauce from the bottom of the pan over the chicken and mushrooms.

Peanut Sauce for Grilled Chicken

*Makes about
2 cups*

1 small onion, minced
2 cloves garlic, minced
2 tablespoons peanut oil
1 tablespoon brown sugar
½ teaspoon crushed red pepper
1 cup chicken stock
1 cup chunky-style peanut butter
2 teaspoons soy sauce
1 tablespoon fresh lemon juice

*Peanut butter was
invented in 1890
by a St. Louis
physician looking
for a healthy, high-
protein food for his
patients. At least
half of America's
peanut crop is used
to make this
popular spread.*

In a 10-inch skillet, sauté onion and garlic in peanut oil until onion is translucent. Blend in brown sugar and crushed red pepper. Cook over low heat 2 to 3 minutes, stirring constantly. Add chicken stock and peanut butter. Cook, stirring constantly, until mixture is completely blended. Remove from heat; add soy sauce and lemon juice. Add more stock or water if sauce is too thick. Stir before serving.

Serve warm over grilled chicken.

NOTE: This sauce is good over unseasoned roasted chicken and also adds a unique flavor to steamed carrots.

Chicken Rutherford Hill

Lila Fletcher Jaeger, Rutherford Hill Winery, St. Helena

Serves 8

*Lila Jaeger
suggests a Merlot
or a
Gewürztraminer.*

2   medium onions, sliced
2   large cloves garlic, minced
4   stalks celery, sliced
3   carrots, sliced
1   large turnip (about ¾ pound), peeled and cubed
2   tablespoons butter
1   tablespoon vegetable oil
½   pound mushrooms, thickly sliced
1   jar (7 ounces) pimiento-stuffed green olives, drained
2   fennel bulbs (about 1 pound), (see Note)*

SEASONED FLOUR:
1   cup all-purpose flour
1   teaspoon salt
1   teaspoon freshly ground black pepper
1   teaspoon paprika

16   pieces of chicken (8 thighs, 8 drumsticks), skinned
¼   cup vegetable oil
1   cup dry Gewürztraminer or other dry white wine such as Chardonnay or Riesling
1   cup chicken stock

Steamed or baked brown rice fluffed with coarsely chopped parsley for accompaniment

*For Lila Jaeger,
life in Northern
California's wine
country is
connected to the
cycles of nature.
This means
growing the vines
that produce
grapes for
Rutherford Hill
wines, and serving
these wines with
meals she prepares
using seasonal
ingredients.*

In a 12-inch skillet, sauté onions, garlic, celery, carrots, and turnip in butter and 1 tablespoon oil over medium heat until almost tender, about 10 minutes. Stir to prevent burning. Add mushrooms and olives and continue to sauté, stirring occasionally, about 5 minutes. Remove from heat and set aside.

Meanwhile, to prepare fennel, remove tough outer stalks, and cut off and discard long stalks and root bottom. Slice fennel bulb in 1-inch-thick rounds. Blanch the slices in boiling water for 3 minutes. Drain and rinse in cold water to stop the cooking process. Drain again. Cut in 1-inch dice and stir into vegetable mixture.

continued

Preheat oven to 350 degrees.

Combine seasoned flour ingredients in paper or plastic bag. Toss the chicken pieces in the flour. Shake off excess.

In a large skillet, lightly brown the chicken pieces in ¼ cup oil over medium-high heat. Remove, drain, and set aside.

In a large, heavy casserole, place half the vegetable mixture, then the chicken pieces. Cover with remaining vegetables.

Combine wine with chicken stock and pour over vegetables and chicken. Cover and bake 1 hour. Add more wine or stock if chicken becomes dry.

When chicken is tender, drain most of the juices into a small saucepan, and cook until reduced to half. Serve chicken accompanied by hot rice and pass the reduced juices to spoon over rice.

NOTE: Fennel is an anise-flavored vegetable resembling celery in appearance and texture.

*Fennel is available at Italian or specialty produce markets and well-stocked supermarkets.

Country Captain Chicken

Marion Cunningham, Author and Cooking Instructor, Walnut Creek

Serves 4

A Gewürztraminer is suggested.

¼ cup all-purpose flour
Salt and freshly ground black pepper

1 frying chicken, cut in pieces

3 tablespoons butter
3 tablespoons vegetable oil
1 large onion, chopped
½ cup chopped green bell pepper
3 cloves garlic, minced
1 tablespoon curry powder
2 cans (10 ounces each) stewed tomatoes, including liquid
1 cup chopped peanuts
½ cup golden raisins

Steamed rice for accompaniment

Food historians suggest that this combination of chicken, tomatoes, and curry originated in India where it was prepared by the Country Captains, officers in the native Indian militia known as the Sepoys. Most likely, a Sepoy captain introduced this dish to the British, who brought it to America.

Combine flour, salt, and pepper in a paper bag. Shake chicken pieces in the flour mixture until coated. Shake off excess flour. In a large sauté pan, combine butter and oil and heat until sizzling. Brown chicken on all sides over medium-high heat. Remove the chicken pieces, reduce heat to medium-low, and allow the fat to cool a little. Add the onion, green pepper, and garlic to pan. Stir until the vegetables are soft, but not browned. Add the curry powder and tomatoes, and stir until blended. Return chicken to pan, cover, and cook over low heat 25 to 30 minutes, or until chicken is tender. Remove chicken pieces to a platter and keep warm.

Turn the heat to high and reduce the liquid until thickened, stirring frequently. Taste and correct seasoning. Stir in peanuts and raisins. Spoon sauce over chicken and serve with steamed rice.

Union Hotel Fried Chicken

Judy Rodgers, former Chef, The Union Hotel, Benicia

Serves 4 to 6

A Johannisberg Riesling is suggested.

1 fresh frying chicken (3 pounds), cut into pieces
1 cup rock salt
A handful of fresh thyme leaves
2 tablespoons cracked black pepper
2 cups cold milk
1¼ cups all-purpose flour
2 cups peanut oil

The small town of Benicia was once the state capital of California. One of Benicia's many historic buildings is the Union Hotel, built in 1882. When the hotel was restored in 1979, a restaurant was opened on its main floor. The menu was comprised of dishes typifying traditional American cookery. Judy Rodgers, its first chef, was instrumental in creating and revitalizing many of the recipes for which the hotel is now known.

In a bowl, toss the chicken pieces in rock salt, thyme, and pepper. Leave chicken at room temperature for 2½ hours. Rinse thoroughly under cold water. Do not soak. Some pepper will cling to the chicken. Drain. Place the rinsed chicken back in the bowl and cover with milk. Allow to soak at room temperature for 2 hours.

At least 2 hours before frying, drain the chicken, then dip the pieces in flour until they are well coated. Refrigerate on a platter for 2 hours. In a large skillet, heat the peanut oil to 365 degrees or until a pinch of flour dropped into the oil sizzles immediately. Fry drumsticks and thighs 5 to 10 minutes, then add the breast pieces and wings. The pieces should be no more than half submerged in the hot fat. Do not crowd pieces. Cook in batches, if necessary. Fry an additional 20 minutes, or until the chicken is nicely browned and crisp. Drain on paper towels.

Serve hot or cold.

Rabbit Stew with White Wine

Serves 4

A White Zinfandel is suggested.

½ pound thick-sliced bacon
8 to 10 small white onions, ends trimmed, and peeled
5 medium red potatoes, cut in eighths
2 carrots, sliced
¼ cup all-purpose flour
1 large rabbit, cut up*
3 cups chicken stock
1 cup dry white wine
3 tablespoons chopped fresh basil leaves, or 1 tablespoon dried
1¼ teaspoons minced garlic
20 peppercorns (see Note)
1 bay leaf
8 to 10 mushrooms, sliced

Crusty French bread for accompaniment

Cut bacon slices crosswise in ¼-inch pieces. In a Dutch oven, sauté the bacon over medium heat for 3 minutes, or until it has rendered most of its fat, but is not yet crisp. Add onions, potatoes, and carrots and sauté with bacon 10 minutes, stirring frequently. Remove vegetables and bacon with a slotted spoon and reserve. Leave the remaining fat in the Dutch oven.

Place flour and rabbit pieces in a plastic bag, and shake until evenly coated. In the Dutch oven, lightly brown the pieces of rabbit in bacon fat over medium heat, about 4 minutes on each side. Move rabbit pieces to expose pan bottom; add the flour remaining in the bag. Cook, stirring to combine with pan drippings, about 1 minute. Add stock, wine, and seasonings. Cook, covered, over low heat for 1½ hours.

Add only the partially cooked onions and continue cooking 30 minutes longer, or until rabbit is tender. Remove meat and bay leaf and reserve stock.

When meat is cool enough to handle, remove from bones and cut in bite-sized pieces. About 10 minutes before serving, return potatoes, carrots, and bacon to the stock and simmer until potatoes are tender. Add mushrooms and rabbit pieces and heat 2 to 3 minutes longer, or until heated through.

Serve in bowls with crusty French bread.

N O T E : If you wish to remove peppercorns after the stew has cooked, before adding to stew tie them in a square of cheesecloth, or put them in a spice infuser.

*Available at many butcher shops.

13.
Leeks
mixed intaglio

Duck with Apples

Serves 2 to 3

A Cabernet Sauvignon is suggested.

Most ducks sold in this country are descendants of nine large, white birds brought here from China by clipper ship in 1873. Now commonly known as "Long Island duckling," the bird was originally called Pekin duck.

6 to 8 green apples (such as Granny Smith or pippin), peeled, cored, and sliced
Juice of 1 large lemon (about ¼ cup)
1 domestic duck (5 to 6 pounds)
Salt and freshly ground black pepper
2 tablespoons butter
10 ounces dry white wine
¼ cup raisins
2 tablespoons Calvados (apple jack) or cognac
1 tablespoon cornstarch
2 tablespoons butter

Place peeled, sliced apples in a bowl of cold water to which lemon juice has been added. Set aside.

Preheat oven to 400 degrees.

Prick duck all over with a fork; sprinkle with salt and pepper. In a roasting pan over direct heat, brown duck on all sides in 2 tablespoons butter. Remove duck and drain fat from the pan. Return duck to the pan and pour the white wine over. Add raisins, cover the pan, and braise in oven for 45 minutes, or until duck is tender and juices run clear. Uncover and continue cooking 5 to 10 minutes longer, or until skin crisps slightly. Remove from oven.

Transfer duck to a serving platter and keep warm. Skim off fat in roasting pan and set pan over direct heat; add Calvados or cognac mixed with cornstarch. Scrape up browned bits from pan bottom and cook over very low heat, stirring to make a smooth sauce. Maintain very low heat to keep sauce warm while preparing apples.

Drain the apples well. In a large skillet, sauté apples in 2 tablespoons butter over low heat 5 to 10 minutes, stirring frequently, until tender-crisp.

Garnish the duck with apple slices, spooning over some of the sauce. Pass remaining sauce separately.

Caper-Dill Swordfish Steaks

Serves 4

*A French
Colombard is
suggested.*

3/4 cup minced onion
1/2 cup butter
1 large carrot, coarsely chopped
1 long stalk of celery, coarsely chopped
1 large lemon, peeled, seeded, and coarsely chopped
3 tablespoons drained capers
Salt and ground white pepper
4 swordfish, halibut, or sea bass steaks (each 1 inch thick and weighing about 8 ounces)
Salt and ground white pepper
2 lemons, thinly sliced
4 tablespoons butter
3/4 cup dry white wine

1 tablespoon chopped fresh dill, or 1/2 teaspoon dried, for garnish

*Capers, widely
used in cooking,
are the pickled
floral buds of the
caper bush, which
grows wild in the
countryside of
southern Europe.*

Preheat oven to 350 degrees.

In a 10-inch skillet, sauté onion in 1/2 cup butter over medium heat until soft, about 5 minutes. Increase heat to medium-high and add carrot, celery, and chopped lemon. Sauté until mixture is thick and glazed, about 10 minutes. Add capers and sauté 1 minute longer. Season with salt and pepper. Spread the mixture evenly in a shallow baking dish just large enough to hold the fish steaks in 1 layer. Arrange steaks on top of the vegetables. Sprinkle with salt and pepper and top each steak with lemon slices and 1 tablespoon butter. Pour wine over fish and cover tightly with foil. Bake 20 minutes. Remove foil and bake an additional 5 to 6 minutes, or until fish flakes with a fork. Dust with dill. Include some of the vegetables with each serving.

Baked Halibut or Tuna with Pesto

Serves 6

A Fumé Blanc is suggested.

½ cup butter
6 halibut or tuna steaks (each 1 inch thick and weighing about 8 ounces)
Salt and freshly ground black pepper
6 lemon slices
¾ cup dry white wine

PESTO SAUCE:
2 cloves garlic, peeled
2 cups packed fresh basil leaves
½ teaspoon salt
¼ teaspoon freshly ground black pepper
½ cup olive oil
½ cup (about 1½ ounces) freshly grated Parmesan cheese
1 tablespoon drained capers, rinsed, and chopped if large

Preheat oven to 350 degrees.

Melt butter in a shallow baking pan large enough to hold steaks in a single layer. Arrange fish steaks in the pan, sprinkle with salt and pepper, and place a lemon slice on top of each. Pour wine over fish. Cover tightly with aluminum foil and bake 20 minutes. Remove foil and bake an additional 5 minutes.

Meanwhile, to prepare Pesto Sauce: In a food processor or blender, finely chop garlic cloves. Add basil leaves, salt, and pepper, and puree. With machine on, add oil in a very thin, continuous stream until incorporated. By hand, stir in Parmesan cheese and capers.

To serve, top each steak with 1 to 2 tablespoons of Pesto Sauce. Serve immediately.

NOTE: To store remaining Pesto Sauce, pack the sauce in a jar, top with a thin film of olive oil, and cover the jar tightly. Pesto can be stored in the refrigerator for one week or frozen for several months.

Salmon and Mushrooms with Hollandaise Sauce

Serves 6

A dry Sauvignon Blanc is suggested.

HOLLANDAISE SAUCE:
- 6 egg yolks
- 4 teaspoons fresh lemon juice
- ¾ teaspoon salt
- ¼ teaspoon dry mustard
- Dash of Tabasco sauce
- ¾ cup melted butter

- ½ pound mushrooms, finely chopped
- 1 small onion, finely chopped
- ¼ cup minced fresh parsley
- 2 tablespoons butter
- 1 tablespoon vegetable oil

- 6 salmon steaks (each 1 inch thick and weighing about 8 ounces)
- 2 cups Chablis or other dry white wine

Lemon twists and fresh parsley sprigs for garnish

To prepare Hollandaise Sauce: In a blender, place egg yolks, lemon juice, salt, mustard, and Tabasco and mix at high speed. With the machine still at high speed, add melted butter in a steady stream until the mixture is emulsified. Set aside.

In a medium skillet, sauté mushrooms, onion, and parsley in 2 tablespoons butter and 1 tablespoon oil over medium heat until onions are golden. By hand, stir mushroom mixture into Hollandaise Sauce and chill thoroughly.

Arrange the steaks in a skillet large enough to hold the fish in a single layer. Add just enough wine to cover the salmon. Poach gently, covered, over low heat about 7 minutes, or until salmon is bright pink and liquid recedes below tops of the salmon. With a slotted spatula, remove fish and place in a baking dish large enough to hold steaks in a single layer. Generously spread steaks with chilled Hollandaise Sauce.

Broil 4 inches from heat about 5 minutes, or until sauce becomes glazed and golden brown.

Garnish with lemon twists and parsley.

NOTE: The chilled hollandaise-mushroom mixture can be made a day in advance.

Cold Poached Salmon with Avocado Sauce

Serves 4

A Dry Semillon is suggested.

2 tablespoons minced shallots (about 2 large cloves)
4 salmon steaks (each 1 inch thick and weighing about 8 ounces)
Salt and freshly ground black pepper
1 tablespoon butter, cut in pieces
1¼ cups poaching liquid (a mixture of water and white wine, or fish stock)

AVOCADO SAUCE:
1 large ripe avocado
½ cup mayonnaise (page 69)
2 tablespoons fresh lemon juice
¼ teaspoon Tabasco sauce
1 clove garlic, minced
1 green onion, finely minced (including green portion)
Salt and freshly ground black pepper

In surprising contrast to its bumpy, leathery skin, the avocado has a very smooth and creamy interior, the result of its high oil content. A ripe avocado will give when gently squeezed; a firm one will ripen to this stage within five days at room temperature. Leaving the pit in an avocado half will keep the flesh from turning brown.

Preheat oven to 350 degrees.

Sprinkle 1 tablespoon minced shallots into a skillet or flameproof baking dish large enough to hold the salmon steaks in a single layer. Place fish steaks in the pan and season lightly with salt and pepper. Dot with butter and sprinkle with remaining shallots.

In a small saucepan, bring poaching liquid to a boil. Pour over fish. There should be enough liquid to barely cover fish; add more, if necessary.

Place a piece of buttered waxed paper, buttered side down, over the fish and bake 15 minutes. Remove from oven and let steaks cool, still covered with paper, in the liquid until they reach room temperature. Discard waxed paper and remove the steaks with a slotted spatula to a serving plate.

While salmon bakes, prepare Avocado Sauce. Mash avocado until very smooth. With a fork, beat in mayonnaise, lemon juice, and Tabasco. Stir in minced garlic and green onion. Adjust seasonings, adding salt and freshly ground black pepper to taste.

Spoon some of the Avocado Sauce over the salmon steaks. Pass any remaining sauce.

NOTE: The buttered waxed paper keeps the fish moist during cooking. A lid or tight cover would retain too much heat, and the fish would overcook.

Sole with Pacific Cream Sauce

Serves 4

*A Fumé Blanc is
suggested.*

½ cup celery, finely chopped
½ onion, finely chopped
½ pound mushrooms, sliced
2 tablespoons butter
4 small fillets of sole (about 1 pound)
8 ounces tiny cooked shrimp

PACIFIC CREAM SAUCE:
¼ cup butter
5 tablespoons all-purpose flour
¾ cup milk
2 egg yolks
½ cup whipping cream
¼ teaspoon fresh lemon juice
½ teaspoon salt
¼ teaspoon ground white pepper
3 tablespoons grated Italian Fontina cheese

Paprika and chopped fresh parsley for garnish

Preheat oven to 375 degrees. Butter a shallow baking dish large enough to hold fillets in a single layer.

In a small skillet, sauté celery, onion, and mushrooms in butter over medium heat until soft. Arrange fillets in a single layer in the bottom of the prepared pan. Spread the vegetable mixture and shrimp on top.

To prepare Pacific Cream Sauce: Melt the butter in the same skillet over medium heat. Stir in the flour until smooth. Turn heat to low and stir constantly for 2 minutes. Do not brown. Remove skillet from heat and slowly pour in milk, stirring constantly to prevent lumps from forming. Return to medium heat. Cook the sauce, stirring constantly, until it just boils and thickens. Remove 2 tablespoons of sauce to a small bowl and stir in egg yolks and cream. Add another 2 tablespoons sauce and stir. Pour the egg mixture into the skillet. Cook, stirring constantly, until sauce thickens enough to coat a metal spoon. Remove from heat and stir in lemon juice, salt, and pepper.

Cover the fillets with Pacific Cream Sauce and sprinkle with cheese.

Bake for 20 to 25 minutes, or until the sauce is bubbly and the cheese is melted and pale golden.

Sprinkle with paprika and chopped parsley for garnish.

Fillet of Sole in Packets

Serves 4

A White Zinfandel is suggested.

Baking food in packets of aluminum foil or parchment is a technique that seals in natural juices and enables a busy cook to produce moist, flavorful, and quickly prepared meals. The aromatic bouquet released when the baked packages are opened is one of the delights of this cooking technique.

4 to 6 stalks celery, cut in ¼-inch dice
    2 leeks (white portion only), cut in ¼-inch dice
    4 medium carrots, cut in ¼-inch dice
    3 (or more) tablespoons butter
      Salt and freshly ground black pepper

    2 pounds fillets of sole
      Salt and freshly ground black pepper
    2 ripe tomatoes, sliced
    1 lemon, sliced
    4 bay leaves
   ¾ teaspoon fresh thyme, or ½ teaspoon dried
    4 squares (12- by 12-inches each) aluminum foil or cooking parchment

Preheat oven to 450 degrees.

In a medium skillet, sauté celery, leeks, and carrots in 3 or more tablespoons butter, for 5 minutes, or until just tender. Season with salt and pepper.

On each foil or parchment square, layer one-fourth of the ingredients in the following order: sautéed vegetables, sole fillets, salt and pepper, tomato slices, lemon slices, bay leaf, thyme. Fold packets securely, tucking edges under, and place on a baking sheet. Bake 20 minutes.

Slit packets before serving, or allow guests to open their own.

Sautéed Scallops in Golden Sauce

Serves 4

A Chardonnay is suggested.

2 pounds scallops, rinsed
Juice of 1 large lemon (about ¼ cup)
3 tablespoons all-purpose flour
¼ cup butter (more, if needed)
3 cloves garlic, minced
¼ cup thinly sliced green onions (including some green portion)
1 cup dry vermouth

Watercress sprigs for garnish

The scallop is the white adductor muscle of a bivalve mollusk. The larger ocean scallop is available all year. The smaller and more costly bay scallop, prized for its delicate, sweet flavor, is harvested and sold only in the fall and winter months. A variety of sea scallop, the calico, is often marketed as a bay scallop.

Marinate scallops in lemon juice at least 15 minutes, stirring once or twice. Drain well and halve scallops if large. Place in a plastic bag with flour. Shake until scallops are lightly coated. In a large skillet, melt butter over medium heat until foamy. Sauté the scallops in butter about 5 minutes on each side, or until opaque and lightly browned. Turn only once. Remove scallops with a slotted spoon. Set aside.

To the warm skillet, add garlic and stir until translucent, adding more butter, if needed. Mix in onions and vermouth. Boil, stirring constantly, and scraping up browned bits from the bottom of the skillet, until onions are soft and liquid has evaporated, about 3 minutes. Sauce will be thick. Return scallops to skillet and stir to coat with sauce. Heat only until scallops are hot.

Serve immediately, garnished with watercress.

Snapper Rancheros

Serves 6

A Petite Sirah is suggested.

6 red snapper fillets (about 8 ounces per serving)
Salt and freshly ground black pepper
All-purpose flour
¼ cup olive oil

RANCHEROS SAUCE:
3 large cloves shallots, minced
2 large cloves garlic, minced
6 ripe tomatoes (about 2½ pounds), cut in ½-inch dice
1 can (4 ounces) diced green chiles
2 tablespoons chopped fresh oregano, or 2 teaspoons dried
Salt and freshly ground black pepper
1 ripe avocado
1 teaspoon fresh lime juice
⅛ teaspoon Tabasco sauce
1 clove garlic, minced
Salt and freshly ground black pepper

Preheat oven to 350 degrees. Butter a shallow baking dish large enough to hold fillets in a single layer.

Sprinkle fillets with salt and pepper and dredge in flour. Shake off excess flour.

In a large skillet, fry fillets in olive oil over medium heat, several at a time, about 2 minutes on each side. Transfer with a slotted spatula to the prepared baking dish. Set aside.

To prepare Rancheros Sauce: In the same skillet, reduce heat and sauté the shallots and 2 cloves garlic in the oil remaining in the skillet until translucent. Add tomatoes and chiles and increase heat to medium. Cook several minutes, or until tomatoes are heated through. Stir in oregano and season with salt and pepper. Spoon the mixture, including the juices, over the fillets. Place in the oven and bake 30 minutes.

Meanwhile, coarsely mash the avocado in a small bowl. Blend in lime juice, Tabasco, remaining minced garlic, salt, and pepper.

When fish is done, use a slotted spatula to carefully remove the fillets to a warm plate, keeping tomatoes and chiles on top. Pour the juices from the baking pan back into the skillet. Boil quickly until the liquid is reduced by about half. Remove from heat and beat in avocado mixture until liquid is incorporated. Adjust seasonings, if necessary.

Spoon avocado mixture over fillets and serve immediately.

Shrimp Madras

Serves 6

A Gewürztraminer is suggested.

½ medium onion, minced
1 small clove garlic, minced
¼ cup butter
¼ cup all-purpose flour
1½ tablespoons curry powder
⅛ teaspoon cayenne pepper
½ cup beef stock
½ cup coconut milk†*
1 cup whipping cream
½ teaspoon fresh lemon juice
1 teaspoon grated lemon peel
1 small green apple, peeled and grated
1 pound cooked shrimp, shelled and deveined

Steamed white rice for accompaniment

CONDIMENTS (CHOOSE ANY OR ALL):
Sliced green onions, chopped chutney, peanuts, shredded coconut, raisins, crumbled fried bacon, chopped hard-cooked egg, chopped ripe tomatoes, chopped candied ginger

The intensity of a curry dish depends on the proportion of spices used in the seasoning. Many families in India and the Middle East pride themselves on their particular blend, never revealing the source of their spices and always varying them according to the dish they are preparing.

In a 2-quart saucepan, sauté onion and garlic in butter over low heat until translucent. Sprinkle with flour, curry powder, and cayenne and stir well. Add beef stock, stirring constantly until thickened. Cook several minutes more, stirring constantly. Blend in coconut milk, whipping cream, and lemon juice. Add lemon peel, apple, and shrimp and simmer, covered, for 20 minutes.

Serve with white rice accompanied by a selection of condiments.

†To prepare your own coconut milk, place ½ cup unsweetened shredded coconut in a blender container and cover with ¾ cup boiling water. Let stand 5 minutes. Cover the container and blend 1 minute. Transfer the mixture to a cheesecloth-lined sieve. Squeeze out as much "milk" as possible. Discard the pulp.

*Available at specialty food stores and well-stocked supermarkets.

Sweet and Sour Sauce for Fish Steaks

Serves 6

6 fish steaks or fillets (each 1 inch thick and weighing about 8 ounces), such as halibut, swordfish, shark, or snapper
Vegetable oil

SWEET AND SOUR SAUCE:

½ cup sugar
½ cup apple cider vinegar
½ teaspoon salt
1 green bell pepper, cored, seeded, and cut in ¼-inch dice
2 ripe tomatoes, cut in eighths
1 small onion, sliced in thin rings
1 tablespoon cornstarch
1 tablespoon water

In a skillet large enough to hold the fish in a single layer, heat a thin film of vegetable oil over medium heat until it ripples. Add fish and fry about 5 minutes per side, or until flesh is opaque throughout. Do not overcook.

Meanwhile, to prepare Sweet and Sour Sauce: In a 1-quart acid-resistant saucepan, bring the sugar, vinegar, and salt to a boil, stirring until sugar dissolves. Add the vegetables and return to a boil. Combine cornstarch and water to form a thin paste. Add to the boiling sauce and stir constantly until sauce thickens slightly and becomes clear, 1 to 2 minutes.

Spoon sauce over the hot fish and serve.

English Cucumber-Dill Butter for Grilled Fish

Phillip Lacock, California Cafe Bar and Grill, Walnut Creek

*Makes about
1 cup*

½ pound unsalted butter, softened
1 tablespoon or more hot water
1 tablespoon finely snipped fresh dill
½ cup English cucumber, peeled and very finely diced (regular cucumber may be used if seeded)
Juice of ½ lemon, strained

In a medium bowl, beat butter with a wooden spoon until smooth. Add 1 tablespoon hot water and dill. Mix until smooth and creamy. Add diced cucumber and lemon juice and stir well. Additional hot water may be added if creamier texture is desired. Refrigerate until ready to serve.
Serve on grilled fish.

NOTE: English Cucumber-Dill Butter can be scooped or spooned cold. Return to room temperature to mold or to roll and slice.

CHAPTER NINE

Desserts

Brandy Milk Shake

Serves 4

1 quart coffee (or espresso) ice cream
¼ cup brandy
¼ to ½ cup milk

Whipped cream and chocolate curls or freshly ground nutmeg for garnish

The term milk shake *first appeared in print at the turn-of-the-century. In the early 1900s the beverage attained popularity, and in time, malt was added to contribute to its sweetness.*

Fill a blender container loosely with ice cream. Add brandy and ¼ cup milk. Blend until smooth. If a softer shake is desired, add more milk.

Serve in oversized wine glasses topped with a generous amount of whipped cream and chocolate curls, or a sprinkling of nutmeg.

NOTE: This recipe can follow the most elegant meal if served in a crystal goblet, or can be whipped up for Super Bowl Sunday and presented in a heavy glass mug.

Banana-Orange Ice

Serves 6 to 8

2 ripe bananas, peeled and cut in chunks
Juice of 2 large oranges (about 1 cup)
Juice of 2 large lemons (about ½ cup)
2 eggs
2 cups water
1 cup sugar

Place all ingredients in a blender and puree. Pour into a non-metal mixing bowl. Freeze until almost firm (4 to 6 hours). With a fork, egg beater, or blender, break up ice crystals. Repeat 2 to 3 times more, at hourly intervals, or until ice is nearly set.

Freeze until firm.

Maple Baked Apples

Serves 6

1 cup pure maple syrup
½ cup fresh orange juice (about 1 large orange)
2 tablespoons butter
1 tablespoon cornstarch
6 McIntosh or Rome Beauty apples
⅓ cup golden raisins
2 tablespoons brown sugar
½ teaspoon ground cinnamon

Whipped cream for garnish (optional)

Of the seven thousand varieties of apples, perhaps best for this recipe is the tart, juicy McIntosh or the subtly sweet Rome Beauty. Both are amply sized for dessert portions and are available throughout California and the West.

Combine maple syrup, orange juice, butter, and cornstarch in a small saucepan. Bring to a boil, reduce heat, and simmer 5 minutes.

Preheat oven to 350 degrees.

Core each apple. Starting at the stem end, pare each apple one-third of the way down. Place apples in a shallow baking dish just large enough to hold 6 comfortably. Combine raisins, brown sugar, and cinnamon and spoon into the center of each apple. Pour hot syrup mixture over apples.

Bake, covered, 30 to 40 minutes, or until apples are still firm, but pierce easily with a toothpick. Baste with syrup at least once during baking.

Serve warm or cold, plain or garnished with whipped cream.

14.
Chocolate Truffles
color pencil, graphite

Lemon Sauce for Blueberries

Serves 8 to 10

5 eggs, separated
¾ cup sugar
   Juice of 2 large lemons (about ½ cup)
1 cup whipping cream, whipped
2 teaspoons finely grated lemon peel

1 quart chilled fresh blueberries, washed and stemmed

To get the maximum amount of juice from a lemon, use the palm of your hand to roll it firmly on a hard surface before slicing and squeezing.

In an acid-resistant double boiler, beat egg yolks with sugar until mixture is light and lemon-colored. Add lemon juice and cook over hot, not boiling, water, stirring with a wooden spoon until the mixture coats the spoon. Do not boil. Remove from heat. Cool.

Beat egg whites until stiff, but not dry. Gently fold egg whites, whipped cream, and lemon peel into the cooled lemon mixture until thoroughly incorporated. Chill until ready to assemble.

To serve, spoon blueberries into champagne glasses or crystal goblets and top with the chilled sauce.

Peach Flambé with Raspberry Sauce and Vanilla Ice Cream

Serves 6 to 8

> 2 cups sugar
> 2 cups water
> 6 to 8 firm ripe freestone peaches
>
> 1 tablespoon sugar
> ¼ cup Cointreau or other orange liqueur
> ¼ cup kirsch
> Grated peel of 1 orange
> Grated peel of 1 lemon
>
> RASPBERRY SAUCE:
> ½ pint fresh raspberries
> ½ cup sugar
> Juice of 1 orange
> Juice of 1 lemon
> 2 tablespoons Cointreau or other orange liqueur
>
> Half-gallon vanilla ice cream
>
> 1 tablespoon Cointreau or other orange liqueur

To ensure a spectacular flambé, slightly warm the liqueur before flaming.

In a 2-quart saucepan, boil 2 cups sugar with 2 cups water until sugar dissolves, 1 to 2 minutes. Poach whole, unpeeled peaches in the sugar water until tender but not mushy, about 4 minutes. Remove with a slotted spoon. Discard poaching liquid. Let the peaches sit until cool enough to handle. Slip off skins. Do not slice.

Place the peaches in a chafing dish if preparing at the table, or in a skillet if to be flamed on the stove. Sprinkle with 1 tablespoon sugar, Cointreau, kirsch, and half of the orange and lemon peels. Reserve remaining grated peel for the Raspberry Sauce. Set peaches aside.

To prepare Raspberry Sauce: Wash berries. Combine in a small saucepan with sugar, orange and lemon juices, and the remaining grated peel. Heat slowly, stirring occasionally. Remove from heat, add Cointreau, and set aside.

When ready to serve, place a scoop of ice cream in individual serving dishes.

Heat the peaches until liquid which has settled on the bottom of the pan is bubbling. Add 1 tablespoon of Cointreau to the chafing dish or skillet and ignite. Spoon flaming peaches onto ice cream. Serve with Raspberry Sauce.

Strawberries with Raspberry Sauce

Serves 6 to 8

1 quart strawberries, washed and hulled
¼ cup sugar
½ pint fresh raspberries
2 tablespoons sugar
2 tablespoons Grand Marnier or other orange liqueur
1 teaspoon fresh lemon juice

The appeal of this warm weather dessert lies in the simplicity of its preparation and the refreshing flavor of the berries.

In a bowl, sprinkle strawberries with ¼ cup sugar. Stir gently and chill.

In a food processor or blender, puree raspberries with 2 tablespoons sugar. Strain and discard seeds. Stir in Grand Marnier and lemon juice. Chill.

At least 1 hour before serving, pour sauce over the berries. Stir just before serving. Serve chilled.

Apple-Cranberry Crumble

Serves 6

CRUST:

1 cup brown sugar
1 cup rolled oats
½ cup all-purpose flour
¼ teaspoon salt
½ cup butter, softened

FILLING:

2 cups fresh cranberries
3 large tart green apples, peeled, cored, and sliced
1 cup granulated sugar
1 tablespoon fresh lemon juice

Vanilla ice cream for accompaniment

Preheat oven to 325 degrees.

To prepare Crust: Combine brown sugar, oats, flour, and salt. Cut in butter until mixture is crumbly. Set aside.

To prepare Filling: Combine cranberries, apples, sugar, and lemon juice. Spread in a 9- by 13-inch baking pan. Spoon crumb mixture over fruit.

Bake 50 to 60 minutes, or until top is lightly browned and bubbly and apples are still tender-crisp when pierced with the tip of a knife.

Serve warm with vanilla ice cream.

Berry Cobbler

Serves 6 to 8

½ cup butter, melted
1 cup milk
1 cup sugar
1 cup all-purpose flour
2 teaspoons baking powder
3 cups berries, or peeled and sliced seasonal fruit such as peaches, apples (sprinkled with 1 teaspoon ground cinnamon), or apricots
½ cup sugar for topping

Vanilla ice cream for accompaniment

Traditional cobblers are made with either apples or peaches. They are similar to a pie or tart, and were especially popular during the nineteenth century.

Preheat oven to 350 degrees.

Pour melted butter into a 2-quart shallow casserole and coat the bottom.

In a mixing bowl, combine milk, 1 cup sugar, flour, and baking powder. Stir until just blended (batter will be lumpy). Pour over melted butter. Do not stir.

Arrange fruit over top. Sprinkle with ½ cup sugar. Do not stir.

Bake 30 to 35 minutes or until top is golden. Serve hot, at room temperature, or cold, with vanilla ice cream.

Rhubarb Betty

Serves 8

CRUST:
½ cup butter
1 cup all-purpose flour
5 tablespoons brown sugar
¼ teaspoon salt

FILLING:
¾ to 1 pound fresh rhubarb

TOPPING:
1½ cups granulated sugar
¼ cup all-purpose flour
¾ teaspoon baking powder
¼ teaspoon salt
3 eggs
⅓ cup whipping cream

Vanilla ice cream or lightly sweetened whipped cream for accompaniment

Rhubarb, or "barbarous root," was discovered by the Europeans during their journeys to the Orient, where it grows wild. In the 1400s, monks learned that the plant could cure simple maladies. In later centuries, rhubarb was cultivated in gardens for its ornamental appeal. Although rhubarb is used in cooking as a fruit, it is actually a vegetable.

Preheat oven to 350 degrees.

To prepare Crust: Mix together crust ingredients until crumbly. Pat into the bottom of a 9- by 13-inch baking pan. Bake 20 minutes, or until lightly browned.

To prepare Filling: While crust is baking, wash and trim off and discard woody ends and all leaves from rhubarb. Split stalks lengthwise and then chop in ½-inch pieces. Set aside.

To prepare Topping: Sift together dry topping ingredients, then stir in eggs and cream until well blended.

Distribute rhubarb over hot baked crust. Pour topping mixture over rhubarb. Bake for 40 minutes, or until lightly browned.

Cool. Cut in squares.

Serve with vanilla ice cream or lightly sweetened whipped cream.

Peach-Berry Cream Puffs

Serves 6

PUFFS:
½ cup water
¼ cup butter
⅛ teaspoon salt
½ cup all-purpose flour
2 eggs

FILLING:
1½ cups whipping cream
¼ cup sugar
2 tablespoons kirsch
3 cups peeled and sliced peaches
1 pint strawberries, washed, hulled, and sliced

SAUCE:
½ pint fresh raspberries
1 tablespoon cornstarch
2 tablespoons kirsch
½ cup sugar
½ cup (5 ounces) red currant jelly

Preheat oven to 400 degrees. Butter a cookie sheet.

To prepare Puffs: In a small saucepan, bring water, butter, and salt to a boil. Add flour all at once and beat with a wooden spoon until mixture pulls away from sides of pan and forms a ball. Remove from heat and cool 5 minutes. Beat eggs. Reserve 1 tablespoon beaten egg for glaze and pour remaining egg into hot mixture; beat until thoroughly incorporated. Spoon batter into 6 equal mounds on prepared cookie sheet. Brush with the reserved egg. Bake for 35 minutes until browned. Remove from oven and poke holes in sides of puffs with a toothpick. Turn off oven, return puffs to oven, and let rest 10 minutes with oven door closed. Remove and cool on a rack.

To prepare Filling: Whip cream, gradually adding ¼ cup sugar. Stir in kirsch. Fold in fruit, reserving some pieces for garnish, if desired.

To prepare Sauce: Puree raspberries in a blender or food processor. Mix cornstarch with kirsch, ½ cup sugar, and jelly. Combine berries and cornstarch mixture in a small saucepan. Bring to a boil over low heat, stirring frequently. Cook until clear and thickened. Strain and discard seeds. Cool sauce before spooning over cream puffs.

To assemble: Split each puff with a knife. Fill centers with cream and fruit. Top with some sauce and garnish with reserved fruit. Pass additional sauce separately.

Blueberry Tart

Serves 8

CRUST:

½ cup butter

3 tablespoons sugar

1⅓ cups all-purpose flour

¼ teaspoon salt

FILLING:

2 pints fresh blueberries

¾ cup sugar

2 tablespoons cornstarch

¼ teaspoon salt

⅔ cup water

1½ tablespoons fresh lemon juice

2 tablespoons butter

TOPPING:

¾ cup whipping cream, whipped

When blueberries are plentiful, try this luscious fruit tart made with succulent berries piled into a simple cookie crust and covered with a mound of whipped cream.

Preheat oven to 375 degrees.

To prepare Crust: With a fork or pastry blender, combine butter and sugar until just blended. Add flour and salt. With a pastry blender, cut together to form a crumbly dough. Press into bottom and up sides of a 9- or 10-inch fluted tart pan with removable bottom. Prick bottom and sides of crust with a fork. Bake 12 to 15 minutes, or until lightly browned. Cool in pan.

To prepare Filling: Wash berries. Place 1 cup of berries in a small saucepan with ¾ cup sugar, cornstarch, salt, and water. Cook over medium heat, stirring constantly, until thick and clear. Remove from heat and stir in lemon juice and butter. Cool. Fold in remaining berries. Mound filling into cooled crust. Chill at least 1 hour.

To serve, remove tart from pan and set on a serving plate. Pile whipped cream in the center, leaving the outside rim of filling exposed, and cut into wedges.

Lemon Tart

Serves 8

PASTRY:

1 cup all-purpose flour
¼ cup confectioners' sugar
¼ teaspoon salt
½ cup chilled butter
1 tablespoon ice water

FILLING:

5 eggs
1 cup granulated sugar
⅔ cup strained fresh lemon juice (about 3 large lemons)
4 teaspoons grated lemon peel
2 tablespoons cornstarch
¼ teaspoon salt
½ cup butter, melted

The California Gold Rush of 1849 brought riches to local farmers who sold lemons to scurvy-prone miners.

Preheat oven to 400 degrees.

To prepare Pastry: Combine flour, confectioners' sugar, and salt in a small bowl. Cut in butter until crumbly. Sprinkle ice water over mixture and combine until well blended. Mixture will be quite dry. (If making dough in a food processor, water may be eliminated.) With fingers, press mixture into bottom and up sides of a 9- or 10-inch fluted tart pan with removable bottom. Bake 8 to 10 minutes; remove from oven. With fingers, press hot crust lightly to ensure an even thickness where bottom and sides of the pan meet. Return tart shell to oven and bake an additional 5 to 10 minutes, or until crust is lightly browned. Set aside to cool.

To prepare Filling: In a food processor or blender, combine eggs, sugar, lemon juice, lemon peel, cornstarch, and salt. Puree until smooth. With machine on, slowly pour in melted butter until just blended. Pour the mixture into a small acid-resistant saucepan. Cook over medium heat, stirring constantly with a wooden spoon, until filling just begins to boil and is quite thick. Place bottom of saucepan in a bowl of ice water and stir until mixture cools to room temperature.

Fill the cooled shell. Chill until ready to serve, then remove fluted metal ring, and slice tart into wedges.

Nectarine Tart

Serves 8

CRUST:

1 cup all-purpose flour
¼ cup confectioners' sugar
½ cup butter

GLAZE:

½ cup (5 ounces) red currant jelly
2 tablespoons cornstarch
2 tablespoons granulated sugar
¼ teaspoon ground mace
⅛ teaspoon ground nutmeg
⅔ cup strained fresh orange juice
Grated peel of 1 orange

FILLING:

4 to 6 ripe nectarines
Juice of ½ lemon
Granulated sugar

TOPPING:

1 cup whipping cream
2 tablespoons confectioners' sugar
1 teaspoon ground nutmeg

The nectarine, a relative of the peach, is aptly named for its nectar. The word is from the Greek—the sweet juice was the drink of the gods on Mount Olympus. More than ninety percent of the nectarines commercially available in America are grown in California's San Joaquin Valley.

Preheat oven to 350 degrees.

To prepare Crust: Combine flour and sugar. Cut in butter until crumbly. Press mixture into bottom and up sides of a 9- or 10-inch fluted tart pan with removable bottom. Bake 15 minutes, or until lightly browned. Cool.

To prepare Glaze: In a small saucepan, combine jelly, cornstarch, sugar, mace, and nutmeg. Stir thoroughly to blend. Add orange juice and peel. Cook over medium heat, stirring constantly, until mixture just comes to a boil and is thick and clear. Set aside.

To prepare Filling: Slice unpeeled nectarines in thin slivers. Toss with lemon juice to prevent discoloring. Arrange in concentric, overlapping circles in the cooled tart shell. Sprinkle with sugar, if desired, to sweeten the nectarines.

Pour the glaze over the nectarines, spreading to be sure all the slices are coated. Refrigerate until serving time.

To prepare Topping: Combine cream, 2 tablespoons confectioners' sugar, and nutmeg. Whip until cream holds its shape.

To serve, remove fluted metal ring, slice tart in wedges, and pass topping separately.

Strawberry Pie

Serves 6 to 8

CRUST:
1 cup graham cracker crumbs (about 18 single crackers)
5 tablespoons butter, melted
½ cup sliced walnuts

FILLING:
2 pints whole strawberries, washed and hulled
½ cup water
1 cup sugar
2½ tablespoons cornstarch
Juice of ½ lemon

8 whole strawberries for garnish
Whipped cream for garnish

Preheat oven to 350 degrees.

To prepare Crust: Mix together the crushed crackers, melted butter, and walnuts. Press into a 9-inch pie pan. Bake 6 minutes. Set aside to cool.

To prepare Filling: Crush 1 pint of strawberries. In a 1-quart saucepan, cook crushed strawberries, water, sugar, and cornstarch over medium-low heat until the mixture boils and is clear and thickened, stirring frequently. Cool, but do not chill. Stir in the juice of one-half lemon.

Arrange the second pint of whole, hulled strawberries in the cooled shell, pointed ends up. Pour the cooled filling over the whole berries. Refrigerate 2 to 3 hours, or until filling is set.

Serve garnished with whipped cream and whole strawberries.

Strawberry Goat Cheese Pie

Laura Chenel and Linda Siegfried, Authors of *Chèvre! The Goat Cheese Cookbook*, Sonoma County

Serves 8

PASTRY:

- 2 cups all-purpose flour
- 2 tablespoons sugar
- ¼ teaspoon salt
- 3 tablespoons vegetable oil
- ½ cup chilled butter, cut in pieces
- 4 to 6 tablespoons ice water

TOPPING:

- 1½ pints fresh strawberries, washed and hulled
- ⅓ cup sugar
- 1 tablespoon fresh lemon juice
- 1 tablespoon cornstarch

FILLING:

- 2 cups goat fromage blanc, softened (see Note)*
- ¼ cup sugar
- ½ teaspoon minced fresh lemon peel
- ¼ teaspoon vanilla extract
- 1 cup whipping cream, whipped

1½ pints fresh strawberries, washed and hulled

Laura Chenel and her cookbook co-author, Linda Siegfried, created this pie when strawberries were ripe and there was an abundance of goat cheese. They are particularly fond of the balance of flavors in this recipe, developed for California Fresh, *as well as the pie's texture and freshness.*

Preheat oven to 400 degrees.

To prepare Pastry: In a food processor, using the steel blade, mix flour, 2 tablespoons sugar, and salt. Add oil and butter. Process until granular. Add ice water and process lightly until dough forms a ball. Wrap in waxed paper and refrigerate 1 hour. On a lightly floured surface, roll out dough to fit a 9½-inch deep-dish pie pan. Fit crust into pan, then line crust with aluminum foil and fill with pie weights, raw rice, or dried beans. Bake 10 minutes. Remove foil and pie weights. Pierce the crust with a fork and return to oven for 10 to 12 minutes, or until lightly browned. Set aside to cool.

To prepare Topping: In a food processor or blender, puree 1½ pints fresh strawberries. Press through a sieve into a small saucepan. Combine ⅓ cup sugar, lemon juice, and cornstarch; add to strained berries. Simmer, stirring frequently, until thickened and transparent. Cool to lukewarm.

continued

To prepare Filling: Combine fromage blanc, ¼ cup sugar, lemon peel, and vanilla. Fold in whipped cream. Set aside.

To assemble pie, fill cooled crust with fromage blanc mixture. Decoratively arrange 1½ pints whole fresh strawberries, pointed ends up, over filling. Gently pour topping over strawberries to cover. Refrigerate at least 1 hour before serving.

N O T E : Goat fromage blanc is strained, unsalted curd made from goat's milk.

*Available at specialty food stores and cheese shops.

Sherry Cream for Fresh Fruit

Elizabeth Martini, Louis M. Martini Winery, St. Helena

Serves 4 to 6

1 cup sour cream
3 tablespoons brown sugar
3 tablespoons Louis Martini Cream Sherry
2 cups fresh blueberries
2 cups fresh ripe nectarines, sliced

In a blender, mix sour cream, brown sugar, and sherry until smooth and creamy. Refrigerate until ready to use.

Stir in fresh blueberries and sliced fresh nectarines or any other combination of fresh fruit desired. Be sure all fruit is coated to prevent discoloration. Chill fruit and cream mixture 3 or 4 hours before serving.

NOTE: The sauce can be prepared a day ahead, if desired.

Orange Sauce for Fruit

*Makes about
2 cups*

1 cup whipping cream
1 egg
½ cup sugar
1 tablespoon grated orange peel
1 tablespoon fresh lemon juice

Whip cream until stiff. Mix remaining ingredients and fold into cream. Serve over any fresh fruit combination.

N O T E : If serving over naturally sweet or presweetened fruit, reduce the sugar to ¼ cup.

Crème Brûlée

Serves 8

3 cups whipping cream
¾ cup granulated sugar
½ teaspoon salt
2 tablespoons vanilla extract
6 egg yolks
½ cup light brown sugar

1 pint fresh raspberries, sweetened with granulated sugar, for accompaniment

Crème Brûlée is an elegant baked custard dessert capped by a caramelized sugar crust. The textural combination of smooth, cool custard and hard, sweet topping is irresistible.

Preheat oven to 300 degrees.

In a double boiler, combine whipping cream, granulated sugar, salt, and vanilla. Heat over simmering water, stirring to dissolve the sugar, until liquid is hot to the touch. It will not be thickened.

Beat egg yolks until thick and light-colored. Slowly add the hot cream mixture, stirring constantly. Pour mixture through a fine sieve into a 9-inch deep-dish ovenproof glass pie pan. Set the pie pan in a larger baking pan and add enough hot water to reach halfway up the sides of the pie pan.

Bake 35 minutes. (A knife inserted in the center is not an accurate test for doneness for this recipe.) Cool the custard to room temperature, then chill thoroughly.

Press brown sugar through a colander onto the surface of the chilled custard. Set custard pan on a bed of cracked ice; broil 4 inches from heat only until sugar begins to bubble and melt. Watch carefully to prevent burning.

Serve with sweetened raspberries as an accompaniment.

15.
Oranges to Cut
graphite

Coeur à la Crème with Bananas Connoisseur

Serves 12

COEUR À LA CRÈME:

1 pound cottage cheese (not low fat)

¼ teaspoon salt

8 ounces cream cheese, softened

6 tablespoons confectioners' sugar

1 cup whipping cream

1 tablespoon vanilla extract

BANANAS CONNOISSEUR:

3 large green-tipped bananas, peeled and sliced diagonally in ½-inch pieces

3 tablespoons fresh lime juice

¼ cup butter

½ cup sugar

¼ cup apricot brandy

To prepare Coeur à la Crème: In a food processor, combine cottage cheese and salt and process until smooth. Add remaining ingredients and blend thoroughly.

Rinse a large square of cheesecloth in water and ring out. Choose a 4-cup coeur à la crème mold, a small wicker basket (not dyed), or a round metal mold pierced like a colander. Line the mold or basket with several thicknesses of dampened cheesecloth, draping excess over sides. Spoon the cheese mixture into the mold and pack firmly. Bring up the edges of the cheesecloth and fold over the cheese. Place the mold on a plate to catch the whey as it drains. Refrigerate overnight.

When ready to serve, open the cheesecloth and invert the mold onto a serving platter. Remove and discard cheesecloth and whey.

To prepare Bananas Connoisseur: Sprinkle banana pieces with lime juice. In a small saucepan or skillet, melt butter over medium heat. Add bananas. Stir in sugar and brandy. Boil briefly to allow alcohol to evaporate. Spoon at once over individual portions of Coeur à la Crème and serve.

NOTE: This slightly sweet, creamy dessert can be prepared as individual servings using foil muffin cups lined with cheesecloth and pierced on the bottom to allow the whey to drain.

Bananas Connoisseur may be flamed at the table in a chafing dish. Place one tablespoon of the brandy in a very small saucepan; warm slightly, ignite, and pour over the bananas. Shake pan or stir until the flame dies.

Almond and Pear Dacquoise

Judith Wahlander, Kären Lode Nady, Two Good Cooks™, Berkeley

Serves 10 to 12

MERINGUES:

6 egg whites, at room temperature
¼ teaspoon cream of tartar
1¼ cups superfine sugar
⅔ cup almonds, blanched, skinned, dried, and finely ground

RASPBERRY SAUCE:

1 pint fresh raspberries
3 tablespoons sugar
1 tablespoon kirsch or amaretto

WHIPPED CREAM FILLING:

2 cups whipping cream
2 tablespoons superfine sugar
1 to 2 tablespoons Poire William or other pear liqueur
1 to 2 fresh ripe pears (depending on size)

Confectioners' sugar
10 to 12 whole fresh raspberries for garnish (optional)

This sophisticated-looking dessert is much faster and easier to make than one would imagine, and is excellent with other fruit fillings too.

Preheat oven to 300 degrees. Line 2 baking sheets with cooking parchment. Draw a 9-inch circle on each sheet.

To prepare Meringues: With an electric mixer, beat egg whites to a froth. Add cream of tartar and beat until stiff but not dry. Add 2 to 3 tablespoons of sugar and beat about 10 seconds. With a rubber spatula, fold in remaining sugar and ground almonds as quickly as possible. Fill a pastry bag fitted with a plain ½-inch tip with meringue and pipe in concentric circles or spread the mixture with a knife to fill the two 9-inch rounds, smoothing the tops if necessary. Bake 60 to 75 minutes, or until meringue is dry but not colored. After 45 minutes baking time, reduce heat to 250 degrees for remainder of baking. Carefully lift meringues on their parchments to a rack. Cool 15 minutes, remove parchment, and let cool completely. The meringue layers should be slightly soft and chewy in the center.

continued

To prepare Raspberry Sauce: In a food processor or blender, puree raspberries until smooth, adding 3 tablespoons sugar. Press through a sieve to remove seeds. Stir in kirsch or amaretto and set aside.

To prepare Whipped Cream Filling: Whip cream until thick. Whisk in 2 tablespoons sugar and pear liqueur. Set aside. Peel pears, then halve, core, and slice crosswise.

To assemble, place 1 meringue layer on a serving plate. Cover with a thick layer of whipped cream. Arrange 1 layer of pear slices over cream. Drizzle a little Raspberry Sauce over pears. Cover with another, thinner, layer of whipped cream. Gently set remaining meringue layer on top. Dust with confectioners' sugar and decorate with rosettes of whipped cream and fresh whole berries. Serve with remaining Raspberry Sauce.

Almond Torte

Narsai M. David, Narsai's Restaurant and Market, Kensington

Serves 8

½ teaspoon sugar
½ teaspoon all-purpose flour

7 ounces almond paste
½ cup unsalted butter
¾ cup sugar
3 eggs
¼ teaspoon baking powder
¼ teaspoon almond extract
1 tablespoon kirsch
¼ cup sifted all-purpose flour

Confectioners' sugar for dusting

TOPPING:
1 cup raspberries, pressed through a sieve

Preheat oven to 350 degrees. Butter an 8-inch round cake pan, then sprinkle with a mixture of ½ teaspoon sugar and ½ teaspoon flour. Tap out excess from pan.

With an electric mixer, cream the almond paste and butter until smooth. Beat in ¾ cup sugar, scraping sides of bowl. Add eggs, one at a time, beating well after each addition. Add baking powder, almond extract, and kirsch. Fold in ¼ cup flour. Spread batter in prepared pan and smooth the top with a spatula.

Bake 30 to 35 minutes, or until a knife inserted in the center comes out clean. Cool and remove from pan. Dust with confectioners' sugar.

Just before serving, top each slice of torte with pureed raspberries.

Almond-Rum Torte

Serves 10 to 12

FROSTING:
- ¾ pound unsalted butter, softened
- 2 cups confectioners' sugar
- 2 eggs
- 2 teaspoons vanilla extract
- 2 tablespoons cold, very strong brewed coffee

- 36 whole ladyfingers
- ⅓ to ½ cup rum, brandy, bourbon, or very strong brewed coffee
- 3½ ounces sliced toasted almonds†

Almonds are grown in abundance in the fertile central valleys of California. They are not a true nut, but the pit of a fruit related to the peach.

To prepare Frosting: With an electric mixer, cream butter and sugar. At low speed, beat in eggs, one at a time, blending thoroughly after each addition. Add vanilla and 2 tablespoons coffee and beat at high speed for 10 minutes, stopping periodically to scrape down sides of bowl. Frosting should be very light and fluffy.

To assemble: On a serving plate, arrange ladyfingers in 2 rows of 6 fingers each, sides and ends touching. Cake will measure approximately 6 by 8 inches. Sprinkle the ladyfingers with one of the liquors or strong coffee. Spread with a layer of frosting. Continue with another layer of ladyfingers, sprinkle with liquor or coffee, then frosting, until all ladyfingers are used. There will be 3 layers. Frost the entire outside of the torte, smoothing with a metal spatula dipped in hot water.

Arrange toasted almonds in overlapping rows to completely cover top of torte. Using the palm of your hand, press remaining almonds into the sides of the torte.

Cut into thin slices. Serve at room temperature.

NOTE: Torte may be frozen before almonds are added. Freeze until frosting is firm, then seal in plastic wrap. Thaw completely before decorating with almonds.

†Toast almonds in a 325 degree oven for 5 to 10 minutes, or until lightly browned. Cool.

Date-Nut Torte

Serves 8

4 egg whites
1 cup sugar
¾ cup graham cracker crumbs (about 12 single crackers)
½ teaspoon salt
1 teaspoon baking powder
½ cup chopped pitted dates
½ cup coarsely chopped walnuts
1 teaspoon vanilla extract

1 cup whipping cream, whipped and flavored with 2 tablespoons confectioners' sugar and 1 teaspoon vanilla extract

Preheat oven to 325 degrees. Lightly butter a 9-inch pie pan.

With an electric mixer, beat egg whites until soft peaks form. Gradually add the sugar and continue beating until stiff peaks form. Mix cracker crumbs with salt and baking powder. Fold into egg whites. When crumbs are partially incorporated, add dates, walnuts, and vanilla. Fold until all the ingredients are well distributed.

Spread into pie pan and smooth out top with a spatula. Bake 40 to 45 minutes, or until the top is pale brown and has formed a thin dry crust. Cool the torte in the pan. Frost with sweetened whipped cream.

To serve, cut in wedges.

Walnut-Prune Torte

Serves 8

TORTE:
5 eggs, separated
¼ teaspoon salt
2 cups confectioners' sugar
2 cups finely ground walnuts

CREAM CHEESE FILLING:
8 ounces cream cheese, softened
½ cup confectioners' sugar
¼ cup butter, softened
1 tablespoon vanilla extract

PRUNE TOPPING:
12 ounces prunes, pitted
¼ cup water
¼ cup brandy
2 tablespoons brandy

The Santa Clara Valley, dubbed "Silicon Valley" in recent years because of its flourishing computer industry, is still the world's leading producer of prunes.

Preheat oven to 325 degrees. Butter a 9-inch springform pan.

To prepare Torte: In a clean bowl, beat egg whites with salt until stiff, about 5 minutes. Set aside. Beat egg yolks and sugar together until light and lemon-colored. Stir in walnuts. Stir about one-third of the egg whites into the walnut mixture; carefully fold in remaining egg whites. Spread evenly in prepared pan and bake about 50 to 55 minutes, or until the top has formed a light brown crust and the center does not jiggle when the pan is gently shaken.

Cool completely in the pan. Run a sharp knife around the rim of the pan to loosen before unmolding. The torte will sink in the center as it cools.

To prepare Cream Cheese Filling: Whip together all ingredients until light and fluffy. Set aside.

To prepare Prune Topping: In a small saucepan, combine prunes, water, and ¼ cup brandy. Boil gently 7 to 10 minutes, or until prunes are soft. Set aside to cool. In a food processor or blender, puree the prunes with any remaining cooking liquid and 2 tablespoons brandy, until prunes are nearly smooth. Some texture is desirable.

Spread the cooled torte with a thick layer of Cream Cheese Filling to the edge of the torte. Carefully spread on the Prune Topping, leaving a rim of white around the edge.

NOTE: To vary, warm Walnut-Brandy Sauce (page 245) can be substituted for the Prune Topping.

Brie Cheesecake with Raspberry Sauce or Caramelized Pears

Albert Katz, The Broadway Terrace Cafe, Oakland

Serves 12

CHEESECAKE:

12 ounces highest quality cream cheese, softened
5 ounces ripe Brie cheese, rind removed
5 ounces ripe St. André triple cream cheese, rind removed
¾ cup sugar
5 eggs
½ cup sugar

RASPBERRY SAUCE:

½ pint fresh raspberries
2 tablespoons Grand Marnier or other orange liqueur

CARAMELIZED PEARS:

2 pounds slightly underripe d'Anjou pears, peeled, cored, and sliced into eighths
¾ cup sugar
½ cup water
2 whole cloves

When Albert Katz prepares this cheesecake recipe for his cafe, he combines a Brie with a St. André or the harder-to-obtain Brillat-Savarin. In the winter when fresh raspberries are unavailable, he serves the cake with Caramelized Pears.

Preheat oven to 350 degrees. Lightly butter a 9½-inch springform pan.

To prepare Cheesecake: In a food processor, combine cheeses with ¾ cup sugar. Process until mixture liquifies, scraping down sides of the bowl. Add eggs and remaining sugar and continue to process until very smooth. Pour into prepared pan. Set pan in a larger ovenproof pan and add enough hot water to reach halfway up the sides of the springform pan. Bake 60 minutes, or until top is just barely browned. Cool. Remove pan sides.

Meanwhile, prepare either Raspberry Sauce or Caramelized Pears.

To prepare Raspberry Sauce: In a food processor or blender, puree the raspberries with Grand Marnier. Press through a sieve and discard seeds. Spoon sauce over individual servings.

To prepare Caramelized Pears: In a saucepan large enough to hold pear slices comfortably, bring sugar, water, and cloves to a boil over medium heat. Add pears and simmer, uncovered, for 20 minutes. Remove from heat, discard cloves, and refrigerate pears in syrup overnight.

The next day, bring pears and syrup to a boil over medium heat. Boil gently, uncovered, until liquid in saucepan has evaporated and pears are light caramel in color. Stir occasionally to prevent pears from sticking. Arrange Caramelized Pears decoratively on Brie Cheesecake before slicing.

Pumpkin Cheesecake

Karen Shapiro, La Viennoise Pastries, Oakland

Serves 12

CRUST:

¾ cup graham cracker crumbs (about 12 single crackers)
½ cup ground pecans
¼ cup brown sugar
¼ cup granulated sugar
¼ cup butter, melted

FILLING:

¾ cup granulated sugar
¾ cup pumpkin puree
3 egg yolks
1½ teaspoons ground cinnamon
½ teaspoon ground mace
½ teaspoon ground ginger
½ teaspoon salt
1½ pounds natural cream cheese, softened
6 tablespoons granulated sugar
1 egg plus 1 yolk
2 tablespoons whipping cream
1 tablespoon sifted cornstarch
½ teaspoon vanilla extract
½ teaspoon lemon extract

Whipped cream and whole pecans for garnish

The pastries at La Viennoise reflect the influence of traditional Swiss and German baking practices and owner-baker Karen Shapiro's insistence on fresh, quality ingredients. The natural cream cheese called for in this recipe produces a lighter cake. Pumpkin puree lends an autumnal flavor.

To prepare Crust: Combine all ingredients and mix well, coating crumbs completely with butter. Pat crumb mixture firmly onto bottom of a 9-inch springform pan. Place in freezer while preparing filling.

Preheat oven to 350 degrees.

To prepare Filling: Mix ¾ cup sugar, pumpkin puree, 3 egg yolks, cinnamon, mace, ginger, and salt in a bowl. Set aside. With an electric mixer, beat cream cheese and 6 tablespoons sugar until smooth. Add the egg plus 1 yolk and the whipping cream. Mix again until smooth. Add cornstarch and blend well. Add vanilla and lemon extracts. Mix again until very smooth. Add spiced pumpkin puree to the cream cheese mixture. Mix until no traces of white remain. (The smooth texture of this cheesecake depends on thorough mixing.)

Pour filling over crumb mixture in springform pan. Bake 45 minutes, or until sides have risen. The center will still be somewhat soft. Remove from oven. Cool to room temperature, then refrigerate until thoroughly chilled. Run a knife around the edge of the pan and release the sides. Remove cheesecake from pan bottom.

Garnish with whipped cream rosettes and whole pecans.

Apple Cake

Makes 12 squares

CAKE:

2 cups all-purpose flour
2 teaspoons baking soda
2 teaspoons ground cinnamon
1 teaspoon ground nutmeg
½ teaspoon salt
1½ cups granulated sugar
4 cups (about 3 large) unpeeled pippin apples, cored and cut in small chunks
1 cup chopped walnuts
1 cup vegetable oil
2 eggs, beaten

CINNAMON FROSTING:

3 ounces cream cheese, softened
½ cup butter, softened
1 cup confectioners' sugar
½ teaspoon ground cinnamon
½ teaspoon vanilla extract

Preheat oven to 350 degrees. Butter and flour a 9- by 13-inch baking pan.

Combine flour, baking soda, cinnamon, nutmeg, and salt in a bowl. Set aside.

Combine sugar and apples in a large mixing bowl. Add walnuts, oil, and eggs. Mix well by hand. Add dry ingredients. Stir until dry ingredients are just moistened. Spoon into prepared pan, spreading evenly.

Bake 50 to 60 minutes, or until toothpick inserted in center comes out clean. Cool cake in pan on a wire rack.

To prepare Cinnamon Frosting: Whip frosting ingredients together with an electric mixer until light and fluffy. Spread on cooled cake.

Frosted Date Cake

Makes 9 squares

CAKE:

1	cup chopped pitted dates
½	teaspoon baking soda
1	cup boiling water
1½	cups all-purpose flour
1	teaspoon baking powder
½	teaspoon ground cinnamon
¼	teaspoon salt
½	teaspoon grated orange peel
½	cup butter
¾	cup granulated sugar
2	eggs
1	teaspoon vanilla extract

FROSTING:

½	cup fresh orange juice
¼	cup brown sugar
¼	cup granulated sugar
¼	cup chopped pitted dates
½	cup butter
1	cup chopped walnuts

California's desert region is the major United States producer of the sweet, sticky fruit of the date palm.

Preheat oven to 350 degrees. Butter a 9-inch square pan.

To prepare Cake: Place dates and baking soda in a small bowl; add boiling water and set aside to cool.

Combine dry ingredients, including orange peel; set aside.

Cream butter and sugar. Beat in eggs thoroughly, then add vanilla. Stir in cooled date mixture. Blend in dry ingredients.

Spread into prepared pan. Bake 30 to 35 minutes, or until toothpick inserted in center comes out clean. Cool cake in pan on wire rack.

To prepare Frosting: While cake is baking, boil orange juice and sugars in a 2-quart saucepan for 10 minutes. Stir occasionally to prevent scorching. Add dates, butter, and walnuts. Simmer 10 minutes longer, stirring occasionally, or until mixture is thick. Cool frosting to lukewarm.

Spread frosting over cooled cake. Cut in nine 3-inch squares.

Chiffon Cake

Serves 12

CAKE:

8 eggs, separated
½ teaspoon cream of tartar
2 cups all-purpose flour
1½ cups sugar
1 tablespoon baking powder
1 teaspoon salt
½ cup vegetable oil
¾ cup water
2 teaspoons vanilla extract

COFFEE OR MOCHA FROSTING (OPTIONAL):

4 cups confectioners' sugar
½ cup butter
2 teaspoons instant coffee powder
¼ teaspoon salt
2 teaspoons vanilla extract
1 egg
⅓ cup whipping cream
½ cup unsweetened cocoa (for Mocha Frosting only)

Preheat oven to 325 degrees.

To prepare Cake: With an electric mixer, beat egg whites and cream of tartar until whites form stiff, dry peaks (about 10 minutes).

Meanwhile, sift together flour, sugar, baking powder, and salt. Make a well in the center and add oil, egg yolks, water, and vanilla. Beat with a spoon until smooth.

With a wooden spoon, gently stir about one-fourth of the egg whites into the yolk batter. Pour yolk batter over the remaining egg whites. Fold together very gently until just blended. Do not stir.

Pour batter into an ungreased 10-inch tube pan and bake 65 to 70 minutes, or until the top springs back when lightly touched and the cake is nicely browned on top. Immediately turn pan upside down and set over the neck of a sturdy bottle to cool. Cool cake completely before removing from pan. Run a knife around the inside edge and center cone to loosen. When out of the pan turn cake right side up and set on a serving plate.

Frost, or serve plain.

To prepare Coffee or Mocha Frosting: With an electric mixer, blend all ingredients and beat at high speed until frosting is light and creamy (about 5 minutes). Spread on top and sides of Chiffon Cake.

Coconut-Pecan Cake

Serves 12

CAKE:

5 eggs, separated
1 cup butter
2 cups sugar
1 cup buttermilk
1 teaspoon vanilla extract
2 cups all-purpose flour
1 teaspoon baking soda
½ teaspoon salt
1 cup shredded unsweetened coconut
1 cup chopped pecans

FROSTING:

½ cup butter, softened
8 ounces cream cheese, softened
1 pound confectioners' sugar
1 teaspoon vanilla extract

1 cup chopped pecans

Preheat oven to 350 degrees. Butter and flour three 8-inch round cake pans.

To prepare Cake: Beat egg whites until stiff. Set aside.

Cream butter and sugar. Add egg yolks one at a time, beating thoroughly after each addition. Beat in buttermilk and vanilla. Sift together flour, soda, and salt. Stir into batter. Mix in coconut and pecans. Gently fold in egg whites until just incorporated.

Divide the batter evenly among the prepared pans. Bake 25 to 30 minutes, or until cakes spring back when touched lightly in the center.

Cool completely on wire racks; remove from pans.

To prepare Frosting: Combine all frosting ingredients except pecans in bowl of an electric mixer. Beat until smooth and creamy.

Cover layers with frosting. Frost top and sides. Press pecans into top and sides of the cake with the palm of your hand.

Slice and serve.

Kahlua Crunch Cake

Serves 16

CAKE:

1¼ cups cake flour
¾ cup sugar
6 egg yolks
3 tablespoons Kahlua
2 tablespoons water
1 tablespoon lemon juice
8 egg whites
1 teaspoon cream of tartar
1 teaspoon salt
¾ cup sugar

KAHLUA CRUNCH:

1½ cups sugar
¼ cup Kahlua
¼ cup light corn syrup
2 tablespoons water
1 tablespoon baking soda

KAHLUA CREAM:

2 cups whipping cream
2 tablespoons Kahlua
1 tablespoon sugar

Infused with the flavor of coffee liqueur, this four-layer cake has a rough coat of candy crumbs pressed into a creamy frosting.

Preheat oven to 350 degrees.

To prepare Cake: Sift flour with ¾ cup sugar into a small bowl. Make a well in the center and add egg yolks, Kahlua, water, and lemon juice. With an electric mixer, beat to a smooth batter.

In a clean bowl, beat egg whites with cream of tartar and salt until foamy. Gradually add ¾ cup sugar, 2 tablespoons at a time; continue to beat until meringue is stiff, but not dry.

Pour cake batter slowly over meringue, folding in gently until blended. Turn batter into an ungreased 10-inch tube pan. Bake 50 to 55 minutes, or until top is golden and springs back when lightly touched. Remove from oven and let cool on a wire rack. Loosen cake with a sharp knife; remove from pan and set aside.

continued

Meanwhile, prepare Kahlua Crunch and Kahlua Cream. Have ready a 9-inch square non-stick pan or line a 9-inch pan with foil.

To prepare Kahlua Crunch: In a 2-quart saucepan, combine sugar, Kahlua, corn syrup, and water; bring to a boil. Cook to the hard-crack stage (290 degrees on a candy thermometer) without stirring. Remove from heat and add baking soda. The mixture will foam rapidly when the soda is added. Stir briskly just until mixture thickens, but do not break down foam by excessive stirring.

Turn Kahlua Crunch into prepared pan without stirring or scraping the sides of the saucepan. Let stand until cool. Knock candy out of the pan and break in coarse crumbs with a rolling pin.

To prepare Kahlua Cream: Whip the cream with Kahlua and sugar until stiff.

To assemble: Cut the cooled cake horizontally into 4 even layers. Reassemble layers spreading with about half of the Kahlua Cream. Sprinkle each layer with Kahlua Crunch crumbs.

Frost the cake on top and sides with the remaining Kahlua Cream. Dust with the remaining Kahlua Crunch. Press crumbs gently into the cream with palm of your hand. Refrigerate until ready to serve.

NOTE: Both cake and Kahlua Crunch can be made a few days ahead. On serving day, cut the cake into layers, crush Kahlua Crunch, whip Kahlua Cream, and assemble.

Persimmon Pudding

Serves 10 to 12

1 cup persimmon puree (2 to 3 very ripe persimmons)
1 teaspoon baking soda
½ cup butter
1 cup sugar
1 egg
3 tablespoons brandy
1¾ cups all-purpose flour
2 teaspoons baking powder
1 teaspoon ground cinnamon
½ teaspoon ground nutmeg
½ teaspoon ground cloves
½ teaspoon salt
½ cup finely chopped almonds
1 teaspoon grated orange peel
1 teaspoon grated lemon peel

Walnut-Brandy Sauce for accompaniment (page 245)

Available in fall and winter, persimmons lend festive color to holiday tables. Their color develops before the fruit is fully ripe, when it still has an unpleasant puckery tartness. If allowed to reach the consistency of a liquid-filled balloon, its sweet, spicy flavor is superb.

Butter a 6-cup lidded tube mold or use a similar capacity metal mold which can be covered tightly with foil (see Note).

In a small bowl, blend persimmon puree with baking soda and set aside.

With an electric mixer, cream butter and sugar; beat in egg, persimmon puree, and brandy.

In a separate bowl, stir together flour, baking powder, and spices. Add to creamed mixture, blend well, then stir in almonds and grated peels.

Pour into prepared mold. Cover and set mold on rack in Dutch oven. Add 2 inches of hot water to the Dutch oven. Cover the Dutch oven tightly and steam the pudding by boiling the water gently 50 to 60 minutes, adding hot water as necessary to maintain water level, until a long cake tester inserted in the center comes out clean.

Cool completely in the mold.

To serve, unmold and cut in slices. Accompany with Walnut-Brandy Sauce.

N O T E : Make sure the Dutch oven is deep enough to accommodate the height of the mold and rack together. If a mold without a center tube is used, cooking time must be increased. Check regularly for doneness.

16.
Seven Persimmons
color pencil, graphite

Walnut-Brandy Sauce

Makes 1 to
1½ cups

1 cup brown sugar
¼ cup butter
¼ cup whipping cream
2 tablespoons light corn syrup
¼ cup chopped walnuts or pecans
2 tablespoons brandy

To the Dutch we
owe credit for
naming a distilled
wine brandy. *A*
distilled American
spirit must be aged
four years,
preferably in an
oak cask, to
achieve the status
of brandy.

In a 1-quart saucepan, combine brown sugar, butter, whipping cream, and corn syrup and bring to a boil over medium heat, stirring constantly. Reduce heat to low. Cook, stirring occasionally, for 5 minutes. Stir in nuts and brandy and simmer 1 minute. Sauce will be thin.

Serve warm over Persimmon Pudding (page 244), Walnut-Prune Torte (page 235), or ice cream.

Apricot Jam Tartlets

Makes about
4½ dozen tartlets

CRUST:
½ cup butter, softened
3 ounces cream cheese, softened
1½ cups all-purpose flour
¼ teaspoon salt
1 egg

FILLING:
1¼ cups apricot jam

Just big enough
for one or two
bites, these
charming
miniature tarts are
made with a cream
cheese crust and a
simple jam filling.

In a food processor or with a pastry blender, blend butter and cream cheese together until well mixed. Add flour and salt and cut together until mixture is crumbly. Stir in egg and blend until dough forms a ball. Wrap in waxed paper and chill at least 1 hour.

Preheat oven to 350 degrees.

Working with half the dough at a time, roll out on a lightly floured surface to ¼-inch thickness. Cut in 2-inch circles and fit in miniature muffin tins (1¼-inch bottom diameter). Gather up the scraps and gently roll again, working dough as little as possible.

Fill each cup with a teaspoon of jam and bake 10 minutes, or until crust edges are lightly browned.

Serve warm or at room temperature.

NOTE: To vary, top each tart with a walnut half after baking, *or* stir ½ teaspoon finely grated lemon peel into jam, *or* stir ¼ cup currants, which have been plumped in warm brandy to cover, then drained, into jam.

Coconut Fruit Tartlets

Makes about 7½ dozen tartlets

TOPPING:
½ cup butter
1⅓ cups sugar
4 eggs
4 cups shredded unsweetened coconut
½ teaspoon vanilla extract

PASTRY:
2½ cups all-purpose flour
2 tablespoons sugar
2 teaspoons baking powder
¾ cup butter, cut in pieces
2 eggs
¼ cup milk

FILLING:
1 jar (10 ounces or 1 cup) raspberry or apricot jam

To prepare Topping: Cream butter with sugar. Beat in eggs thoroughly. Stir in coconut and vanilla. Set aside.

To prepare Pastry: Combine dry ingredients. In a food processor or with a pastry blender, cut butter into flour mixture until crumbly. With a fork, beat eggs with milk; stir into flour mixture until moistened. Form into a ball.

Preheat oven to 400 degrees.

To assemble: Using thumb and forefinger, press about 1 teaspoon of dough into the bottom and sides of the cups in miniature muffin tins (1¼-inch bottom diameter). Keep unused dough lightly covered to prevent it from drying out.

Place a level ½ teaspoon of jam in the center of each tartlet. Cover the jam with 1 level teaspoon of coconut topping, spreading to the edge of the tartlet so the jam will not leak out during baking. Do not overfill.

Bake 10 minutes. Tartlets will be puffed and golden. Allow to cool slightly. Gently loosen top edge with a sharp knife. Cool tartlets on wire racks.

NOTE: The tartlets can be made ahead and frozen.

Cheesecake Cookies

Makes 25 bars

CRUST:

½ cup chilled butter, cut in pieces
½ cup brown sugar
1¼ cups all-purpose flour
⅛ teaspoon salt
½ cup finely chopped walnuts

FILLING:

12 ounces cream cheese, softened
½ cup granulated sugar
1 egg
2 tablespoons milk
2 tablespoons fresh lemon juice
1 tablespoon vanilla extract

Preheat oven to 325 degrees.

To prepare Crust: In a food processor, combine butter, brown sugar, flour, and salt; blend until mixture is crumbly. Add walnuts and process just to blend. Remove 1¼ cups of this mixture and refrigerate. Press remainder into bottom of a 9- by 9-inch ungreased baking pan. Bake 12 to 15 minutes, or until lightly browned and slightly crusty to the touch. While crust bakes, prepare filling.

Remove crust from oven when done. Increase oven temperature to 350 degrees.

To prepare Filling: In a food processor or with an electric mixer, blend filling ingredients until smooth. Pour over hot baked crust. Sprinkle with reserved crumb mixture and bake 30 minutes. Cool, then chill.

When chilled, cut in 25 squares. Serve cold.

Cherry-Nut Cookies

Makes 6 to 7
dozen cookies

1 cup butter
1 cup confectioners' sugar
1 egg
1 teaspoon vanilla extract
2¼ cups all-purpose flour
1 cup (about 5 ounces) red or green glacé cherry halves
1 cup pecan or walnut pieces

With an electric mixer, cream butter and sugar. Blend in egg and vanilla, scraping down sides of bowl with a rubber spatula. Blend in flour, cherries, and nuts. Dough will be stiff and sticky. Chill 30 minutes. Roll dough into 3 logs, each about 1½ inches in diameter, in sheets of waxed paper. Freeze, wrapped, until firm.

Preheat oven to 325 degrees.

Slice frozen logs in ¼-inch-thick rounds and bake on ungreased cookie sheets for 13 minutes, or until tops look dry but are not browned.

Cool on wire racks. Store in airtight containers.

NOTE: Since the dough must be frozen before baking, it can be prepared weeks in advance.

Grand Marnier Bars

*Makes about
40 bars*

DOUGH:
1 cup chilled butter
1 cup sugar
1 egg yolk
2 tablespoons Grand Marnier
1 teaspoon vanilla extract
2 cups all-purpose flour

TOPPING:
½ cup whipping cream
½ cup sugar
2 tablespoons Grand Marnier
¼ teaspoon almond extract
¾ cup (about 2¼ ounces) sliced almonds

Preheat oven to 350 degrees.

To prepare Dough: With an electric mixer, cream butter and sugar. Beat in egg yolk, 2 tablespoons Grand Marnier, and vanilla. Stir in flour. Spread in an ungreased jelly-roll pan. Dampen fingers in water to help spread dough out and prevent sticking. Leave shallow fingertip impressions in the dough; set aside.

To prepare Topping: In a small saucepan, combine cream and ½ cup sugar. Over low heat, cook and stir the mixture until transparent and sugar is dissolved; remove from heat. Add 2 tablespoons Grand Marnier and almond extract. Pour evenly over the dough. Sprinkle with almonds.

Bake 15 minutes. Increase oven temperature to 400 degrees and bake an additional 10 minutes, or until pale golden brown. The top may still appear damp. While still warm, cut in rectangles with a sharp knife. Cool cookies in pan.

Date-Oatmeal Cookies

*Makes about
3 dozen cookies*

1 cup all-purpose flour
2 teaspoons baking powder
½ teaspoon ground nutmeg
¼ teaspoon salt
1 cup chopped pitted dates
½ cup butter
1 cup sugar
1 egg
2 teaspoons finely grated orange peel
2 tablespoons fresh orange juice
1½ cups rolled oats
⅔ cup chopped walnuts

Preheat oven to 375 degrees. Butter a baking sheet.

Sift together flour, baking powder, nutmeg, and salt. Stir in dates to coat and separate. Set aside.

With an electric mixer, cream butter and sugar. Beat in egg, then orange peel, orange juice, and dry ingredients with dates. Stir in oats and walnuts.

Drop by level tablespoons 2 inches apart on prepared cookie sheet. Bake 12 to 15 minutes, or until just lightly browned. Cool on wire racks. Cookies will have soft centers, but will crisp when cooled.

Shortbread

Makes
8 to 12 wedges

1¼ cups all-purpose flour
½ cup chilled butter, cut in pieces
3 tablespoons cornstarch
¼ cup sugar

Additional sugar for topping

Preheat oven to 325 degrees.

In a food processor, combine all ingredients and process until crumbly. Spread mixture in a 9-inch round pan with removable bottom. Press dough firmly into pan.

Using the tines of a fork, make decorative impressions all around edge of shortbread. Prick surface evenly.

Bake 30 to 40 minutes, or until edges begin to turn golden. Remove from oven; while still hot, use a sharp knife to cut shortbread into wedges and then sprinkle with additional sugar.

Cool before removing pan rim and bottom. Store in an airtight container.

Walnut-Spice Bars

*Makes about
12 dozen
small bars*

1 cup butter, softened
2 cups sugar
3 eggs
1 teaspoon baking soda
2 teaspoons water
1 package (10 ounces) chopped pitted dates
3 cups all-purpose flour
1 teaspoon ground cinnamon
1 teaspoon ground nutmeg
¼ teaspoon ground cloves
¼ teaspoon salt
1 cup chopped walnuts
Sugar

With an electric mixer, cream butter and sugar. Add eggs, one at a time, beating well after each addition. Dissolve baking soda in water and combine with creamed mixture. Add dates. Sift flour and spices together and beat into creamed mixture. Stir in chopped walnuts.

Cover the dough with waxed paper and chill several hours or overnight. Preheat oven to 350 degrees.

Divide chilled dough into 6 equal portions for easier handling. On a lightly floured surface, work dough with palms into 10-inch ropes, about ¾ inch in diameter. Then flatten the ropes with fingers to form a ½-inch-thick ribbon.

On an ungreased baking sheet, place 2 ribbons far apart (they will spread). Sprinkle tops with sugar. Bake on the center rack of the oven 20 to 25 minutes until light brown, dry on top, and barely moist on the inside. Cool about 2 minutes. While still hot, gently cut in half lengthwise, then slice crosswise diagonally into 1-inch bars. Remove bars to wire rack to cool. Cookies will harden as they cool.

Repeat with remaining dough. Store in airtight containers.

Jane's Chocolate Chip Cookies

*Makes 4 to 5
dozen cookies*

1⅓ cups butter
1 cup granulated sugar
1 cup brown sugar
2 eggs
2 teaspoons vanilla extract
3 cups all-purpose flour
1 teaspoon baking soda
1 teaspoon salt
1 cup chopped nuts
2 packages (12 ounces each) semisweet chocolate chips

*Everyone has a
food that comforts
the spirit and
nourishes the soul.
This classic
chocolate chip
cookie recipe has
cheered three
generations of one
Oakland family.*

Preheat oven to 375 degrees.

With an electric mixer, cream butter and sugars. Beat in eggs one at a time, then add vanilla. Add remaining ingredients and beat until well combined.

Using a small ice-cream scoop, drop cookie dough in golf ball-sized mounds, about 2 inches apart, on ungreased baking sheets. Bake 8 to 10 minutes, or until lightly browned. Cool slightly before removing from baking sheets.

Cool completely on wire racks. Store in airtight containers.

Florentines

*Makes about
7 dozen cookies*

¾ cup all-purpose flour
½ teaspoon baking powder
½ teaspoon salt
1 cup sugar
¼ cup milk
¼ cup light corn syrup
½ cup butter, melted
1 teaspoon vanilla extract
1 cup rolled oats
1 cup chopped walnuts
1 cup (about 5 ounces) red or green glacé cherry halves
10 ounces semisweet chocolate, cut in pieces

*In the sixteenth
century, florentines
were usually
savory pies or
tarts. Now the
word is associated
with these delicate,
lacy cookies which
originated in
Florence.*

Preheat oven to 375 degrees. Butter and flour 2 baking sheets.

Sift dry ingredients into a bowl. With an electric mixer, beat in milk, corn syrup, melted butter, and vanilla until smooth. Blend in oats and walnuts.

Drop batter by level teaspoonfuls, at least 3 inches apart, onto prepared baking sheets. Place a cherry half in the center of each cookie.

Bake 8 minutes, or until edges are brown. The cookies spread into a lacy pattern. Cool the cookies 1 minute, then quickly and carefully remove to wire racks to finish cooling. Butter and flour the baking sheets again as necessary.

When cookies are cool, melt chocolate over hot, not boiling, water and spread the undersides of the cookies thinly with chocolate. Chill upside down until the chocolate loses its sheen, about 5 minutes. Store in airtight containers to preserve crispness.

Creamy Pralines

*Makes about
36 pieces*

2 cups sugar
¾ cup whipping cream
½ cup light corn syrup
¼ teaspoon baking soda
¼ cup unsalted butter, cut in pieces
1 teaspoon vanilla extract
2 cups pecan halves

*During the reign
of Louis XIII of
France, Count
Plessis-Praslin
distinguished
himself both in
battle and in
romance. To
sweeten one of his
many proposals,
he had his chef
prepare a
"praline," and the
confection thus
created still bears
his name.*

Lightly butter 2 baking sheets with unsalted butter.

In a 4-quart saucepan, combine sugar, cream, corn syrup, and baking soda. Cook over medium heat, stirring constantly, until sugar is dissolved. When mixture begins to boil, cover and boil undisturbed 2 to 3 minutes, or until sugar crystals clinging to the sides of the pan are dissolved.

Remove cover and boil gently to soft-ball stage (240 degrees on a candy thermometer), stirring if the mixture starts to burn. Syrup will be a light caramel color.

Remove saucepan from heat. Drop butter on surface of syrup but do not stir. Let pan sit, undisturbed, until candy reaches 110 degrees, or the pan cools just enough to place the palm of your hand on the bottom (about 30 minutes).

With a wooden spoon, beat in the melted butter and vanilla. Continue to beat until the candy thickens and becomes rope-like (it will hold its shape briefly). Do not scrape hardened candy from the sides of the pan. Stir in the pecans and use a tablespoon to drop candy onto prepared cookie sheets. Candy will be quite sticky. Let sit until firm enough to handle.

Wrap individual candy pieces in plastic wrap or foil and store in airtight containers. Allow the candy to age overnight. It will lose its sticky texture and become very creamy.

CHAPTER TEN

Chocolate

Fudge Flummery

Steven Poses, Proprietor of The Commissary, Philadelphia

Serves 8 to 10

½ cup strong brewed coffee, or 1 teaspoon instant coffee powder dissolved in ½ cup boiling water
8 ounces sweet chocolate, cut in pieces
1 cup granulated sugar
1 cup unsalted butter
4 eggs

TOPPING:
1 cup whipping cream
¼ cup confectioners' sugar
¼ teaspoon vanilla extract

At any one time, there are thirteen bakers working at The Commissary. One of their most popular specialties is this Fudge Flummery, also known as Chocolate Mocha Cake. This dessert is a cross between a Decadence, a type of torte, and a pudding—yet distinctly different from both. Perhaps it is most aptly described as a chocolate-lover's delight. A member of our League visiting Philadelphia thought this recipe was special enough to include in California Fresh.

Preheat oven to 350 degrees. Cut aluminum foil or cooking parchment to fit a 1-quart loaf pan, charlotte mold, or 8-inch cake pan; line pan. Butter the foil or parchment.

In a small saucepan, combine coffee, chocolate, sugar, and butter. Cook over medium heat until chocolate and butter are melted, stirring occasionally. Stir in eggs. Combine well and pour into the prepared pan.

Bake 30 minutes, or until cake cracks around the sides and is crisp on top. Cool in the pan. Cover, then refrigerate overnight, or for as long as one week.

At serving time, invert the chilled cake on a serving dish and carefully peel off the foil or parchment.

Whip the cream with confectioners' sugar and vanilla until it holds soft peaks. Frost cake with whipped cream. Slice thinly and serve.

Chocolate Pie with Pecan Meringue Shell

Serves 6

SHELL:

2 egg whites
½ teaspoon red wine vinegar
¼ teaspoon ground cinnamon
¼ teaspoon salt
½ cup sugar
½ teaspoon vanilla extract
½ cup chopped pecans

FILLING:

6 ounces semisweet chocolate, cut in pieces
2 egg yolks
¼ cup water
¼ teaspoon ground cinnamon

1 cup whipping cream
½ teaspoon vanilla extract
¼ cup sugar

Preheat oven to 325 degrees. Butter a 9-inch pie pan.

To prepare Shell: Combine egg whites, vinegar, cinnamon, and salt. With an electric mixer, beat until egg whites are stiff but not dry. Gradually add ½ cup sugar and beat until stiff, glossy peaks form. Fold in vanilla and pecans. Spread meringue over bottom and sides of prepared pie pan. Bake 45 to 50 minutes, or until meringue is golden. Cool.

To prepare Filling: In a double boiler, melt chocolate over hot, not boiling, water. Blend in egg yolks and water; stir until smooth. Add cinnamon. Cool slightly. Spread ½ cup of chocolate mixture in bottom of cooled meringue. Refrigerate.

Meanwhile, whip cream with vanilla and ¼ cup sugar until soft peaks form. Spread half the cream over chilled chocolate layer. Fold remaining chocolate mixture into remaining whipped cream. Spread evenly over top of pie to cover bottom whipped cream layer, leaving meringue rim uncovered.

Chill the pie at least 4 hours before serving.

November Torte

Alice Medrich, Cocolat, Berkeley

Serves 8 to 10

TORTE:

6 ounces semisweet or bittersweet baking chocolate, cut in pieces
½ cup unsalted butter, cut in pieces
3 eggs, separated
½ cup sugar
¼ cup all-purpose flour
⅔ cup ground toasted hazelnuts†
¼ cup Grand Marnier
   Dash of salt
¼ teaspoon cream of tartar
3 tablespoons sugar

CHOCOLATE GLAZE:

4 ounces unsalted butter, cut in pieces
6 ounces semisweet or bittersweet baking chocolate, cut in pieces
1 tablespoon light corn syrup

Optional garnish: Chocolate leaves (page 263), candied orange peel, or caramelized hazelnuts†

The story of this torte begins in Paris. It was there in the early seventies that Alice Medrich was introduced to the finest European pastries and her landlady's family recipe for rich chocolate truffles.

Preheat oven to 375 degrees. Butter and flour an 8-inch round cake pan or line the bottom with waxed paper or cooking parchment.

To prepare Torte: Melt chocolate with butter in a double boiler placed over not-quite-simmering water. Stir frequently until smooth and melted. Remove from heat and set aside.

Whisk egg yolks and ½ cup sugar together until pale yellow. Whisk in chocolate mixture, flour, and toasted hazelnuts. Add liqueur. Set aside.

In a clean mixing bowl, with an electric mixer, beat egg whites, salt, and cream of tartar at high speed until soft peaks form. Continue to beat, gradually adding the remaining 3 tablespoons sugar, until stiff and glossy.

Fold about one-third of beaten egg whites into chocolate batter to lighten. Fold in the remaining egg whites quickly, but gently.

Turn batter into prepared pan and bake 30 to 40 minutes, or until a toothpick inserted about 1 inch from the edge of the cake shows moist crumbs. The center of the cake will test very moist. Cool cake in the pan.

Meanwhile, to prepare Chocolate Glaze: Place butter, chocolate, and corn syrup in a double boiler and warm gently over low heat, stirring until chocolate and butter are completely melted and smooth. Cool glaze until almost set but still spreadable.

continued

*When Alice
returned to
Berkeley, she
opened her first
European-style
pastry and
chocolate specialty
shop—Cocolat.
From this shop,
Alice introduced
us to chocolate-
glazed genoise
cakes lightly
steeped in Grand
Marnier, and to
her landlady's
chocolate
truffles—now a
Northern
California
staple—which
trace their lineage
to an apartment in
the Sixteenth
Arrondissement.*

When cake has cooled, run a knife around the edges of the cake. Cooled cake will have settled in the center leaving a higher rim; press this rim down gently with your fingers to flatten and level the cake. Unmold cake upside down onto an 8-inch, stiff cardboard circle. Spread edges of cake with just enough cooled Chocolate Glaze to smooth out any imperfections. Be careful to keep the glaze pot free of cake crumbs.

Gently reheat remaining glaze in a double boiler over low heat until it is smooth and pourable. Strain glaze through a fine strainer. Place cake on a turntable or plate and pour all of the glaze onto center of cake. Using a clean metal spatula, and with as few strokes as possible, spread glaze over the edges of the cake. Lift cake up off the plate and set it on a rack to dry before removing to a serving platter.

Serve plain or decorated with chocolate leaves, slivers of candied orange peel, or caramelized hazelnuts. Store and serve this cake at room temperature; refrigeration will dull the glaze.

†Toast shelled hazelnuts on a baking sheet in a 350 degree oven for 15 minutes. Cool. Rub off most of the skins. In a food processor, grind nuts in short pulses; do not overprocess. Two-thirds cup whole hazelnuts produces an equal amount of ground nuts.

To caramelize hazelnuts, skewer each of 10 or more perfect hazelnuts (skins may be left on) on the ends of wooden skewers. In a small saucepan over medium heat, dissolve ½ cup sugar in ½ cup water. Cover, bring to a boil, and cook 4 to 5 minutes. Uncover, but do not stir. Wash sugar crystals from the sides of the pan with a wet pastry brush. Continue to cook without stirring until syrup is a medium-dark amber color. Remove from heat and quickly dip each skewered nut in the syrup. Set the dipped, skewered nuts on the rim of a cake pan to drip, cool, and harden. Remove each nut from the skewer, snip off any caramel tails that may have formed, and place nuts evenly spaced around the top of the glazed cake.

Chocolate Cake with Butter Rum Sauce

Serves 12

CAKE:

2 ounces unsweetened chocolate
½ cup butter
2 eggs
1 cup granulated sugar
1 teaspoon vanilla extract
¼ teaspoon salt
½ cup all-purpose flour

SAUCE:

1 cup whipping cream
¾ cup light brown sugar
½ cup butter
3 tablespoons dark rum
½ teaspoon vanilla extract

Preheat oven to 325 degrees. Butter a 9-inch springform pan.

To prepare Cake: In a double boiler, melt chocolate and butter over hot, not boiling, water, stirring occasionally until smooth. Remove from heat and cool to room temperature.

With an electric mixer, beat eggs at high speed 3 to 4 minutes. Gradually beat in sugar and continue to beat until very thick, about 5 minutes. Beat in vanilla, salt, and cooled chocolate mixture. On low speed, blend in flour. Pour into prepared pan.

Bake 30 to 35 minutes, or until toothpick inserted in center comes out clean. Cool completely in pan on wire rack.

To prepare Sauce: In a saucepan, combine cream, brown sugar, and butter. Cook over low heat, stirring frequently, until mixture boils. Boil 5 minutes, stirring occasionally. Remove from heat. Stir in rum and vanilla.

To serve, spoon a moderate amount of warm sauce on a rimmed dessert plate. Top with a wedge of cake.

Chocolate Mousse Cake

Elizabeth Thomas, Elizabeth Thomas Cooking School, Berkeley

Serves 6 to 8

8 vanilla wafers, finely crushed
8 ounces semisweet chocolate, cut in pieces
¼ cup boiling water
1 tablespoon instant coffee powder
1 teaspoon vanilla extract
8 egg yolks
⅔ cup sugar
4 egg whites
A pinch of salt
1¼ cups whipping cream
1 tablespoon confectioners' sugar
¼ teaspoon vanilla extract

9 stiff leaves (such as camellia) and additional semisweet chocolate for making Chocolate Leaves†

The concept for this chocolate cake began many years ago with a recipe for chocolate mousse given to Elizabeth Thomas by a Swiss friend. It has since evolved into this delicious, rich dessert.

Preheat oven to 350 degrees. Butter a 9-inch springform pan. Coat with cookie crumbs.

Place chocolate in a double boiler. Add boiling water to instant coffee and pour over chocolate. Cover and set over hot, not boiling, water. When chocolate has melted, beat in vanilla with a wooden spoon. Cool, uncovered.

With an electric mixer, beat egg yolks until pale and thick. Gradually add sugar and continue to beat for about 5 minutes. Add cooled chocolate mixture to yolks. Mix well and place half the mixture in another bowl.

In a clean bowl, whip egg whites with salt until stiff, and fold into one of the bowls of chocolate. Pour into prepared cake pan, gently leveling top with a spatula.

Bake for 25 minutes. Cool in the pan on a wire rack. The center will fall, leaving plenty of space for the filling. When completely cool, remove to a serving platter.

Whip the cream, reserving ¼ cup for garnish. Fold the rest into remaining chocolate mixture. Fill cake, leveling top with a spatula.

To serve, mix reserved whipped cream with confectioners' sugar and ¼ teaspoon vanilla. Pipe whipped cream rosettes on top of cake. Decorate cake with Chocolate Leaves. Refrigerate.

†To prepare Chocolate Leaves, gather 9 stiff leaves, such as camellia. Melt semisweet chocolate in a double boiler over hot, not boiling, water. Wash and dry leaves. Spread the underside of the leaves with a thin coating of melted chocolate. Refrigerate until hardened. Peel off green leaves and decorate cake with chocolate replicas.

Triple Chocolate Cake

Serves 10 to 12

CAKE:

½ cup butter
4 ounces unsweetened chocolate, cut in pieces
½ cup butter, softened
2 cups granulated sugar
3 eggs
1 teaspoon vanilla extract
¼ teaspoon salt
1 cup all-purpose flour

FILLING:

4 ounces unsweetened chocolate, cut in pieces
4 ounces semisweet chocolate, cut in pieces
1½ teaspoons vanilla extract
3 egg whites
⅓ cup superfine sugar
2 cups whipping cream

GLAZE:

8 ounces semisweet chocolate, cut in pieces
⅓ cup water

Leaves or flowers for garnish

This is definitely a triple-threat dessert for chocoholics— chocolate cake, chocolate filling, and chocolate glaze!

Preheat oven to 350 degrees. Lightly butter a jelly-roll pan. Line bottom and sides of pan with waxed paper. Butter waxed paper and dust with flour; shake off excess flour. Lightly oil an 8-cup charlotte mold or soufflé dish.

To prepare Cake: In a double boiler, melt ½ cup butter and chocolate together over hot, not boiling, water. Stir until smooth. Set aside to cool.

With an electric mixer, cream ½ cup butter and 2 cups sugar. Beat in eggs, one at a time, until incorporated. Stir in vanilla, salt, and cooled chocolate mixture. By hand, stir in flour. Spread batter into prepared jelly-roll pan and bake 20 to 25 minutes, or until toothpick inserted in center comes out clean. Remove from oven. Invert cake onto a wire rack. Carefully peel off waxed paper and cool completely. When cool, trim and discard crusty edges.

continued

Using prepared charlotte mold or soufflé dish as a guide, cut rounds of cake to fit bottom and top of the mold and a strip to fit around sides. It will be necessary to piece the sides, but glaze will cover the seams. Fit a round of cake into bottom of mold. Line sides with remaining cake. Set top round aside.

To prepare Filling: In a double boiler, melt the chocolates over hot, not boiling, water. Stir until smooth. Set aside to cool. Stir in vanilla.

In a clean bowl, beat egg whites until foamy. Add superfine sugar, a little at a time, continuing to beat until stiff, glossy peaks form.

In a separate bowl, whip cream until stiff. Carefully fold egg whites and cooled chocolate into whipped cream until no trace of white remains. Fill the cake-lined mold. Cover with the reserved cake round. Cover with plastic wrap and chill for several hours or overnight.

To prepare Glaze: Melt chocolate with water in a small saucepan over very low heat, stirring frequently until smooth. Cool until thickened, but not set.

To serve, loosen sides of cake with a sharp knife, if necessary, and unmold cake onto a serving plate. Pour cooled glaze over top and let drizzle down sides and seams. Chill again until glaze is set.

Cut in thin wedges to serve. For color, ring the cake at its base with fresh leaves or colorful flowers.

Hot Chocolate Sauce

Makes about
1½ cups

½ cup butter
1 package (6 ounces) semisweet chocolate chips
¼ cup unsweetened cocoa
¾ cup sugar
½ cup whipping cream

In a small saucepan, combine all ingredients. Boil 2 minutes, stirring occasionally.

Serve warm over meringue shells, white or chocolate angel food cake, or peppermint ice cream.

NOTE: The sauce keeps for a week in the refrigerator, but will harden with chilling. To soften, melt in a double boiler over hot, not boiling, water, or in a glass dish in a microwave oven.

White Chocolate Mousse

Serves 6 to 8

8 ounces white chocolate, cut in pieces
2 egg yolks
5 tablespoons Grand Marnier or other orange liqueur
1⅓ cups whipping cream, whipped
4 egg whites, beaten until stiff

Orange or tangerine peel roses (coiled strips of peel), or dark chocolate leaves (page 263) for garnish

To understand the difference between white chocolate and chocolate, it is important to know the difference between cacao and cocoa. Cacao refers to the cacao tree, pods, and beans. When the cacao bean is processed, two ingredients remain: a creamy, yellowish cocoa butter and a brown cocoa liquid. Both white chocolate and chocolate are made from cocoa butter. White chocolate, however, does not contain cocoa liquid, which gives chocolate its color and also its stimulating effect.

Melt chocolate in a double boiler over hot, not boiling, water. Stir occasionally. Remove from heat and stir in egg yolks and liqueur. Fold in whipped cream, then fold in egg whites. Pour into serving bowl. Chill until firm.

Garnish with orange or tangerine peel roses, or dark chocolate leaves.

Mocha Truffles

Makes 5 dozen

12 ounces semisweet chocolate, cut in pieces
4 egg yolks
1½ cups confectioners' sugar
1 cup butter, softened
2 teaspoons instant coffee powder
¼ cup brandy
2 teaspoons vanilla extract
2 cups finely chopped pecans

Americans consume nine-and-one-half pounds of chocolate per person each year!

In a double boiler, melt chocolate over hot, not boiling, water. Cool.

In a medium bowl, beat egg yolks. Add sugar gradually, beating until smooth. Beat in butter, a little at a time. Dissolve coffee in brandy and vanilla. Combine with egg and butter mixture. Add cooled chocolate and mix thoroughly. Chill 4 to 5 hours.

Shape candy in ½-inch balls. Roll in pecans. Place in paper candy cups or on a serving plate.

Refrigerate or freeze until ready to serve.

Chocolate-Orange Ice Cream

*Makes about
1½ quarts*

1 package (10 ounces) chocolate-covered orange stick candy (with soft centers)
2 ounces semisweet chocolate
3 cups whipping cream
1 cup milk
½ cup sugar
1 tablespoon vanilla extract
½ teaspoon salt
6 egg yolks

In a double boiler over hot, not boiling, water melt chocolate sticks and chocolate. Orange centers of the candy will not melt completely. Set aside.

In a 2-quart saucepan, bring the cream, milk, sugar, vanilla, and salt just to a boil over medium heat. Remove from heat. Add chocolate mixture and stir well.

Meanwhile, whisk egg yolks thoroughly. Gradually add a cup of the hot chocolate mixture to the yolks, whisking vigorously. Return yolk mixture to the saucepan, stirring constantly. Cook gently until mixture thickens, about 5 minutes. Do not boil. Set aside to cool.

Chill, then freeze in an ice-cream freezer according to the manufacturer's instructions.

NOTE: The ice cream can be frozen in a tray in the freezer instead of in an ice-cream maker, but it will not be as smooth.

INDEX

Numbers appearing in italics indicate margin notes.

ABOUT M.F.K. FISHER

For almost fifty years Mary Frances Kennedy Fisher has chronicled her love of fine food and wine with passion, wit, and beautifully crafted prose. Her stories are intimate, personal recollections of her own experiences that at the same time speak of universal human concerns. The acclaimed author of seventeen books and numerous magazine articles, she is considered America's greatest food writer. Her contributions have appeared in *The New Yorker, House and Garden, Gourmet, Vogue,* and *The New York Times.* Originally from the Midwest, she moved with her family when she was a young girl to the small town of Whittier in Southern California. She then lived abroad for many years, mainly in France and Switzerland. Her home is now in Sonoma County, part of the famous wine-producing region north of San Francisco.

ABOUT BETH VAN HOESEN

The controlled, yet wonderfully expressive, linear quality of Beth Van Hoesen's fine drawings and prints finds an antecedent in the art of Dürer and Rembrandt. Although first trained as a painter, Ms. Van Hoesen turned to printmaking as the medium to express her interest in line and space. She is nationally recognized for the individuality and personality of her portraiture, still-life, and animal studies, which are always drawn from a model. Her meticulous attention to every aspect of the printmaking process is also well known. The artist has exhibited in many individual and group shows, and her work is part of prominent private and public collections including the Achenbach Foundation for Graphic Arts, San Francisco; the Art Institute of Chicago; the San Francisco Museum of Modern Art; The Oakland Museum; the Smithsonian Institution, Washington, D.C.; and the Victoria and Albert Museum, London. She and her husband, artist and tapestry designer Mark Adams, have their home and studio in a converted 1909 San Francisco firehouse.

ABOUT GORDON CHUN

Graphic designer Gordon Chun created the elegant and contemporary appearance of *California Fresh*. Specializing in the design of museum publications and institutional graphics, Mr. Chun has received numerous national awards for his work. Born in Honolulu, he graduated from the University of California, Berkeley, with a degree in fine arts. His design office is in Berkeley, where he also lives with his wife, Suzanne, and their son and daughter.